A

HISTORY

OF

LOUISIANA.

BY

. GRACE KING,
Author of "Bienville," etc.

AND

JOHN R. FICKLEN,
Professor of History in Tulane University.

NEW ORLEANS:
L. GRAHAM & SON,
PRINTERS.

PREFACE.

In presenting this History of Louisiana to the people of the State, the authors find it necessary to say a word of preface. Their intention has been to write a history that would give the children of Louisiana a simple and true account of the progress of the State from the earliest times of discovery down to the present era. It is hoped, however, that the work will not prove uninteresting to older persons as well.

Every effort has been made to secure accuracy of detail; but as some errors may have crept in, the authors will be glad to receive notice of any that meet the eye of the critic.

If a subsequent edition is demanded, the authors expect to enrich their work with further illustrations. Especially do they hope to obtain portraits of all the State governors—a task which it has been found impossible to accomplish in time for this edition.

It may be added that all the artistic and mechanical portion of the work was done in New Orleans—the book is entirely a home product.

The authors desire to thank the librarians of the Fisk, the Howard, and the State Libraries for uniform courtesy and kindness in putting at their disposal the rich historical treasures from which the materials of this work are drawn.

Among these treasures the authors wish to acknowledge their special obligations to the Histories of Louisiana by the Hon. Charles Gayarré and Judge Martin; to Fiske's Discovery of America; to Margry's Documents; and to the official documents relating to the French and the Spanish Domination.

Grateful acknowledgment is also made to E. H. Farrar, Esq., for the privilege he kindly granted of borrowing books and maps from his valuable library.

The authors owe special thanks to Messrs. L. Graham & Son, printers, for the care they have taken in the execution of their share of the labor.

In conclusion it is proper to state that Miss King wrote the first part of the history (as far as the end of the Spanish Domination), and that Mr. Ficklen completed it,

CONTENTS.

HISTORY OF LOUISIANA.

ERRATA.

Page   6—For *Manvilla* read *Mauvilla*.
Page   6—For *points* read *point*.
Page 12—Insert *the* before pioneer.
Page 20—For *was stuck* read *were stuck*.
Page 21—For *gladened* read *gladdened*.
Page 23—For *abie* read *able*.
Page 25—Insert *they* before *waylaid*.
Page 27—For *Chanteaugnay* read *Chateauguay*.
Page 142—For *huricanes* read *hurricanes*.
Page 204—For *1811* read *1812*.
Page 222—For *necessities* read *necessaries*.
Page 225—For *Armand* read *Armant*.

history of the discovery of the Mississippi river and valley, and the struggle for its possession by the three great European powers, Spain, France and England.

entered it. He found the Indians friendly and eager to trade. They lived in great towns composed of many small villages, and wore ornaments of gold.

Pamphilo de Narvaez. 1529.—The reports of these great Indian villages and the gold ornaments excited the greed and cupidity of Pamphilo de Narvaez. He saw in Florida a country rivaling Mexico and Peru for rich plunder. With four hundred men and four ships he set sail for it from Cuba. He landed at Appalachee Bay and marched inland, ordering his fleet to remain on the watch for him in the gulf. At first they found fields of corn and Indian villages; but afterward they journeyed for days through forest solitudes. Their cruelty to the Indians who fell into their hands kindled the fiercest retaliation against them. They were compelled to fight every step of their way forward. Their food gave out, and they suffered the tortures of famine. Some of their captives, forced to act as guides, led them only into the thickest of swamps and forest, out of which they had barely strength to extricate themselves. Their search was now, not for gold, but for food. Finally, weak, faint and dispirited, they returned to the seashore. Their ships were nowhere in sight. After wandering along the coast aimlessly they, in despair, set to work to build boats to get away from their terrible condition. They constructed a bellows and forge. All their iron, even spurs and stirrups, were made into hatchets and nails. Their shirts they made into sails. Cordage was twisted from their horse's hair and palmetto fibre. They made pitch of pine rosin and oakum of palmetto bark. Every man joined in the work. Every three days a horse was killed for food. At length, five vessels were finished and all embarked, crowding the boats to the water's edge. After six weeks they came to a river so great that it freshened the sea water into which it flowed, so that they could drink it. It was the Mississippi, the Espiritu Santo, of Pineda. In the rough water off its mouth, two of the boats capsized and all on board drowned, among them, Narvaez. The other three boats were driven ashore somewhere on the coast of Texas. Ten years afterward, four gaunt, haggard men, looking more like animals than human beings, arrived in Mexico. They were all of the Narvaez expedition which had survived the massacre of the Indians, starvation, and the hardships of their wanderings.

Hernando de Soto. 1539.—The last and most celebrated of the Spanish explorers of Florida was Hernando de Soto. De Soto had been with Pizarro in Peru, and had seen the vast wealth of the Indians. Like Pamphilo de Narvaez, he thought what Pizarro could plunder in Peru, he could plunder in Florida. He set sail from Havana in 1539, with 570 men, and 233 horses, in nine vessels. Never had so brilliant, so well armed, so well provided an expedition started from Spanish shores.

HERNANDO DE SOTO.

They landed at Tampa Bay, then called the Bay of Espiritu Santo. Here, with great pomp, De Soto took possession of the country for the Spanish king, and pitched his camp, confident of his future triumphs and booty.

But before daylight, the Indians, who had been secretly watching him, attacked him in vast numbers, with terrific yells. Many of his men were killed before he could retreat to his boats.

He commenced his march. The Indians, with the cruelty of Narvaez fresh in their memories, met the new invaders with all the fierceness of their savage nature. Learning that one of the men of the Narvaez expedition was a slave in a neighboring tribe, De Soto obtained possession of him as interpreter and guide.

But Florida held no better fate for him than for Ponce de Leon and Narvaez. The country was poor. Instead of great Indian cities, with temples filled with treasures to sack, he found only moderately sized and sparsely scattered Indian villages, and in the naked, poorly armed Indians the fiercest and most vindictive of foes, who fought like demons, and neither gave nor sought quarter. More than once, De Soto's coolness and courage alone saved his own life and the lives of his army from utter destruction. Hoping always to find the gold and treasures and triumphs further north, he marched day after day, on and on. Through the wild territories of the present States of Georgia and South Carolina he led his band, until they reached the Tennessee river. Turning then, upon his steps, he countermarched and journeyed toward the south, until the great village of the Manvilla or Mobile Indians rose before him. In a fierce battle here his men were killed in great numbers.

But almost as deadly as the Indian arrows, were the fevers that broke out in the army and thinned his ranks day by day. Leaving Mobile behind him, he pushed forward again to the northwest, opening his way through thickets and forests, climbing over steep hills, fording morasses, and crossing innumerable streams that cut through the country.

The Mississippi. 1541.—At length, after three years, he came to the banks of a mighty stream, over a mile wide, whose swift, turbid currents carried down great forest trees, which they had uprooted and torn away from their native soil. It was such a river as none in the army had ever seen before.

De Soto named it El Rio Grande de la Florida; the great river of Florida. He crossed it on rafts, at some points above the Arkansas, and led his army still forward toward the west. But he found in the west only what he had found in the east and in the north and in the south; sickness, misery, hardships, and Indians who pursued him like wolves. He came at last to the end of his hope and endurance. Retreat was ordered. Once more the army was turned; and they marched until they came again to the banks of the Mississippi. De Soto could march no further. The iron will and constitution which had seemed superhuman sank under the accumulated hardships, disappointments and ill health. Seized with a fever, he expired on the banks of the great river, surrounded by the gaunt, worn men who had followed him so trustfully and loyally.

With his dying breath he appointed as successor Louis de Muscoso, his faithful lieutenant. To insure the dead body of their leader from Indian outrage, his followers wrapped it in skins, enclosed it in a hollow tree trunk, and in the silence and darkness of midnight they conveyed it to the middle of the mighty stream and sank it under the depths of its yellow currents.*

Muscoso made an attempt to reach Mexico by land; but he was forced to return to the Mississippi, where he and his men built boats, and so reached the mouth of the river. The vindictive Indians pursued them to the last, ambushing them from the banks and killing them with their deadly arrows. Setting sail upon the gulf, they reached, at last, the Spanish settlement on the coast of Mexico. More than half of their number had perished.

QUESTIONS.

How did Louisiana first become known to Europeans? Did Columbus know anything of the Mississippi? Who was Americus Vespucius? What coasts did he probably explore on the first voyage? When is the Mississippi first seen on a map? Was the exploration of Florida followed up? What was Bimini? Relate Indian stories about it? Who was Ponce de Leon? Why did he call the country Florida?

---

* The precise locality has never been determined, but it is supposed to be near the mouth of the Red river.

Relate his voyage? Who was Pineda? What did he name the Mississippi? Give an account of the expedition of Pamphilo de Narvaez? Who was Hernando de Soto? What did he hope to gain in Florida? Give an account of his march? When did he come to the Mississippi? What did he name it? Continue his march? Who was his successor? How was De Soto buried? What of Muscoso?

———•◆•———

CHAPTER II.

FRENCH EXPLORERS.

Re-discovery of the Mississippi. 1669.— One hundred and thirty-two years the Mississippi flowed over the dead body of De Soto, before another white man came into touch with its history. The fact of its existence had passed from memory, and lived only in old charts and records stored in Spanish archives.

And now its chronicle takes us to a different country, and to a different nation. Instead of Spain and Spaniards, we have to do with France and the French, and instead of Cuba and the Gulf of Mexico, we must start from distant Canada and the Great Northern Lakes of America.

Let us study it on the map.

It will be seen that the French had entered and taken possession of the St. Lawrence river. They had founded the cities of Quebec and Montreal upon it, and made settlements in the neighboring regions. Little by little their missionaries and pioneers were advancing west, planting the cross and the standard of France in the territory of the great lakes, Ontario, Erie, Huron, Michigan and Superior. From the Indians that visited these mission houses and trading stations came the account of the vast country lying still further west and south; a country unknown and unexplored yet by the white men. The accounts were not those by which the cupidity of the Spaniards had been aroused and they lured to

OLD MAP OF THE MISSISSIPPI VALLEY.

disaster. These Indians described no fabulous kingdom filled with gold and silver and precious stones. They spoke only of the wonders of nature; grand scenery, gigantic mountains, huge cataracts, immense forests and prairies, and boundless hunting fields swarming with game. But above all, they described a great river that they crossed to come to Canada, a river they called the Mississippi, which they said flowed the entire length of the continent, through a valley teeming with riches and peopled with innumerable savage tribes to convert to the Christian faith and subdue to France. These stories, drifting to Montreal and Quebec, came to the ears of the Governor of Canada and of his intendant. But before reaching Montreal the stories had to pass through the settlement of the most celebrated pioneer France ever possessed in this country, Robert Cavalier de la Salle.

La Salle. 1669.—Robert Cavalier de la Salle was born in the city of Rouen, in Normandy, France. He was

educated in the religious schools of the time, and came to Canada at the age of twenty-three, determined to make a name and fortune in New France, as it was called. He obtained a large grant of land on the St. Lawrence, a few miles above Montreal. Here clearing the forests and superintending the building of houses for his settlers, he would, at the close of the

LA SALLE.

day, look out to that part of the heavens bright with the rays of the setting sun, and he would think about the vast un-

known region that lay between him and the west, and about
the Indian stories of the great river that flowed through it to
the sea on the other side of the continent; a river so long, the
Indians said, that it would take nine months to reach the
end.

La Salle, like most men of his day, thought that China lay
just on the other side of this continent, consequently any
river that flowed straight west to the sea would furnish a
new, short and easy route between Europe and Asia. To
be the first explorer of this route would indeed gain him
fame and fortune.

He hastened to Quebec and laid his plans to explore it before the governor, who gave his consent but no money. La
Salle, without hesitation, sold his settlement and with the
money bought canoes and hired men. The expedition started
from his settlement, which, as though it were really the first
step on the road to China, received the name of "La Chine."

They paddled up the St. Lawrence to Lake Ontario and
stopped at an Indian village to get a guide to the head waters
of the Ohio, which would conduct them into the Mississippi.

Louis Joliet.—Here La Salle met the man whose name
with his own was to be inseparably connected with the Mississippi. This was Louis Joliet. He was a young man of
about La Salle's age, and like him full of energy and ambition. He was a fur trader and pioneer, and was just returning from an expedition to Lake Superior. He also had
heard of the Mississippi, but knew nothing beyond what the
Indians had told him.

La Salle proceeded on his way through Lake Erie, into the
Ohio river, which he explored a long distance. Then returning he passed through Lakes Huron and Michigan, and
crossed into the Illinois river and explored it. He was gone
on his expedition two years. He never reached the Mississippi; but he had learned the way to get into it. He returned

to Canada for a larger expedition to carry out the larger schemes he had formed.

Joliet and Marquette. 1672.—In the meantime a new governor was put over Canada; the Count de Frontenac. The intendant, relating to him all the stories about the Mississippi, advised him to pursue its discovery and exploration, and named Joliet as the proper man to be employed for it. Frontenac accepted both the advice of the intendant and the man of his choice, and Louis Joliet was commissioned to discover and explore the Mississippi. Father Jacques Marquette, a Jesuit priest at Michilimakinak, was selected to accompany him.

Marquette. 1673.—Jacques Marquette was one of the noblest and purest missionaries that ever came to this country. Born of good and honorable family, in France, he sailed to Canada before he was thirty, to devote himself to the conversion of the savages. He learned six of their languages, and cheerfully braved all the dangers of their barbarous tempers, and the hardships of frontier life, to carry on his work among them. Far out on the great lakes he had advanced his missions, but an unexpected outbreak of the savages had driven him back to Michilimakinak. Here it was that Joliet found him and gave him the governor's commission. Marquette, in his lonely post, had heard much from the Indians about the Mississippi. As he thought over its majestic size; of the mildness and fertility of its great valley, and of the number of Indian tribes living in it, it became the dearest wish of his heart to christianize so favored a region. With joy, therefore, he consented to accompany Joliet. Their preparations were soon made. They consisted of two birch bark canoes, five men, and a supply of smoked meat and Indian corn. They started in the most beautiful time of the year in that region; in the spring, the month of May.

Joliet and Marquette. 1672.—As we followed La Salle, let us follow Joliet and Marquette also on the map. They

journeyed around the mouth of Lake Michigan until they
reached the mission of Father Claude Allouez.* Here
they turned into Fox river, which led them across Lake
Winnebago, and through a vast prairie country filled with
wild rice, in which great flocks of birds fed. They
passed villages of Kickapoo Indians to whom the priest and
Joliet explained their expedition. The Indians stared with
wonder at their temerity and tried to dissuade them from so
perilous a journey, by telling them the most horrible tales of
the cruelty and treachery of the Indians along the Mississippi.

The priest and pioneer were not to be frightened, however. They asked for guides and set out as soon as possible.
They followed Fox river to the end, carried their canoes over
to the Wisconsin, and launched them in that river.

Mississippi Discovered.—For ten days they paddled
down the Wisconsin, until from their right a broad, rapid
current dashed across their course. It was the Upper Mississippi! Into it they turned their canoes. It bore them
rapidly along. They gazed with wonder and awe at the
panorama which nature here unfolded to them, hour after
hour and day after day, as they advanced. The banks,
covered with gigantic virgin forests, now rose into perpen-
dicular heights, now sank into undulating plains. Wild
animals darted in the thickets; from the edge of illimitable
prairies buffalo stared at them from under their shaggy
manes. They hauled up all kinds of strange fish in their
nets. They no longer camped on the shores at night. Mind-
ful of the Indians of the region, after cooking their supper
on land, they carefully extinguished their fires, and, paddling
out into the stream, anchored and slept there, with sentinels
on watch. But no human being was to be seen. At last,
one day, on the western bank, footprints in the mud caught
their eyes. They were found to lead to a well beaten path,

---

*A devoted Jesuit priest, who founded as early as 1670 this mission at St
Francis Xavier, as he named Green Bay.

across the forest towards a prairie. Leaving their canoes in charge of the others, Marquette and Joliet set out to follow the path. They walked until they saw seven Indian villages in the distance. Then creeping cautiously along, they came near enough to hear talking in the wigwams. With a shout they made themselves known, and paused in anxious doubt whether their reception would be that of friends or foes. The Indians swarmed out of their wigwams like wasps out of their nests. For an instant all was wild excitement and confusion. Then calumet bearers were seen advancing with their peace pipes. Marquette and Joliet received them thankfully.

The Indians proved to be the Illinois. Far from being foes they were most friendly to the French. A grand reception was at once held, which all the warriors, squaws and children attended. Marquette, standing forth among them, proclaimed his sacred message of the Christian faith, and the nature of the enterprise upon which he and Joliet were engaged. The chief of the tribe responded in a speech, in which he expressed his joy at seeing the white men and his admiration of them, but implored them to proceed no further in their hazardous undertaking.

All sat down now to a great feast, served in the highest Indian style. First there was a wooden bowl of sagamity or hominy, seasoned with bits of meat and grease, which the Indians fed to their guests with wooden spoons, as though they were infants. Then came fish. The Indians carefully removing the bones and blowing on the morsels to cool them, placed them with their own fingers in the mouths of their guests. The greatest savage luxury, roast dog, was then presented, but learning that it was not palatable to the priest, the Indians politely substituted buffalo meat in its stead. The night was passed talking and sleeping, stretched out on buffalo skins on the ground. The next morning an escort of six hundred followed Marquette and his friend to

their canoes, and waved them farewell as they pushed from
the bank and paddled out of sight down the stream.

The canoes passed the mouth of the Illinois, and shortly
afterwards came to a huge towering rock, on the face of
which the Indians had painted hideous monsters in red,
green and yellow. The good priest, terrified at what he
considered the work of the devil, hurried away from it, with
many prayers and signs of the cross.

And now, the great, rushing, yellow torrent of the Missouri
poured into the stream before the travelers, turning the currents into a muddy brown. Their canoes almost upset in
the sudden whirlpool and eddies. On they paddled, past the
site of the present city of St. Louis and the mouth of the
Ohio. The highland scenery changed into lowland scenery;
mosquitoes made their appearance. A few miles above the
mouth of the Arkansas they came to the village of the Kappas Indians, who at first sight gave furious war cries and
seized bows and arrows and made most terrific demonstra-
tions. They were pacified, however, and feasted the voyagers and permitted them to pursue their way unharmed.

At the mouth of the Arkansas was a large village of the
Arkansas Indians. These received the travelers well and
entertained them hospitably.

Marquette and Joliet decided that this should be the end
of their exploration. They had found out that the Mississippi flowed south, not west, and that it emptied into the
Gulf of Mexico, not into the Gulf of California. Thinking
themselves much nearer the mouth of it than they really
were, they feared if they went further they might fall into
the hands of the Spaniards or of some hostile Indians, and so
not be able to return at all.

The canoes headed up stream, and they retraced their
·rse to the Illinois, which they entered and so reached Lake
·higan and the mission house at Green Lake. But mid-
ımer heat and the long voyage were too much for the deli-

cate body of the priest. He fell ill, and on reaching Green Bay was too weak to continue the journey. It was then the end of September. Joliet proceeded to Quebec alone. He gave the governor the account of his and Marquette's voyage. Frontenac, delighted with the success of it, ordered public rejoicings, and, in sign of the French triumph, changed the name of the great river from Mississippi to Colbert, after the enlightened minister of Louis XIV.

The saintly Marquette remained at Green Bay a year. Thinking then that his health was sufficiently restored, he returned to the beautiful country of the Illinois to found a mission there. He was received like an angel from heaven by the Indians, and was entering on his pious work, when his disease came upon him again. He hastened his departure, but he was not able to arrive at Green Bay; his sufferings increased so violently that he was forced to stop on the shores of Lake Michigan, where he expired and was buried.

QUESTIONS.

How many years after De Soto before the Mississippi was again visited by white men? Describe the advance of the French into Canada. How did they hear of the Mississippi? Who was La Salle? How did the idea of exploring the west come to him? What country did he think to reach in crossing the continent to the west? Relate what followed. Who was Joliet? Continue with La Salle's expedition. Did he get into the Mississippi? Who was the new governor of Canada? Who was named to accompany Joliet? Who was Marquette? How did Marquette and Joliet get into the Mississippi? What Indian village did they pass? What did the Indians tell them of the Indians along the Mississippi? Describe the upper Mississippi. Relate the journey of Joliet and Marquette. Arrival of Joliet in Canada? Death of Marquette? After whom did Frontenac name the Mississippi?

CHAPTER III.

FRENCH EXPLORERS CONTINUED.

La Salle meanwhile had not been idle. Having thoroughly explored the two ways to the Mississippi, he had set about to make his plans and preparations to take possession of the river itself. His plans, as a look at the map will show, were very grand and of vast importance to France. He proposed not only to explore the Mississippi to its mouth, but to build forts and trading posts as he went along in all favorable places, particularly at the mouths of those great rivers that flowed into the Mississippi.

As France already possessed the great lakes at the north, this would make her mistress of all the great waterways of the country and give her the monopoly of all its trade. It was a scheme that instantly found favor with Frontenac, and as a first step toward accomplishing it he gave to La Salle the new fort he had just built, Fort Frontenac, and all the trading privileges attached to it. But to carry out such a scheme required a great outlay of money. La Salle went to France, where he secured the favor of the king and raised money for the enterprise, and in addition gained a friend and companion whose loyal faithfulness was never to swerve from him. This was Henri de Tonty, an Italian officer, surnamed the "Iron Hand," from an artificial hand of metal which he wore to replace the one he had lost in the wars.*

For a year after his return to Canada La Salle was busily engaged making his preparations. An expedition of this size could not be carried in canoes; large vessels were needed to convey the supplies of men, arms, ammunition, provisions and building material across the great lakes, and to bring back to Canada the large stores of furs which La Salle ex-

---

*Tonty wore a glove over it, and made good use of it afterwards to astonish and keep the Indians in awe of him; sometimes, with a slight tap from it cracking their skulls or knocking out their teeth.

pected to get from the Indians. He got his party together and started from Frontenac, and advanced to Niagara river, where they stopped to build a fort, and a vessel which was named the Griffin. They embarked again, and, sailing through Lakes Erie and Huron, and Lake Michigan, came to the mouth of the St. Joseph river. Here they stopped and built a fort, Fort Miami.

But it is one thing to plan expeditions and another to carry them out. La Salle, for all his courage and fortitude, was no leader. Proud, haughty, reserved and suspicious, ✓ his men, instead of loving him, learned to dislike and fear him. They deceived him, and stole from him; they deserted at every opportunity; they even tried to assassinate him.

From Fort Miami the Griffin was sent back to Canada loaded with a wealthy cargo of furs gathered from the Indians.

Nothing was ever afterward heard of the vessel or cargo. La Salle always thought that the captain had scuttled her and made away with the furs, which in those days were as good as gold. He pushed on in canoes up the St. Joseph to its end, and carried his canoes over the portage to the Kankakee, which flowed into the Illinois. But the Illinois Indians, so gentle and hospitable to Marquette, were distrustful of and savage to La Salle. French traders, jealous of La Salle's fur monopoly, had poisoned the minds of the natives against him. He built his third fort on the Illinois river, a few miles above the Indian village on Lake Peoria. From messengers from Canada he heard here, besides the loss of the Griffin, that his creditors had seized his property at Fort Frontenac. From his griefs and disappointments in the enterprise he gave this stronghold the appropriate name of "Creve-Cœur" (Broken Heart).

With the Griffin and all his furs lost, his property in Canada seized, his men deserting and mutinous, provisions exhausted and no means at hand to replace them, La Salle saw himself forced to go to Canada for new supplies. He left

Fort Creve-Cœur in command of Tonty and set out with four men and an Indian guide. It was in early spring, the deep snow lay white upon the ground, the rivers and lakes were frozen over. He made the journey, over a thousand miles, mostly on foot with snow shoes, dragging his canoe after him.*

He hastened through his business in Canada, and in the autumn he once more paddled his canoe through the waters of the St. Joseph, towards his fort. But what a different scene met his eye as he advanced. Fort Miami deserted and destroyed; the great towns of the Illinois a shocking sight of rapine, cruelty and outrage; blood and corpses, fire and havoc everywhere. He pushed on to Fort Creve-Cœur and Tonty. The fort was demolished, no human being visible. The bloody Iroquois had passed over the country, and nothing but the silent forests were left to bear witness to the thoroughness of their work.

But the indefatigable explorer was only the more resolved not to give up. He had to return to Canada again and make a new start on his journey. He searched in every direction for traces of Tonty. He had given him up as massacred, when from some Indians on Green Bay he heard that the " Iron Hand " was still alive among the Indians of Lake Ontario. La Salle sped on, found him, and together they commenced at the very beginning again to form their expedition.

Success of La Salle. 1682.—They set out in the early winter, fifty-four of them, in canoes. Following the route with which they were now familiar, they got into the Illinois, and from it into the Mississippi.

---

* Before starting from the fort, La Salle sent a priest in the expedition, named Hennepin, to explore the sources of the Illinois river. Hennepin was captured by the Sioux Indians and carried far up in the northwest. At the Falls of St. Anthony, which he named after his patron saint, he was rescued by a Canadian "coureur de bois" (adventurer). Hennepin did not return to Fort Creve-Cœur, but went on to Canada, where he published an account of his adventures. After La Salle's death, Hennepin claimed that, besides going up to the Falls of St. Anthony, he had descended to the mouth of the river, and that he, not La Salle, was entitled to the honor of its first exploration. His claim was proved to be false, and he untrustworthy.

They paddled down the Mississippi, gazing, as Marquette and Joliet had done, with awe and wonder on the mighty stream turning and twisting before them through its forest-covered heights and slopes. Camping on the Chickasaw bluffs they built a fort which they named Fort Prudhomme, after one of the men who went hunting in the woods and did not return. After six days' continual searching for him, La Salle concluded he must have been killed and was proceeding without him, when he was found and brought to camp, almost dead from hunger and fatigue.

They stopped at the Kappas and Arkansas villages at the mouth of the Arkansas river, which had formed the limit of Marquette's and Joliet's explorations. The Indians showed themselves gentle, kind hearted and hospitable. When the smoking, feasting and entertainment following their reception was over, La Salle, with great pomp and ceremony, erected a cross bearing the arms of the king of France. The priest chanted a Latin hymn, the soldiers shouted " Vive le roi!" and La Salle in a loud voice proclaimed that he took possession of the whole country in the name of the king of France. The Indians standing around stared in wonder and admiration.

Arkansas guides piloted the party the rest of their way down the river. They showed La Salle on the right hand side of the river the path that led to the great Tensas village, on Lake Tensas, a few miles inland. While the rest of the expedition waited at the river landing, Tonty with some of the men went on a visit to it.

Great Tensas Village. 1682.—It was indeed a great village; greater and handsomer than any Tonty had ever seen in America. The wigwams were large and well built; their shape round. The walls were of pickets plastered with mortar, made of clay and moss; the roofs were conical shaped, formed of split canes fastened together, with a hole in the pointed centre for a chimney. The temple of the sun and the lodge of the chief were built like the other wigwams, only larger and handsomer. On the roof of the temple and on each side the entrance were daubed rude pictures of animals. The inside was a dark, gloomy bare room, in which stood a kind of altar; before it burned a perpetual fire from three logs placed end to end. The temple was surrounded by a palisade on which was stuck the heads of the victims sacrificed to the sun god; and before the door was a block of wood on which lay braids of hair, also from the sacrificed. The chief and dignitaries of the village wore white mantles woven from the bark of the mulberry tree. They all came in state to visit La Salle at the bank of the river and returned loaded with presents which the generous French-man had bestowed upon them.

Down to the Mouth of the Mississippi. 1682.—The explorers next stopped at the Natchez village, which in size and appearance was very like the Tensas. La Salle erected another cross here. The Houmas village, which came next, was passed in a fog without being seen.

Then came Red river, rolling from the west, churning up the Mississippi into eddies and whirlpools and emptying into it great floating trees and masses of driftwood. The canoes glided unknowingly over the spot where the dead body of the unfortunate De Soto had been sunk in midnight burial, and sped unmolested between the banks from which the ambushed warriors had sent their deadly arrows into Muscoso's flying band. At the Quinipissas village, warlike sounds broke into their peaceful, calm advance. But La Salle, anxious to avoid strife and bloodshed, hastened by unheed-ing. He stopped at a village he saw on the left bank of the river. It was deserted, and some of the cabins were filled with corpses. It was the village of the Tangipahoas, destroyed by their enemies only a few days before.

Now the river divided into three channels. The canoes paddled into them—and now the bright gleaming gulf opened out before them. Eyes gladened—Voices rose in shouts—The journey was ended—The task at last accomplished—The Mississippi explored to its very mouth!

Taking Possession of the Mississippi. 1682.—La Salle jumped to the land. By the grace of God and his own indomitable will the plans formed at La Chine thirteen years before, while his eyes looked across the forest toward the setting sun, had been realized.

After sounding and exploring all around the mouth of the river, the canoes filed up stream again and paddled along until they came to where the banks rose dry and firm above the muddy current. Here all landed—La Salle, Tonty, priests, Frenchmen, Canadians, Indians. After prayers and hymns of thanksgiving and praise, a great column was made and erected, bearing the arms of the king of France. La Salle, standing beside the column, made the following proclamation in a loud voice:

"In the name of the most high, mighty, invincible and victorious
"Prince, Louis the Great, by the grace of God King of France and of
"Navarre, fourteenth of that name, I, this 9th day of April, 1682, in
"virtue of the commission of his Majesty, which I hold in my hand, and
"which may be seen by all whom it may concern, have taken, and do
"now take in the name of his Majesty and of his successors to the crown,
"possession of this country of Louisiana, the seas, harbors, ports,
"bays, adjacent straits, and all the nations, peoples, provinces, towns,
"cities, villages, mines, minerals, fisheries, streams and rivers within
"the extent of the said Louisiana, from the mouth of the great river,
"St. Louis, otherwise called the Ohio, as also along the river Colbert,
"or Mississippi, and the rivers which discharge themselves thereinto,
"   . . . from its source as far as its mouth at the sea or Gulf of
"Mexico . . . from the assurance we have from the natives of
"this country that we were the first Europeans who have descended
"or ascended the said river Colbert; thereby protesting against all
"who may hereafter undertake to invade any or all of these aforesaid
"countries or lands to the prejudice of the rights of his Majesty, ac-
"quired by consent of the natives dwelling therein; of which and
"of all else that is needful, I hereby take to witness those who hear
"me, and demand an act of the notary, here present.

The cross was then planted with further ceremonies and near it was buried a leaden plate engraved with the arms of the king of France, and the inscription, *Ludovicus Magnus regnat:* Louis the Great reigns.

La Salle fell ill on the return voyage and was forced to stop at Fort Prudhomme, while Tonty carried the report of the expedition to Canada. By the middle of summer he was able to go to Fort Miami. There he remained for a year with Tonty, arranging plans for a new expedition. He then went to Canada and sailed to France.

QUESTIONS.

What was La Salle doing meanwhile? Give an account of his schemes? What friend did he gain in France? Continue La Salle's operations, start and journey? What fort did he build on the St. Joseph? Continue account of journey? What was the location and name of his third fort? Why was La Salle forced to return to Canada? Relate his return? Who and what was Hennepin? Continue account of La Salle? Where is Fort Prudhomme? Describe Kappas and Arkansas village? Describe the great Tensas village? Quinipissas village? The deserted Tangipahoa village? Describe the act of taking possession?

CHAPTER IV.

FRENCH EXPLORERS CONTINUED.

La Salle's new expedition was to be an entirely different enterprise from the last. Instead of undertaking again the long, difficult and dangerous journey from Canada, La Salle decided to sail direct from France, and found a colony at the mouth of the Mississippi, fetching at once all the settlers and materials necessary. When the colony was fairly established he intended to open communications with Canada, and build his line of forts and trading posts along the way to it. The Mississippi, it is true, did not lead to the west and to China, but it flowed south, leading to the mines of Mexico and the trading centres of Spanish America and the West Indies. He had visions of discovering in Louisiana gold and silver mines as rich as those in Mexico, and of monopolizing all the commerce of the Gulf of Mexico and the Carribean Sea. He even looked forward, in case of a war between France and Spain, to the invading and capturing of Mexico itself.

The court of France granted all that was needed for the new colony and forts, and La Salle, confident and full of hope, sailed with two hundred and eighty colonists, in four ships, from La Rochelle, in July, 1684. But from its beginning the enterprise seemed doomed to disaster and misfortune.

The same unhappy faults of temper which made La Salle unpopular with his subordinates and companions before, produced dissensions again. His jealousy and tyranny became unbearable. Before he was half way across the ocean his men hated him; he was in dispute with every officer in the squadron, and in open quarrel with Mr. de Beaujeu, the officer of the royal navy sent to escort him. At St. Domingo many of his men deserted. The rest suffered cruelly from an epidemic of fever then raging there. La Salle himself fell dangerously ill of it, and while he was slowly recovering he heard of the capture of one of his vessels and valuable cargo by the buccaneers. The news gave him a relapse, from which he came near dying. Finally he was able to set sail in the month of December.

On the Gulf Coast. 1685.—On New Year's day, 1685, they came to anchor in sight of land.

When he was at the mouth of the Mississippi, La Salle had taken its latitude, but not its longitude; consequently he had to steer his ships with only half knowledge of the location of the point he was steering for. Had he sailed due north from the channel into the gulf, he would have hit it,

but he heard such exaggerated accounts of the easterly currents of the Gulf of Mexico that he thought he must take a
westerly course to counteract them.   A look at the map will
show the result of his error.   Instead of landing near the
mouth of the Mississippi he landed four hundred miles away
on the coast of Texas.

The low sandy shore was the same as the shore around the
Mississippi, and its configuration was not unlike the delta. La
Salle was convinced that it was the delta of the Mississippi
and would hear no contrary opinion from any of his officers.
The ships sailed along the coast until they came to Matagorda Bay; there the colony disembarked. One of the freight
vessels wrecked entering the harbor and most of her cargo
was lost. De Beaujeu, the royal escort, with his vessel, sailed
back to France. A fort was built named Fort St. Louis, and
the emigrants struggled along heroically for two years in their
forlorn condition, building lodgings and fortifications and
tilling the ground.   But the seasons were against them, provisions and the supplies of clothing gave out, and sickness
attacked them.   The little graveyard filled, fuller and fuller.
Worst of all, the last remaining vessel was wrecked and lost,
and all communication with the mother country, all hope
from the outside world, was cut off. Despair settled over the
fort and its inmates. During this trying period, La Salle,
always great in misfortunes, showed marvelous patience,
courage and fortitude, day and night devoting himself to
to those who had trusted their future to him.   He was the
last of the band, however, to open his eyes to the facts of
his desperate situation, that instead of being on the Mississippi, he and his colony were castaways on an unknown and
unexplored shore, out of reach of help of any French settlement.

End of La Salle. 1687.—La Salle adopted the only re-
ͺurce left him—to go on foot to Canada and fetch back
ᵻ to the colony. He assembled what was left of his

wretched companions, only about forty now, and announced
his resolution to them. He selected those who were to accompany him, about twenty, among them his brother, the
Abbe Cavalier, and his two nephews, a priest, and the young
Frenchman, Joutel, who afterward wrote an account of the
journey. The parting was sad and solemn, the women and
young girls weeping bitterly.

La Salle, still, notwithstanding the desperate nature of his
mission, could not lay aside his haughty demeanor to his
companions. The men under him, naturally lawless, had become savage with suffering and disappointment. They were
not disposed to stand any discipline from their superiors. A
dispute between some of them and La Salle's nephew resulted in the assassination of the nephew. The assassins
then, for their own safety, forced all the men to join them,
and to make themselves perfectly secure, and satisfy their
long hatred against La Salle, waylaid him and murdered
him.

Joutel, the priest, and La Salle's brother made their escape from the assassins. Reaching the Arkansas, they got
into the Mississippi, and from thence to Canada and France,
where they arrived eighteen months after leaving the coast
of Texas. Their appeal to the king in behalf of their companions of Fort St. Louis was in vain. Louis XIV would
do nothing for them. Their fate was indeed most tragic.
The Indians fell upon the fort and slaughtered all the inmates with the exception of two children and one man, whom
they kept prisoners. The Spaniards, who claimed this part
of the country, sailing over there not long afterwards to drive
the French away, found nothing but dilapidated walls and
buildings and mutilated corpses. One man, however, had
made a life-saving effort for La Salle. This was Tonty. In his
distant fort on the Illinois river, he heard from Indians and
Canadian tramps that La Salle was in the mouth of the river,
shipwrecked and a prey to the Indians. Raising a band of

Canadians, he with all speed journeyed there.   He found, of course, no trace of La Salle nor of his expedition.

QUESTIONS.

How was the new expedition to be different from the last? What were La Salle's plans when the colony was established? When and with how many did he sail? What appears from the very beginning? What happened at St. Domingo? What did he do when the truth broke upon him? What happened? Who escaped? What did they do in France? What was the fate of the colony? Who made an at-tempt in behalf of La Salle?

CHAPTER V.

FRENCH EXPLORERS CONTINUED.

France was at the time plunged in war, fighting Spain, England, and the other principal powers of Europe com-bined against her in the league called the Holy Alliance. The Mississippi, the grand new territory of Louisiana, and the baandoned massacred colony of Matagorda Bay, were for-gotten in the excitement of great battles and sieges nearer home.   But as soon as the peace of Ryswick was signed (1697), Louis XIV showed himself eager enough to take up and push La Salle's great scheme.

Louis XIV, however, was not the only king of Europe who had his eyes fiexd on the rare prize of the Mississippi and Louisiana.   There was, besides, William III, king of England, anxious to gain it to add to his possessions in America.   And there was also Charles II, king of Spain, determined that no power except his should be established over the gulf, and near his precious mines of Mexico.

Louis XIV's minister of marine was the Count Louis de Pontchartrain, a man of great moral worth and enlighten-nent. The Count de Pontchartrain's secretary and assistant ras his son, Jerome Count de Maurepas, a young man of brilliant qualities, filled with ambition for himself and for the glory of France. It was to these two men that France owed her triumphs over England and Spain in the contest for the possession of the Mississippi and Louisiana.

When Louis XIV announced, after the peace of Ryswick, his determination to continue La Salle's enterprise, Pontchartrain, with energy and vigor, fitted out the expedition for it, and Maurepas produced the man to lead it. This man was the great Canadian seaman, Pierre Lemoyne d'Iberville.

Iberville. 1698.—Iberville was the son of Charles Le Moyne, of Dieppe, Normandy, one of the earliest and most

IBERVILLE.

noted settlers of Canada. He was one of nine brothers, all of whom distinguished themselves working and fighting for their country.* Of all the nine, Iberville was the most glorious, and it is with pride that Louisiana points to h i m as her founder.

Before he was fourteen, he had become a good sailor by cruising in a vessel of his father's in the Gulf of St. Lawrence. After that he voyaged on the Atlantic, sailing with skilful navigators, to and fro, between Canada and France. Strong, active, daring and handsome, he never failed to please his superiors and secure the good fellowship of his subordinates; and there seemed no enterprise on land or sea perilous enough to daunt him. His

---

* The names of these famous brothers were Charles, Sieur de Longueuil; Jacques, Sieur de Sainte Helene; Paul Pierre, Sieur d'Iberville; Paul, Sieur de Maricourt; Francois, Sieur de Bienville; Joseph, Sieur de Serigny; Louis, Sieur de Chateaugnay I; Jean Baptiste, Sieur de Bienville II; Francois Marie, Sieur de Sauvole. Three of them, Sainte Helene, Chateaugnay, and Bienville I, were killed in battle. Four, Longueuil, Bienville II, Sauvole and Serigny, became governors of cities or provinces.

most famous exploits were against the English in Hudson's Bay and on the coast of New Foundland. In canoe or in snow shoes, brandishing gun, hatchet or cutlass, we see him ever in the front of his hardy band of Canadians and Indians, and always leading to success. From 1686, the year that the unfortunate La Salle was making his life and death struggle on the coast of Texas, until 1697, when the Peace of Ryswick put an end to the war with England, he was the hero of one brilliant action after another, until his name in the reports from Canada to France became the sure sign of French victory and English defeat.

When Maurepas, therefore, sent for Iberville and confided to him the mission of completing La Salle's work, he well knew that his man was one who had never disappointed expectations of a friend or foe.

Iberville's Expedition. 1698.—La Salle's failed plan was to be carried out. A colony was to be transported directly from France to the Mississippi and settled there ; communications afterwards opened by river to Canada, and forts built at the mouths of all the important streams emptying into the Mississippi.

Pontchartrain and Maurepas threw themselves heartily into pushing forward the preparations. Two frigates, the Badine and Marin, were fitted and manned with a picked crew; and two freight ships were purchased and filled generously with stores of ammunition, arms, provisions, presents for the Indians, etc. Iberville himself superintended everything on the spot; selected his men, tried, tested his arms, and examined the provisions and presents for the Indians. For in all his enterprises Iberville never left anything to the chance of another man's sense of duty.

Joutel was, after all his adventures, living peaceably in his native city of Rouen. Pontchartrain tried to induce him to join the expedition, but Joutel refused. He sent, however, to Iberville the journal he had written of La Salle's expedition. It contained only the accounts of a great failure, but there is no surer way to success than by studying the reasons of another's failure.

Everything being completed on the morning of the 24th of October, 1698, Iberville fired the signal from his frigate, the Badine, and led the way out of the harbor of Brest, followed by the Count de Surgeres in the Marin; the heavily loaded freight ships sailed slower behind them.

With Iberville sailed his young eighteen-year-old brother, Bienville, a midshipman; with the Count de Surgeres sailed, as lieutenant, the Sieur de Sauvole,* both destined to be governors of Louisiana.

One of the freight ships disappeared in a gale, off Madeira, and after a short search was given up as lost. The rest of the squadron, after a quick and uneventful voyage, arrived at St. Domingo, where they made a hasty stay for supplies of fresh water and food. Here the royal escort, the Marquis de Chateaumorant, on the warship Francois, joined them, and shortly afterwards, much to the delight of the whole squadron, the lost freight ship made her appearance, with her mast broken, but not otherwise injured by the gale.

Before he left France, Iberville had heard of an English expedition being fitted out also to discover and take possession of the mouth of the Mississippi, and he had made up his mind, if it were to be a race, to be the first at the goal; if a contest, to hold good, by ruse or force, his reputation against his rivals.

Some English vessels had been sighted off St. Domingo; fearing that they might belong to the English expedition, he hastened his departure, setting sail from the island on the last day of December. He took with him as pilot, Lawrence de Graff, one of the most noted buccaneers of the time and

---

* The Sieur de Sauvole is sometimes confounded with Sauvole, the brother of Iberville and Bienville. He, however, was no relation to them.

region, a man who had lived upon the Gulf of Mexico and knew it thoroughly.

They sailed through the channel of the Yucatan, and steered due north, across the Gulf of Mexico. Anchoring every night and sounding their way as they went along by day, they advanced slowly. It was not until the afternoon of the twenty-third day that land was sighted. Taking his bearings, Iberville found that he had struck the coast of Florida as he expected, just south of Apalachicola Bay.

De Graff had spoken of a beautiful harbor on the coast of Florida, well known to buccaneers, who went there for mast timber and to get shelter from storms. Iberville, anxious to find and take possession of it, commenced a systematic search for it. He sent a barge to row in and explore close along the shore, while he brought the ships in as near as their draught permitted, and scanned the land with his glasses. Mile after mile was thus passed. Suddenly the barge signaled a bay ahead with the masts of vessels in it. Iberville thought the vessels must be English. He fired the signal to halt. The vessels in the bay, taking it for a warlike demonstration, answered with a volley of musketry. Then a fog fell and the vessels saw nothing of one another for hours. When it lifted, Iberville sent a party ashore and found out that the harbor was the one he was in search of, but that the Spaniards were in possession and had named it Santa Maria de Galvez de Pensacola.

The disappointed French squadron remained at Pensacola several days and then set sail for Mobile Bay.

Fearing opposition from the Spaniards, Iberville concealed from them the real object of his expedition, giving out instead that he was in search of some roving coureurs de bois, to whom he was carrying the king's orders to return to Canada.

Mobile Bay. 1699.—The ships anchroed in front of Mobile Bay. Iberville, with his young brother, Bienville, crossed

to the long, narrow island that lay like a breakwater
between the gulf and the bay, and explored it, At one end
they came to a ghastly heap of human bones, left from some
ruthless Indian massacre ; so they named the island Massacre
Island.   A terrific storm broke over the fleet here. Iberville,
engaged in sounding the channel, was driven with his men
to one of the near little islands for shelter.   For three days
they were held there, storm-bound, the driving rain, mists
and spray shutting them off from even the sight of their vessels in the gulf.

When the storms had subsided and fair weather set in,
Iberville explored the shores of Mobile Bay.   Returning to
the ships, anchors were raised and sails set for another
stage of the search.

Mobile Point and Massacre Island dropped in the distance
behind them.   Before them, in the beautiful blue, glistening
waters to the north and northwest, other islands came into
view ; dots of white sand and green trees that seemed to float
on the dancing waves.   Iberville sent Bienville to look for
harborage in them from the south wind that was threatening
another storm.   Bienville returned after an unsuccessful
search and the ships sailed on anxiously in the stiffening
breeze.   Other islands appeared in the northwest, and nearer,
in the south, two flat, sandy surfaces.   Iberville ran into these
and found the shelter he needed.   It was Candlemas day, and
the islands received the name of Chandeleurs Islands.   In
the morning, Bienville was again sent out to look for a harborage among the islands to the north and a pass between
them.   This time his search was successful.   At daylight,
Iberville, leading the way in the Badine, steered his fleet
through the pass between the two islands and anchored safely
in the harbor of Ship Island.

His men, freed at last from their long confinement on ship-
board, spread themselves gladly over the small place, delight-
ing in the rare abundance of fish and oysters. The live stock

was landed; the swine were put on the adjoining island, which the sailors named Cat Island, on account of the quantities of little animals upon it, which they took for cats. The little animals were really raccoons, and it is said that in a few years the swine destroyed them all.

QUESTIONS.

What was the condition of France at the time? What followed after the Peace of Ryswick? Who, besides Louis XIV, wanted Louisiana? Who was the Count de Pontchartrain? Who the Count de Maurepas? Who was Iberville? How many brothers had he? When were his most famous exploits performed? Whose plan was to be carried out? When did Iberville sail? Who sailed as midshipman under him? Who as lieutenant under Surgères? Relate the voyage to San Domingo? What did Iberville hear before sailing from France? Whom did he take with him as pilot? How did he steer across the gulf? What part of the Florida coast was first sighted? What had De Graff spoken of? What harbor was it? Why did Iberville conceal his designs from the Spaniards? For what point did he set sail? Why was the island named Massacre? How was Chandeleur Islands named? Why was Cat Island so named?

CHAPTER VI.

FRENCH EXPLORERS CONTINUED.

North of Ship Island, about twenty miles away, the low, scalloping shore line of the mainland could be seen, and upon it, with glasses, Iberville could distinguish the forms of Indians moving about. He lost no time in sailing over there in a sloop, well provided with presents for the Indians and well protected by a crew of Canadians. Bienville accompanied him in a canoe. Landing, they followed the tracks of the Indians, and came to where they could see canoes full of them busily crossing to and fro between Deer Island and Biloxi. At sight of the white men the natives abandoned their canoes and fled in terror. The Canadians pursued, but were only able to come up with one of them, a poor old man who lay helpless on the beach, unable to move on account of a putrefying sore on his leg. He was moaning and shivering with cold and pain and seemed to expect instant death from the white men. The Canadians reassured him by signs, took him in their arms and carefully carried him higher up the beach—laid him on a buffalo skin and kindled a fire to warm him. They put a handsome present of tobacco near him, and, to show that they did not intend anything unfriendly, drew up the abandoned canoes of provisions on the beach and left them. A squaw, as old and almost as wretched as the man, seeing that the white men did nothing warlike, crept out of the woods where she had been hiding and watching, and joined the group. The Canadians withdrew and left them together.

During the night the old woman slipped away to carry the news and some of the tobacco to her tribe. In the morning the Canadians found a piteous spectacle; the fire had caught on the weeds and grasses around the old man, and the poor wretch lay half burned. The Canadians did what they could to ease his pains, but in a few moments he died.

The old squaw returned, bringing some of her tribe with her, and later in the day many more came slipping out of the forest to join in the smoking and feasting of the white men, and received some of the tobacco, hatchets, knives, beads and paint which Iberville distributed with a generous hand. He finally succeeded in gaining their good will and confidence sufficiently to induce three of the chiefs to go with him on a visit to the ships, Bienville and two Canadians being left behind as hostages.

Ship Island. 1698.—As the boats approached the ships the chiefs stood up and began to chant their peace songs. Their reception gratified their vanity exceedingly. Iberville had cannon shot off, and the ships put through their manœuvres and gave them a great feast with sagamity made with

prunes. He gave them, also, brandy to drink, which astonished them greatly, burning their stomachs so long after it
was swallowed. But what excited their greatest wonder and
admiration was the spy glass, by which they could see so far
with one eye, while the other eye stayed at home. They examined everything on the floating houses, as they called the
ships, with the greatest curiosity. They belonged to the
Annochy and Biloxi tribes and lived on the Pascagoula
river. They did not know anything of the Mississippi, nor
of any of the tribes met by La Salle.

When Iberville returned with them to the mainland, he
found Bienville making friends with a new set of Indians.
These were a party of Bayougoulas and Mongoulachas warriors who were out on a hunt, but hearing the sound of cannon
they had hastened to the seashore to find out what it was.
Much to Iberville's gratification they lived on the banks of
the Mississippi, which they called the Meschacébe, and knew
the tribes met by La Salle. Iberville gave them a store of
presents, among them a calumet or peace pipe, such as they
had never seen before. It was of metal, shaped like a ship
under full sail, flying the lily banner of France. The evening
was passed in a great jollity, with singing and dancing and
telling of stories around the camp fire. In the morning the
warriors left to continue their hunt, promising to return in
three days and guide Iberville by the little river they traveled
on into the Mississippi. They were to light a fire at the camp
on the seashore, as the signal of their return, and Iberville
was to answer by a cannon shot. Iberville sailed back to his
ships, elated. Once guided into the river, all that he had to
do to accomplish his task, was to follow it to its mouth, fix
the exact latitude and longitude, make his way to Ship
Island, get his vessels and sail there.

Twenty-four hours later, a day too soon for the appointment, the signal fire was descried on the mainland. Iberville,
with all haste, sailed over to the spot. But he found only

the forest ablaze from the fire; not an Indian was to be seen. He returned disappointed to Ship Island.

Looking for the Mouth of the Mississippi.—The next day, however, he had another expedition ready to execute his first plan. Two sloops were manned with a good force of Canadians, sailors and filibusters,* and provided with ample supplies of ammunition and food for six weeks and each carrying a canoe in tow. Iberville commanded one, Sauvole the other. They sailed from the ships, and steered south, where in clear water low lying groups of bare, sandy islands could be seen.

In the Mississippi Delta.—It was Friday, the 27th of February. The wind was from the southeast, with rain and fog. The sea tossed restlessly. Running the length of the first island, the boats entered the strange scene of the Mississippi delta. Far as the eye could reach, islands small and great rose before them. Some standing high and dry, others rippled over by the slightest wave. Here the water broadened out into deep, handsome bays; there it crested and curled into sheets of foam, over rising bottoms and sand bars. No vegetation was to be seen except willows and osiers. The men struggled with sail and oar to find a way through the watery maze; consuming hours to get around one island only to find another blocking their path. Well tired out at night, they pitched their camp on the nearest dry land. They made now and then catches of fish and gathered oysters to add to their fare. The only game they saw was wild-cats; great rough, red-furred animals. On Sunday such a furious storm broke over them that they could not leave their camp. The thunder pealed as they had never heard it before; the lightning flashed fearfully; the rain descended in torrents. The water rose until it stood two inches over the highest part of their island, and the waves swept it from end to end.

*The term filibuster is derived from "flibote," a small, fast sailing vessel used by the Dutch. It was applied to roving adventurers who formerly sailed the Gulf of Mexico in search of conquest and plunder.

The day was passed cutting osiers and piling them up to
stand on, catching rain for drinking water, and during the
showers hanging shivering over the smouldering fire to protect it.

Finding the Mississippi. Monday, March 2, 1699.—
On Monday the weather permitted an early start. Steering
always south and southeast, the sloops kept the irregular
shore line to the right in view, so as not to pass any river
that might be there. The northeast wind rose to a gale and
the sea broke over the small barks. The canoes were taken
up and shipped inside, and the men took turns holding their
gummed cloths down over the deck by main strength, to
keep the water from pouring in and swamping them. Tack-
ing this way and that, first off the shore for fear of being
beached, then on, for fear of being engulfed in the raging
sea, the sloops fought their way along. For three hours they
battled gallantly to double a rocky point that rose grim and
threatening before them. The night was coming on. The
bad weather showed no signs of abatement. Iberville saw
before him no hope. He must either be wrecked ashore or
perish at sea during the night. Determined to seize the one
chance of daylight for himself and his men, he grasped the
tiller, put his sloop about, and, with the wind full astern,
drove her upon the rocks. The other sloops followed his
example. But, to his wonder, as he approached, the rocks
opened out before him and through the openings whitish
muddy water gushed into the gulf. He steered into it, tasted
it; it was fresh; the Mississippi was discovered!

The murderous rocks were only driftwood, piled in huge,
fantastic shapes, covered with deposits of Mississippi mud,
hardened into cement by sun and wind! They looked indeed
like the palisades which made the Spaniards call the river the
Palissado.

The boats advanced up the river until they came to a good
camping place. Then landing, lighting their fires, and put-

ting their supper to cook, the men threw themselves upon the rushes and enjoyed the rest they had so richly earned.

It was the last Monday of the carnival; as the stars came out, and the savory fragrance of their homely repast stole upon the air, they could not help contrasting their day's work with the masquerading and frolicking of friends and relatives in the old world. And they exulted in the dangers they had run, and the brave success they had met, for, as Iberville said, it was a gallant task, discovering unknown shores in boats that were not large enough to keep to sea in a gale, and yet were too large to land on a shelving shore, where they touch and strand a mile out.

QUESTIONS.

What lay to the north of Ship Island? Relate what followed. Give episode of the old Indian. Describe the reception and entertainment of the Indians at Ship Island. To what tribe did they belong? Did they know anything of the Mississippi or of the Indians met by La Salle? What did Iberville find on his return to the mainland? To what tribe did these Indians belong? Where did they live? What did they promise Iberville? What followed? Continue with the start on Monday. What course did the boats pursue? Why? Describe the gale. Relate what followed. What were the murderous rocks at the mouth of the river? What had the Spaniards called the river? What day was it?

CHAPTER VII.

FRENCH EXPLORERS CONTINUED.

The next morning Mardi Gras, mass was celebrated, the Te Deum sung, and a cross and the arms of the king of France erected. The boats pushed off from the shore for the exploration of the river. Like De Soto and La Salle, Iberville gazed with awe at the mighty stream which rolled before him, whose currents bore down what appeared to be floating forests. The boats had hard work to make any head-

way with such a current against them; they needed a new
wind for every turn, and could not make much use of
their sails, and the men at the oars declared they rowed six
miles to progress one. Their first day's journey ended at the
little bayou named Mardi Gras for the day.

The low, grass covered banks began to rise higher and
higher as they advanced. Instead of willows and sedges,
oaks and magnolias and thickly grown forests gradually
made their appearance.

Bienville, paddling ahead to reconnoitre, would sometimes
startle up flocks of ducks and sarcelles; and sometimes deer,
wild beeves, raccoons and opossums running along the bank,
would tempt the Canadians into a hunt; and great was the
rejoicing around the camp fire when fresh game was brought
in to add to their larder. Several alligators were killed and
the meat cooked, but it was not exactly enjoyed. Every
afternoon when the camp was pitched the cannon was fired
off to attract the attention of any Indians thereabouts, and
Iberville would climb to the top of a tall tree to take obser-
vations of the new country about him. They saw no Indians
until the fifth day, when turning a bend the explorers came
upon two in a pirogue. But in a flash, they leaped to shore
and disappeared in the woods. A gun shot further on, five
pirogues full of Indians were seen. Iberville succeeded in
speaking with them. These Indians belonged to the Annochy
tribe, which lived, as we have seen, along the lake shores.
They gladly traded their stores of dried meat to the Frenchmen. One old fellow in particular was most enterprising;
spreading out his entire stock and sitting behind it in market
style, bargained the whole of it—a hundred pounds—for two
knives. The Annochys knew the Bayougoula hunters who
were met by Iberville and they gave him a guide to their village.

Site of New Orleans.—That night the camp was pitched
close to the spot selected by Bienville twenty years afterwards

for the site of New Orleans. Near by was a deserted Indian village formerly inhabited by the Quinpissas. It consisted of ten cabins, thatched with palmetto. On a tall point of the bank commanding the river, was a fortified oval shaped cabin, surrounded by a palisade. A few miles higher up the guide conducted Iberville to the portage used by the Indians in their journeys between the river and the lakes· Taking their pirogues out of the river, they had only to drag them over a short road to launch them into a bayou that ran into the lake. Both banks of the river in this locality were covered with canebrakes of enormous height and thickness.

At, Bayou Plaquemines, then called Bayou Ouacha, from the Ouacha Indians living on it, two large pirogues of Ouachas and Bayougoulas were met. As soon as the Bayougoulas heard that the French intended visiting their village, they turned back in their pirogues to announce the news, so that a reception could be prepared. The next day, when the boats arrived in sight of the landing, a pirogue of Bayougoula and Mongoulacha warriors came out to meet them, chanting peace songs and brandishing their calumets, gaily adorned with brilliant feathers. At the landing the white men, according to Indian notions of politeness, were tenderly helped from their boats, supported under their elbows, and conducted to where the chief sat, surrounded by the squaws and warriors of the united Bayougoula and Mongoulacha tribes. Mats of cane and skins were spread on the ground in a cleared space for the guests. In the centre, resting on two forked sticks, guarded by two warriors who never took their eyes from it, was the precious calumet presented by Iberville on the lake shore.

Traces of Tonty.—The chief, a man of great pride and dignity, wore a coat of blue French serge. Iberville's first question was to find out where it came from. The chief answered that it had been given him by Tonty, of the Iron Hand, who had paid his tribe a visit in passing along

the river. The next day, when Iberville went over to the
village, a few miles inland from the river, he discovered
among the treasures of the temple a glass bottle, which the
Iron Hand had also left in the tribe.

The Bayougoulas and Mongoulachas. 1699.—The village of the Bayougoulas and Mongoulachas resembled almost
identically that of the Tensas. There were only one hundred and fifty inhabitants in the village, a great many having
died off in a recent epidemic. The cabins were cleanly kept.
The bed frames, about two feet above the ground, had bark-
covered branches the size of a man's arm, laid close together
for mattresses, cane mats for sheets, and skins for covering.
The only other furniture was earthen pots which the women
made very nicely. The women tied their hair high on top of
their heads and wore girdles of cloth woven from the fibres
of trees, colored red and white and fringed with long cords
that fell to the knee and shook with every movement of the
body. The little girls wore girdles of moss. The men went
naked except on grand occasions, when they tied around
them a kind of sash made of feathers strung together and
weighted at the ends with bits of stone or metal, which
jangled and tinkled gaily when they danced. The warriors
were handsome, well made and active, but very lazy. The
fields for corn and pumpkin were small, and were tilled
with implements of bone. When the crops were gathered
they were used as play grounds by the tribes. There were
a few chickens in the tribe which were said to have come
from tribes in the far west, evidently from some of the Spanish possessions. The dead, wrapped in straw mats, were
placed on little conical, covered platforms, raised all around
the village, attracting great crowds of buzzards and dissem-
inating loathsome odors.

The tribe regarded the opossum with particular venera-
tion, but the French found it only a hideous combination of

ugliness, with its pig's head, rat's tail, badger's skin and pouched stomach.

To requite the hospitality and friendliness of these Indians, Iberville spread upon the ground before them a dazzling array of presents—scarlet doublets embroidered in gold, scarlet hose, blankets, shirts, mirrors, beads, hatchets and knives. The Indians gave also of their best in return; feasts and entertainments, abundant supplies of corn and twelve large dressed deer skins.

From accounts that he had of La Salle's Mississippi exploration, Iberville understood that there was a fork about here in the river. His plan was to return to the gulf by this fork. But when he questioned the Bayougoulas they denied that there was any fork in the river, and said that when Tonty went to rescue La Salle he had paddled the same way both up and down the Mississippi. Fearing that the Bayougoulas might be deceiving him and concealing one of the outlets of the Mississippi, Iberville decided to go on to the next tribe, the Houmas, and interview them. One of the Bayougoula chiefs and a party of warriors accompanied him as guides and introducers to the Houmas.

Manchac.—On the way the Bayougoula chief pointed out on the right a small stream, which he said was the only stream he knew that ran from the Mississippi into the gulf. It was called Ascantia, now Bayou Iberville or Manchac. Some miles further on, on the right bank, they came to a small river celebrated for its fish, that formed the boundary line between the hunting grounds of the Houmas and the Bayougoulas.

Baton Rouge.—Here Iberville saw a tall, red, leafless corn stalk, hung with offerings of fish and game by the Indian hunters. The Frenchmen called it a " Baton Rouge," and thus named the spot afterwards to become the capital of Louisiana.

Pointe Coupee.—The next day the chief pointed to a tiny stream running into the river on the left, and said if the boats could only get through it, they would cut off a whole day's journey. Iberville was not the man to be stopped by an " if." He put his Canadians at once to work. A huge drift pile was cut away, the bottom of the stream was deepened and cleared, and the boats were slowly towed through and launched into the Mississippi, just eighteen miles above the point where they had left it. The Mississippi in course of time adopted this cut-off also, and in a few years abandoned its old channel entirely for it.

The Houmas. 1699.—The Houmas' reception was even more cordial than that of the Bayougoulas and Mongoulachas. A delegation of them were waiting to welcome Iberville at their landing, and there was no end to their ceremonies and professions of friendship. Iberville, who did not smoke, complained of the number of times he had to smoke the calumet. When it was at last over the officers of the party and the delegation set out for the Houma village, some eight miles inland. The Indians kept up their peace songs all the way, leading their guests up and down hill, through canebrakes and swamps, at such a pace that the heavily clad Frenchmen were severely tasked to follow them.

At the entrance to the village the chiefs and principal warriors advanced, brandishing crosses made of white wood. All assembled in the open space in the centre of the village, where presents were exhibited, speeches made, more calumets smoked, and a great feast served. In the afternoon the handsomest of the young warriors and squaws, in all their finery of paints, feathers and jingling girdles, bounded from behind the trees and danced until late in the evening, to an orchestra of gourd rattles.*

Then all adjourned to the great cabin of the chief, where, lighted by huge blazing fagots of cane, the frolic was kept

---

* Called Chichieconchy, made of hollow gourds with pebbles inside.

up till midnight. The French officers retired to the couches prepared for them, but not to sleep, for the chiefs harangued one another with interminable addresses until daylight.

The Houma village was large and well built, like that of the Bayougoulas, but the tribe had also been very much thinned by a recent epidemic. They knew Tonty, who had passed several days with them, leaving his boats at the same landing where Iberville left his. But they said also that they knew of no fork in the river. Thinking that, like the Bayougoulas, they might have some reason for deceiving him, Iberville determined to bring his visit to an end and hurry on to the Tensas and question them. Some of the Houmas and a Tensas Indian visitor consented to go with them.

Turning Point. 1699.—The boats pushed away from the landing; the oarsmen showing fatigue and discouragement after their long, hard pull up the river, on no better rations than sagamity with an occasional treat of dried beef. Stopping for dinner, Iberville cross-examined all the Indians again, separately, about the fork in the river. They all agreed that the Mississippi flowed without a break to the gulf and that La Salle and Tonty had never traveled but one way to the gulf and back. He was forced to believe them. The Bayougoula chief, to prove his veracity, confessed to Iberville that Tonty had left a letter in his tribe to be delivered to a Frenchman, who was to come up from the sea (evidently meaning La Salle). The letter had been kept a secret from Iberville out of the suspiciousness and distrust natural to the Indian in treating with the white man.

As he was pushed both for time and provisions, Iberville concluded that a further journey would be unwise and useless. He gave the orders; the boats were turned around.

Rowing down stream, the men easily put mile after mile behind them. Arrived at the bayou called Ascantia, Iberville decided to go through it to the gulf. He left Sauvole in command of the expedition, and charged Bienville to obtain

at any price Tonty's letter from the Bayougoula village; and
with two canoes, four Canadians and an Indian guide, he
pushed his way through the tangled opening of what was
called henceforth Bayou Iberville.

Bayou Iberville. 1699.—It proved to be but ten feet
wide and three feet deep at most, and so choked up as to be
almost impassable for even a pirogue. The first day they
traveled twenty-one miles and made fifty portages over fallen
trees and rafts. After a few days the Indian guide deserted.
Iberville continued without him, resolved to show the natives
that he was not dependent upon them. Then one of the
Canadians fell ill, and Iberville had to take his place, not
only paddling the pirogue, but in carrying an end of it over
the portages. He noted with delight the beautiful country
through which the Ascantia flowed. He said it was one of
the finest he had ever seen—rich soil, handsome forests, and
no canebrakes. The river was filled with fish, and alligators
were so thick in it that at times he seemed to be paddling
through a solid mass of them. He heard wild turkeys in
quantities, but he did not succeed in killing any.

The first lake he came to he named after his young protector, the count de Maurepas; the second after the count de
Pontchartrain.

Camping at night on the low grassy points or islands
around the lakes, he made acquaintance with those pests of
hunters and fishermen, mosquitoes; "terrible little animals,"
he calls them, "to men in need of rest."

Traveling from twenty to thirty-six miles a day, he soon
came to the shores opposite Ship Island. He crossed over
and mounted the deck of the Badine, just one month and
two hours after he had started on his expedition. Eight
hours later Sauvole and Bienville were seen speeding their
way across the gulf.

Bienville brought the precious letter left by Tonty. He
had bought it for a hatchet. It was addressed to M. de la

Salle, Governor General of Louisiana, and contained the
account of the loyal pioneer's efforts to rescue his friend.
He said he had found the cross erected by La Salle eight
years before, lying half buried in the sand, and had set it up
again twenty-one miles higher up the river. He had left
another letter for De La Sallè concealed in the hollow of a
tree near the cross. As we have seen, no cross was found
by the Iberville expedition, either going up or coming down
the river; it had disappeared, and with it all clue to the
other letter.

QUESTIONS.

What took place Mardi Gras morning? Account of journey up the
river? The meeting with the Indians? Where did the French camp
that night? What of the portage? Describe arrival and reception at
Bayougoula and Mongoulacha landing? What did the chief wear?
What was this trip of Tonty's? Describe Bayougoula and Mongoulacha village? What of the Ascantia? Relate origin of the name of
Baton Rouge? What about Pointe Coupee? Describe Houma reception? Welcome of French? Did the Houmas know of the fork in
the river? What did Iberville do at noon? What did Mongoulacha
chief confess? What did Iberville conclude? What did he decide
about the Ascantia? What was the Ascantia henceforth called? When
did he arrive at his ships? What did Bienville bring?

FRENCH DOMINATION.

CHAPTER VIII.

ESTABLISHMENT.

Iberville had intended to take possession of the mouth of
the river by making an establishment there. But now, with
time and provisions running short, he saw that he must select
some spot nearer Ship Island and his vessels. His choice lay
between a site on Lake Pontchartrain; the mouth of the

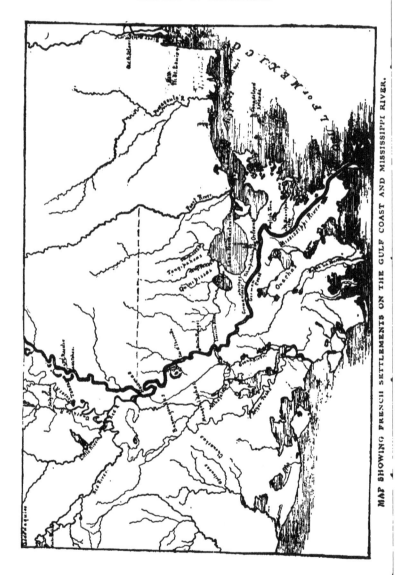

MAP SHOWING FRENCH SETTLEMENTS ON THE GULF COAST AND MISSISSIPPI RIVER.

Pascagoula river, and the Bay of Biloxi. The advantages of the latter were found so superior to those offered by the other two places that he decided in favor of it.

The spot selected for the fort was the highest point on the rising ground on the eastern shore of the bay. Work was commenced upon it immediately. Trees were cut, a space cleared and the fort laid out. The barges and small boats plied incessantly between it and the ships, fetching over the supplies of tools, implements, provisions, arms and ammunition, and the details of workmen drawn from the crews. The logs for the bastions and stockades were cut a mile and a half away and boated to the building. Corn and peas were sown in the clearings. In six weeks enough was completed to justify Iberville's leaving for France. He put the Sieur de Sauvole in command, and Bienville second in command under him. Then taking with him only the men and provisions necessary for his own ships, he sailed for France.

Sauvole vigorously carried on the work left him to do. He finished the fort, maintained discipline among his men, and made friends with his Indian neighbors. Almost every week brought a visit from some of them, prompted by curiosity or greed.

The first to make an appearance was their old acquaintance, Autobiscania, the Bayougoula chief, with a party of his warriors. They were received with military honors, which duly terrified them, as was intended ; but the presents reassured them, particularly the shirts, which to their great delight were fitted upon them. They looked with wonder at the fort, astonished that the French could get together and pile up such a number of great logs in so short a space of time. All went well until the sentinel came at nightfall to get the watchword from the sergeant. The whisperings threw the Indians into lively fears of treachery, out of which Sauvole had to calm and soothe them.

At daylight they confessed that their wives were on the side of the bay, and they would also like to see the fort. Permission being given, the savage dames were sent for. They landed; Autobiscania, anxious that the show should be equal to female expectations, made signs to Sauvole to put his men under arms, and ran himself to hunt up the drummer. The visit terminated to the satisfaction of all.

Bienville's Explorations.—After Iberville's departure from Biloxi, while Sauvole was regulating the affairs of the fort, Bienville proceeded to make acquaintance with the natives and country about him. He visited the Quinipissas, who lived on the shores of Lake Maurepas, and sought out the villages of the Moctobys, Biloxis, and Pascagoulas along the Pascagoula river. From there he went to Mobile Bay again and explored it, and made a reconnoissance on foot of Pensacola and its surroundings. On his return to Biloxi, he, with two pirogues and five Indians, set out once more to retrace Iberville's journey through the lakes and Bayou Iberville into the Mississippi, and to explore Bayou Plaquemine. But he found the Indians living on Bayou Plaquemine, the Ouachas, Chouachas and Opelousas, so ferocious and menacing that he was glad to beat a retreat to the Mississippi again.

Paddling his way confidently along to within twenty-three miles of its mouth, he rounded a bend and was arrested by a sight which startled and transfixed him. A corvette lay anchored mid-stream before him. He sent his companion pirogue forward to speak the vessel. It proved to be English. Bienville then advanced and went aboard. The captain, named Banks, turned out to be one of Iberville's old Hudson Bay prisoners, and therefore an acquaintance of Bienville's. The ship belonged to the expedition of which Iberville had heard, and for which he had been so anxiously n the look-out. It was one of three vessels loaded with nigrants which had sailed from England to make an establishment on the banks of the Mississippi about the very time that Iberville, with his squadron, sailed from France. They had passed the winter in Carolina, where the greatest number of colonists, pleased with the climate, had chosen to remain. One ship had returned to England, leaving the other two to pursue the search for the mouth of the Mississippi. The captain said they had cruised fruitlessly for thirty leagues round about, when he found this stream and entered it. As it was the only one large stream he had discovered in his cruise on that shore, he doubted not it was the Mississippi. Bienville convinced him that the river and country were in the possession of the King of France, who had force sufficient at hand to protect his rights. He had the satisfaction of seeing the captain raise anchor and head the corvette down stream. "The English Turn" in the Mississippi still commemorates the bend in the river where the young lieutenant and his five Canadians obtained this triumph over the Englishman.

Return of Iberville.—Iberville returned shortly after the new year, 1701. He brought with him supplies of money, provisions and reinforcements of men, among them sixty tried Canadians, who had been with him in Hudson Bay. His seventeen-year-old brother, Chateaugnay, accompanied him, and his relations the Sieur de Boisbrant, and the noted pioneer, Jarchereau de St. Denis; a noted geologist, the Sieur Le Sueur, came over also with men and means to exploit certain copper mines that were said to be in the upper Mississippi country.

Iberville stayed only long enough at Biloxi to get an expedition ready to build a fort on the Mississippi, which the visit of the English captain warned him as necessary. During the search for a proper situation, Iberville, coming to the deserted village of the Quinnipissas, made a planting of sugar cane there from seed he had brought from St. Domingo. But the seed, already yellow and sour, came to naught.

Fort Maurepas. 1700.—The location selected for the fort was on the left bank of the river, about fifty-four miles above its mouth.   A strong log building twenty-eight feet square was put upon it; and a powder magazine, five feet above the ground, well banked with earth.   During the building a pirogue of Canadians came down the river and stopped at the landing.   Iberville greeted the leader, Tonty, "the Iron Hand," with warm welcome.   The loyal man had heard of the French settlement and had traveled down the river to offer his services. Iberville gladly accepted them, for an exploration he wished to make into the Red river country, to find out the number of tribes of Indians living there, and the exact limit of the Spanish possessions. They set out at once.   Stopping at the Houmas' on their way up the river, Iberville gave them some apple, orange and cotton seed to plant.   Louisiana thus owes to him the first plantings of her two great staples.

The Natchez. 1700.—At the Natchez landing Iberville despatched a messenger to announce his presence to the Natchez chief.   The chief responded by sending his brother, escorted by twenty-five men, with the calumet of peace and an invitation to the village.   Climbing to the summit of the steep bluff, covered with magnificent forest trees, Iberville gazed with joy upon the beautiful rural landscape.   "It was a country," he says, "of plains and prairies, filled with little hills and groves of trees, with roads intercrossing from village to village, and from cabin to cabin—a country resembling France not a little."   Half way to the village the chief appeared, ceremoniously advancing, surrounded by his body guard—twenty large, well made men.

The village differed from the other villages visited only in being handsomer and better built.   The cabin of the chief stood on a spacious mound ten feet high.   Facing it was the temple; around stood the cabins, enclosing a handsome open space.   A small running stream near by furnished the water.

The Natchez were the most enlightened and civilized of the Mississippi river Indians. They worshipped the sun, and their chief was called after their deity the Great Sun; his brothers the Little Suns. The government was an absolute despotism. The Great Sun was master of the labor, property and lives of his subjects. He never worked. When he wanted provisions he sent out biddings to a great feast, and the invited were required to attend, bringing sufficient supplies for the entertainment and for the after support of the royal family. None were allowed to approach him without observing an elaborate deferential ceremony. He selected his servants from the most noted families, and when he died these servants were strangled to death, to accompany him to the next world. When an heir was born, each family that had a new-born infant appeared with it in the royal presence ,and a certain number were selected to be his attendants. If the heir died, all thus chosen, were strangled. The chieftainship was hereditary, but it was not the son of the Great Sun, but the son of his nearest sister or nearest female relative, who succeeded to the government. The royal princesses were not allowed to marry in the royal family, but were forced to take their husbands from the common tribe. No women except the mother and sisters of the Great Sun, were ever allowed to enter the temple.

The Tensas. 1700.—The Indian guides all advised Iberville and Tonty not to attempt to go up Red river, which was much rafted and difficult of navigation. They persisted that the easiest and best way of getting into the Red river lands was by going up above Red river and striking across the country from the great Tensas village. The advice seemed reasonable, and it was followed. Iberville, with his party, paddled up to the Tensas landing and made their way on foot through the woods to Lake Tensas, where they found pirogues for the rest of the journey. They were well received by the Tensas, but during the night were witnesses of such a scene of barbarity as turned their hearts from the tribe. A terrific storm broke out. Lightning struck the temple, setting it on fire. In a few moments it was entirely consumed. The Indian priest, or " medicine man," as he was called, attributed the disaster to the wrath of their god, because after the recent death of the great chief the tribe had not made the human sacrifices demanded of their faith.

Standing by the furious flames, with the storm raging about him, he called out repeatedly in a loud, commanding voice: " Women, bring your children and offer them in sacrifice to the Great Spirit to appease him!" Five squaws responded, and five papooses, strapped in their swaddling clothes, were thrown into the heart of the burning pile. Proud of his victory over them, the priest led the unnatural mothers in triumph to the cabin of the new chief, where all the village assembled to praise, caress, and do them honor. A painful trouble in his right knee prevented Iberville, at the last moment, from leading the exploration into the Red river country. He turned the command over to Bienville and journeyed back to Fort Maurepas. On his arrival he fell very ill of fever, which kept him for some time from proceeding to Ship Island, where quite a notable event was happening to enliven the monotony of the officers' lives.

Visit from the Spaniards. 1700.—De la Riola, governor of Pensacola, came in all the panoply of his power with three armed vessels and several hundred men to protest against the French settling in a country which he claimed belonged to the King of Spain. The French, no ways intimidated by the Spaniard's pomp and arrogance, determined to make as brave a show as he. During the four days of his visit all traces of sickness and privation were carefully hidden; men and officers wore their gala uniforms; wine flowed and banquets were served with reckless prodigality and the ort and garrison kept up one continual round of gaiety nd frolic. De la Riola sailed away as majestically as he came, but was very much impressed with the abundance and stability of the new French establishment. He was soon to be still more impressed with it.

Seven days afterwards the officers at Ship Island saw an open boat approaching from the sea, with figures of men in distress in it. They proved to be the stately Spanish commander and his officers, naked and famishing. A gale in the night had struck their squadron shortly after leaving Biloxi, and every vessel had been wrecked on Chandeleurs Islands; they had not had time even to clothe themselves, and for five days had only had a small bit of chocolate to eat and nothing but sea water to drink.

Again the French proved themselves equal to the occasion. Messengers were despatched with the news to Pensacola; boats were sent to rescue the miserable crews perishing on the exposed sand bars; food, drink and clothing were prepared. De la Riola was equipped from tip to toe out of Iberville's wardrobe; the officers were supplied by the other French officers, and French boats conveyed them all to Pensacola.

QUESTIONS.

Where did Iberville intend to make his settlement? What of Sauvole after Iberville's departure? What of Bienville? What Indians lived on Bayou Plaquemine? Give the meeting with the English vessel? What commemorates the circumstance? When did Iberville return? Who accompanied him? What was his next expedition? What of Fort Maurepas? Planting of cane? What expedition did Iberville and Tonty undertake? What seed did Iberville give the Houmas? Describe Natchez village and the Natchez? Give an account of Spanish commander's visit?

CHAPTER IX.

FURTHER ESTABLISHMENT.

Bienville left the Tensas village with his party; twenty-two Canadians, with six Tensas and one Ouachita for guides. It was early March, the severe winter still lingered, and the country was beginning to overflow from rising water. Not only was every little bayou swollen into a rushing stream, but great tracts of land lay under the water from knee to breast deep; in many places over the head. As they had no pirogues they crossed on foot-logs when they could find them (they were generally hidden under water), and sometimes they would fell a tree for a bridge. But most of the times they swam or waded across, pushing their clothes before them on rafts; always firing off their guns first, to scare away the alligators. As Bienville was only of medium height, he was at a great disadvantage, and many times had to swim, when his companions only waded. The water was icy cold and the Indians soon turned back, saying they did not like walking naked all day in cold water. At night the camp was pitched on any dry spot to be found. Sometimes the travelers would come to a good hunting place and a day would be given up to supplying their bags with game; but days would often pass when all the meals consisted only of sagamity. They would make from ten to twelve miles a day, crossing from six to a dozen bayous and swamps. Hardy as the Canadians were, many of them fell ill from the hardships and exposure. Often in the water they would be seized with chills and cramps, and were forced to climb trees and stay in the branches until they recovered. Once four men thus passed a whole day in the trees until rafts were sent to fetch them away. To add to their discomfort rain set in, and every day drenching showers would again and again wet them to the skin. But Bienville says they never stopped sing-

ing and laughing, to show the Indians they met that Frenchmen, unlike Spaniards, did not mind such fatigue.   They
met only a few Indians journeying to get out of the high
water, or carrying salt from the salt springs in the Ouachita
country to sell to the Indians along the Mississippi.

They came to Red river, but found most of the villages
inundated and abandoned. What Indians remained were living on rafts and scaffoldings, and their supplies of corn were
too meagre for the French to buy any.

Bienville visited some villages of the Natchitoches, Sou-
chitionis, Nakasas, and Yataches, living above the water, and
there he met some Caddodaquious Indians,   They gave him
so discouraging an account of the road and distance to their
village that Bienville decided not to push his sick, disabled
and half-starved men any further to get there.   Procuring
pirogues, he brought them down Red river to the Mississippi.*   On his arrival at the settlement, Iberville put him
in command of Fort Maurepas and sailed to France.

Fort Maurepas. 1700.—Bienville took up his position at
Fort Maurepas, which soon, with its fields of corn and vegetables, formed a bright picture on the banks of the great,
savage river.   Canadian coureurs de bois learned the way
down there from the north and west; and every now and
then bands of them would paddle up to the landing, their
pirogues almost sinking under the heavy loads of peltry,
dried meat and bears' grease ; the sombre forests resounding
with the echoes of their loud frolicking.   More quietly
and humbly, missionaries, who had already begun to establish themselves along the Mississippi, would come, with a few
attendants only and Indian guides, to the new settlement of
their faith and country to greet their compatriots and get
tidings from France.   .

---

* Jachereau de St. Denis the following year explored the same country as far as
the Caddodaquious ; and a few years afterward founded a post at Natchitoches. St
Denis' attempts to open an overland trade from the French colony to Mexico led
to a series of romantic and thrilling adventures of which he was a most interesting
hero. St. Denis may be called the father of the Natchitoches country.

Biloxi. 1700.—At Biloxi Sauvole struggled through trying experiences. The Canadian settlers proved themselves
unruly under discipline; they liked no work but hunting and
fighting, and were much given to drinking, saving up their
daily allowance of spirits until they accumulated enough to
get intoxicated. Then the Indian visitors came in such numbers that he was hard pressed to give them the food and
presents they expected, and without which they might turn
into enemies; in addition to this, great pirogues of Canadians
would come to Biloxi from Fort Maurepas, and they would
quarter themselves on the garrison until asked to leave. The
ship of supplies promised from France did not arrive. Sauvole had to send to St. Domingo and buy the necessaries of
life. There was a drought which killed all vegetation and
dried up all the springs. This was followed by a season of
great rain. Fever broke out and soon became epidemic.
Soldiers and Canadians died in numbers.

Death of Sauvole. August, 1701.—The gallant young
commander himself was stricken with it and died in August,
1701, leaving his uncompleted journal for a record of his
faithfulness and conscientiousness in duty. At the news of
his death, Bienville hastened over from Fort Maurepas to
Biloxi and took command.

Arrival of Iberville. 1701.—In December, couriers from
Pensacola brought news of Iberville's arrival at that port,
accompanied by De Serigny, his brother, a mariner of great
repute in the royal navy. He was unable to move from Pensacola, being confined to his bed with an abscess in his side,
which caused him great suffering, and for which he had been
operated on ship-board. The fever which he had caught on
the Mississippi had continued in France, almost causing his
death there, and preventing his return sooner to the colony
with the supplies he had promised.

Impressed with the necessity of a port directly on the gulf
coast as a protection to his position on the Mississippi, and

still unreconciled to the possession of Pensacola by the Spaniards, Iberville had, during his long stay in France, endeavored to procure its cession from Spain. He wrote an able
paper to the court of Spain on the subject, assuming as warrant for his presumption the new and near relations between
the thrones of France and Spain (the grandson of the king of
France being heir to the throne of the king of Spain). The
paper was submitted to the Spanish Junto, or council of
state, who, far from approving his designs, warned him, as
an interloper, off the coast which they claimed still as Spanish.

Iberville's answer to this was the determination to settle
Mobile. That would give France a close and definite boundary line on the east against the Spaniards, assure her of the
possession of the Mobile river, the next important stream of
the country after the Mississippi, and secure to her the continuous stretch of Gulf Coast all the way to La Salle's western
limit, Matagorda Bay. Without loss of time, he sent orders
to Bienville to transport the colony from Biloxi to Mobile.

Mobile. 1702.—The new fort, named Fort St. Louis de la
Mobile, was to be situated on the right bank of the Mobile
river, about fifty miles above its mouth. The work of
removal from Biloxi was pushed forward vigorously. De
Serigny brought over from Pensacola his ship laden with
the supplies for the colony, and all the small boats and men
to be spared from Iberville's ship. Tents were erected on
Massacre Island for the storage of freight until flat-boats
could be built to convey it across the bay and up the river.
As soon as Iberville was well enough to come to Mobile and
superintend the work, Bienville was sent out to establish relations with the tribes of the country round about. On the
island at the mouth of the Mobile he found only deserted
habitations, and on one of them the carefully hidden gods of
one of the vanished tribes. They were rude figures of men
and animals, which the Indian guides would only approach by

walking backwards, and which they warned Bienville not to touch on pain of death.

Bienville, to the Indians' astonishment, carried them without suffering any disaster to Iberville, who examined them and pronounced them relics of some of the old Spanish explorers.

Eighteen miles above the fort were the Mobile Indians, the descendants of the fierce warriors who had given De Soto so warm a reception. Six miles above the Mobiles lived the Tohomes, a small but industrious tribe, whose corn crops often stood between the French garrison and hunger. On the Alabama river were the Alabamas, a fighting, refractory tribe, whose warriors were ever on the war path against their neighbors, white and red. On the Apalachicola river were the Apalaches, or Conchaques; a peaceful tribe subdued to the Spaniards, but suffering such ravages from the inroads of the Indians incited by the English of Carolina that they soon moved into the neighborhood of the French for protection. To the northwest, between the Tombigbee and the Mississippi, was the territory of the Choctaws, the largest and most powerful tribe of the region. Cunning, brave and well skilled in their savage warfare, they formed the great safeguard of the French against the vindictive and unconquerable Chickasaws. The lands of this celebrated tribe lay to the north of the Choctaw, between the French and English possessions, and the French found them in course of time more redoubtable foes than the English themselves.

It was with great satisfaction that during the building of the fort Iberville received forerunners from Tonty, announcing his speedy arrival, with chiefs from both these important tribes. A grand reception was at once prepared, and presents selected. These were exposed in full view; two hundred pounds of powder, the same quantity of balls and bird shot, twelve guns, a hundred hatchets, fifty knives, a number of cauldrons, and quantities of small articles, such as beads, flints, awls, etc. With so tempting an array spread before them, the chiefs smoked all the calumets and made all the treaties desired by Iberville, and departed from the fort well promised to France and laden with booty.

Mobile. 1702.—Iberville sailed away from his anchorage at Massacre Island on the last day of March, 1702; neither his brother nor his colony ever saw him again.*

QUESTIONS.

Describe Bienville's expedition. What of the Indians he met? Did he go to the Caddodaquious? What of life at Fort Maurepas? When did Sauvole die? What followed? What news came from Pensacola? Who accompanied Iberville? Describe the removal from Biloxi. What was the new fort named and where situated? Give an account of the Indians of the Alabama country.

CHAPTER X.

MOBILE. 1702-1711.

Mobile.   1702-1711.— Bienville was left in command. The charge committed to him by Iberville was no light one. He was not only to maintain himself in his present position, but with his handful of men to hold Iberville's great grasp of country, with the mouth of the Mississippi, firm to the crown of France. The Spaniards to the east and the English to the north were to be kept in check, and all the warring, restless savage tribes under him to be fastened together in tractable submission to his authority and armed into an efficient force to oppose against the colonies of France's rivals.

---

* The gallant Canadian died of yellow fever at Havana, in 1706, four years later. His last effort at arms, like his first, was against the English. He was preparing, with a large armament, to attack the British islands in the Antilles and their settlements on the Carolina coast. Landing at Havana for reinforcements of Spaniards and filibusters, he was attacked by the prevailing epidemic, and died. Iberville had advanced large sums to the government for Louisiana, so left little to his widow and children. His widow afterward married a French nobleman, the count de Bethune.

Let us give a glance at the life and character of the twenty-two-year-old governor.

Jean Baptiste Le Moyne Sieur de Bienville was the ninth son of his father and the sixth brother of Iberville. Left

BIENVILLE.

an orphan when a child, he lived with his eldest brother, the Baron de Longueuil, in the chateau de Longueuil, near Montreal. At fourteen he followed Iberville to sea, and before he was eighteen had taken part in all the thrilling dangers of the struggles in Hudson Bay. Quiet, gentle and reserved, he yet possessed an indomitable will and inflexible courage; well proven in the course of this history. Even at an early age he knew how to gain a powerful influence over his friends and men under his command. The Canadians were ever devoted to him, and formed an unfaltering clan behind him, ready for any service of offence or defence. The Indians respected and revered him and called him father. He knew the Indians, indeed, as few white men ever knew them, and in his dealings with them acted with a judgment which they never questioned. He boasted that he never broke his word to them, always conformed to their manners and customs, and talked to each tribe in its own dialect. In Canada, he spoke with ease the language of the natives, and on his arrival in Louisiana he acquired the dialect of every tribe with which he came in contact, a capital of infinite advantage him in his after career.

Fort St. Louis de la Mobile. 1702.—With all its de-
pendences, the fort was soon completed. Standing eminent
on the bank of the river it was an imposing edifice for the
times in that wild country. It measured three hundred and
sixty feet square, and held at each corner a battery of six
guns. Inside were a chapel, the guard house, officers' lodgings and a parade ground. The barracks for the soldiers
and Canadians were outside, some fifty paces to the left, on
the bank of the river. Later, also, on the left of the fort, a
residence for the priest was erected.

The Indians from all the neighboring country flocked to
sate their wonder at the marvelous structure, always leaving
well impressed with French power and wealth, and feed with
their presents. The Spaniards from Pensacola came also as
often as the Indians; and Bienville claimed that these neighbors were even more costly to him than the Indians. The
garrison at Pensacola seemed always in a state of famine,
their supply ships from Vera Cruz being ever delayed or lost
at sea, and hardly a week passed that a boat was not sent to
Mobile to borrow provisions. As Bienville complained they
would many a time have been forced by starvation to abandon their settlement, if he had not kept them up from his
scant stores, not daring to refuse on account of the new alliance and kinship between the French and Spanish monarchs.

War with England.—The war* declared by England
against France and Spain, on account of this very kinship,
made itself felt before he was firmly established in his fort.
Indian war parties, equipped by the English, in Carolina,
over and over again ravaged the corn fields and burned the
villages of the Indians of Florida, and attacked the Indians
in the French territory, while an English fleet, hovering in
the gulf, kept the seaboard from St. Augustine to Mobile in
a constant state of alarm.

---

* War of the Spanish Succession, 1700, over the succession of the grandson of
Louis XIV to the throne of Spain. England, Germany, Holland, Portugal and
Prussia opposed this aggrandizement of the royal house of France.

Bienville flew to the rescue of his Indian allies, distributing arms and ammunition to their warriors, and equipping
them into equality with the English Indians. The flying
bands of Apalaches were received and settled along Mobile
river.* The Spaniards at Pensacola, instead of assisting him
in these crises, only increased his burdens. As ill provided
with munitions of war as with provisions, they knew no better means of defence, when threatened, than to shut themselves in their strongholds and send appeals to Bienville, and
he was forced to respond with men, arms and boats.

Indian Troubles.—And along the Mississippi, wherever
English traders could insinuate themselves in the Indian
tribes, the savages would break into revolt, and the tomahawk would be raised to spread destruction and carnage up
and down the river. The humble, pious missionaries and
their attendants were always the first victims. And almost
as often Spanish barks, long pointed pirogues, from the
river countries would come flying across the gulf bearing
news of assassination and murder, and fetching a load of
wounded praying for protection and medical help.

So, one day came good father Davion,† fleeing from the
Tunicas, telling the story of the murder of the aged priest
Foucault and his attendants, by their Coroas‡ guides, as they
were peacefully descending the river to visit Mobile; and so,
later, Father Gravier§ arrived, his arm pierced with five
arrow-heads, shot by the Indians of his mission on the Illinois.

* Here, under the spiritual charge of M. Huvé, they built themselves a church,
and became so edifying a religious example that the colonists used to jaunt out on
Sundays and feast-days to see them perform their devotions and hear them sing the
Latin hymns.
† Father Davion had originally settled at Natchez, but making no converts, he
went to the Tunicas, and erected a cross on the highest bluff, where he said mass
every morning. The bluff was called Roche a Davion until 1764, when it became
known as Locus Heights, and afterwards and ever since as Fort Adams.—Claiborne's Mississippi.
‡ Nicholas Foucault had a mission among the Arkansas, where he had accomplished much good, when, in 1702, he set out for Mobile with three attendants and
a Coroas guides. The guides killed them for the plunder of their luggage.
§ Father Gravier, a Jesuit, had succeeded to the mission at Kaskaskia, among
Ilinois, continued by Allouez after the death of Marquette. He was appointed
General by the Bishop of Quebec. An accomplished as well as a devoted
, he has left valuable descriptions of the Indians and early settlements by the
ch. He was always an earnest friend of Bienville.

War with the Alabamas. 1702.—Bienville intrusted the punishment of the Coroas to the Arkansas, who gladly undertook it, while he prepared to inflict upon the Alabamas what they merited for an act of treachery which had incensed the whole colony.

Some of their chiefs came to the fort with such plausible stories of the plenteousness of corn in their village that Bienville sent five men home with them to purchase. After some weeks, one of them came back alone to tell of the treachery of the savages. The party had traveled to within two days' of the Alabama village. Here the chiefs begged the white men to remain while they went in advance to notify their people, so that a reception could be prepared. That night, while the white men slept, the Indians returned and tomahawked four of them. One escaped by leaping into the river and swimming for his life. A hatchet thrown after him inflicted an ugly wound on his arm; this he dressed with pine gum, gathered from the trees, chewed, and applied as he fled through the forest.

Bienville, raising a levy amongst his Indian allies, mustered, with his Canadians, a force of nearly two hundred men, of which Tonty and St. Denis shared with him the command.

The plan was to ascend the Mobile river and the Alabama to some convenient point, to land, and marching rapidly across the country, fall a surprise upon the foe. The Mobilians were to act as guides and baggage carriers. But it was soon seen that they were in secret sympathy with the Alabamas They conducted the little army so cunningly that at the end of eighteen days it was spent with marching and very little if any nearer the enemy than when it set out. Then, upon some trivial pretext, all the Mobilians, Choctaws and Tohomes deserted in a body.

The French commanders were forced, without striking a blow, to return also to the fort, which they reached (by marching in a straight line) in four days. But in a few days

they quietly led forth another expedition, composed of white
men only. They made the entire journey by water. As
they neared the spot where their companions had been assassinated, scouts were sent to spy out the camp. It was found
a short distance above on a bluff upon the bank of the river.
Bienville was for attacking it at once; but his companions
prevailed in favor of a surprise at night. They waited in
their hiding places through the rest of the day until darkness fell and the camp fires dimmed to a dull smouldering
glow, when the savages, as they judged, would be in a heavy
sleep. Then the command was given and the stealthy advance begun. With all their precautions a dry twig crackled
under some foot. The war cry rose in the air. The old men,
women and children broke from the camp and ran into the
forest. The warriors retreated slowly after them, firing their
guns at the invaders. All escaped with the exception of four;
two killed and two wounded. The French also had two men
killed, and had, for the rest of their vengeance, to content
themselves with destroying the Alabamas' camp, breaking
up their pirogues and throwing their hunting booty into the
river.

On his return to Mobile, Bienville put the scalps of the
Alabamas in the market, offering a gun and five pounds of
powder and ball apiece for them.

The war sputtered along like a slow fire for nine years.
The Mobilians a few years afterwards were detached from
the Alabamas by Bienville's generosity in restoring to them
some captive Alabama women and children taken prisoners,
whom the Mobilians claimed as kinspeople. Their gratitude
to Bienville for the restoration maintained them in unswerv-
ing loyalty to the French ever afterwards.

The 1st of February, 1705, tidings came to Mobile that
the Chickasaws had seized and sold as slaves to the English
several Choctaw families who had come to visit them in good
faith, and that the act of treachery had caused a rupture be-

tween the two nations. As there were in Fort St. Louis at that time more than seventy Chickasaws of both sexes, they were very much troubled about returning to their villages, which they could not do without passing through the territory of the irate Choctaws. At their solicitation, Bienville sent twenty-five Canadians under De Boisbriant to escort them. They arrived on their route at the Choctaw village about the end of the month. The Choctaw chief assured De Boisbriant that they would not oppose the return of the Chickasaws, but that it was only just to reproach them with their perfidy in the presence of the French. Therefore, the Chickasaws were invited to assemble in the open space in the centre of the village, and the Choctaw chief, with his calumet in his hand, began his harangue to them. He reproached them with their injustices and want of good faith; told them if the French took any interest in them, it was because of ignorance of their real character. The Chickasaws listened with more uneasiness than contrition. Around, a circle of Choctaws had gradually closed them in. When the orator had reached his-point that they were too vile to live, and therefore it was proper they should die, reversing the calumet in his hand, there was no hope of escape from the sentence, which was executed at the instant. Only the women and children were spared. Several Choctaws were killed in the *melee*, and De Boisbriant accidentally received a ball in trying to get out of the way. He was placed upon a litter and carried to the fort by a numerous escort of Choctaws.

It was a blow which staggered the Chickasaws. They sent deputation after deputation to Bienville, praying his good offices in favor of peace After a year's hostilities and losses had somewhat mitigated the resentment of the Choctaws, Bienville was able to bring them to terms and persuade them to smoke the pipe of peace with their adversaries. The reconciliation proved a mere truce, however, and Bienville's hope of uniting the two powerful tribes for the French an illusion.

In the summer of 1703-1704 ships came from France, fetching everything that a growing colony could need; emigrants, money, soldiers, missionaries, provisions, a commissary, clothing, live stock, and most important of all, under charge of two Gray Sisters, twenty-three young girls, to be married to worthy young men.

The emigrants received their allotments of lands along the river; the cattle were set at large, the goods and provisions stored in the magazines, and the outstanding accounts of soldiers, and their employés, paid.

All seemed to bid fair for the happiness and prosperity of Mobile. But the last ship, touching at Havana for live stock, brought yellow fever into the colony. The plague raged pitilessly; priests, sailors, soldiers, and the new emigrants sickened and died of it. The place was almost depopulated; and, most grievous and serious of all to Bienville and to the colony, was the loss of the brave, loyal, efficient Henri de Tonty.

Dissensions. 1706.—Almost as fatal as the epidemic were the discords that broke out among the officers of the colony. The priest De la Vente,* and the royal commissary, De la Salle,† were barely installed in their positions, when they began to chafe and fret under the authority of the young commander. Their criticism of and opposition to him produced a most bitter and active animosity, which inflamed the whole garrison into partisanship. Accusations and recriminations passed from side to side. Letters were written to France by De la Salle and De la Vente, charging Bienville with illicit trade with the Spaniards and unlawful use of the royal stores and provisions. Bienville retaliated with

---

* Louisiana belonged to the diocese of Quebec. On the 20th of July, 1703, Saint Vallier, Bishop of Quebec, formally erected Mobile into a parish, uniting it to the Seminary of Foreign Missions in Paris and Quebec, who agreed to supply it with clergy. Rev. Henry Roulleaux de la Vente was appointed parish priest, Rev. Alexandre Huvé, curate.—*Colonial Church in America, Shea.*

† De La Salle, son of a naval officer at Toulon, was not related to the great xplorer.

general charges of incompetence, untruthfulness and mischief-making.

As the years passed without a vessel coming from France, Chateaugnay, "the sea courier," of Mobile, and his transport were kept busy plying between Mobile, Cuba, St. Domingo and Vera Cruz, bringing provisions and carrying the mail for both the French and Spanish establishments. Pensacola caught fire and burned to the ground, and the vice admiral's ship sank to the bottom at her moorings, which reduced the Spaniards to greater misery and dependence on Bienville than ever before, and once more threatened by the English Indians, Bienville .himself had to lead a company to their relief.

Government's Dissatisfaction with Bienville. 1708.— The repeated letters from the priest and commissary reiterating their charges against Bienville made at last an impression on the government. Jerome de Maurepas was now Compte de Pontchartrain and Minister of marine, having succeeded to his father's position and title. The confidence which he felt in Iberville extended to Bienville only so long as Iberville lived. After the death of his brother, the young governor found out that he was to be judged without favor, and that from Pontchartrain all that he could expect was strict justice.

Bienville Dismissed. 1708.—After three years of waiting, a ship with the sorely needed supplies arrived from France. By it Bienville also received a letter dismissing him from office, informing him of the charges against him. A new governor, M. de Muys, was sent out, and a new commissary general, M. Diron D'Artaguette. De Muys died at Havana, on his way to the colony.

De Muys was not only to supersede Bienville; he was, with D'Artaguette, also to institute a strict inquiry into his conduct, and if the charges against him were found true they were to arrest him and send him prisoner to France, on a

lettre de cachet.* The captain of the ship was given an
order to take charge of Bienville, conduct him to France,
and deliver him up to the commander of the first port at
which he landed.

Bienville demanded that some one be put immediately in
his place, that he might return to France and answer the
charges against him. D'Artaguette, however, concealing
the harsh orders given him and De Muys insisted that he should
remain at his post until the king appointed another governor.
He made an examination into Bienville's administration, and
wrote a report to the Minister of Marine, not only exonerat-
ing him from charges against him, but praising him highly
for the ability with which he had met and overcome his difficulties. Far from Bienville and his brothers making money
out of the colony, they were all poor, not having for several
years received a cent of their salary.

Three years again passed after the last vessel and no relief came from France. The colony made brave efforts
to be independent of the mother country. A brisk little
trade in peltry, bears' grease and other forest produce sprang
up between it and Florida and the West Indies and Central
America. Massacre Island throve and prospered with the
sure persistency of a port town. Inhabitants drifted to it
from the fort, from the country, and dropped upon it from
vessels. Houses were built, stores opened, trees set out and
gardens planted, until, as Bienville said, it was a pleasure
to see it. And the property accumulated was considered so
valuable that the loss inflicted by a raid from an enterprising
British privateer was estimated at £50,000.

Up the river, affairs were not so flourishing; provisions
and clothing became exhausted, and what was worse the
supply of gunpowder threatened to give out—a timely loan
from St. Domingo alone preventing this calamity. With the

* Lettre de cachet," a warrant for the arrest of a person under the old régime
government) of France.

able-bodied men always under arms, and with no oxen to
assist in tilling the ground, dependence had to be placed on
the Indians for bread food.   Successive overflows destroyed
the corn crops of these, and the garrison was often reduced
to acorns for nourishment.   In 1711 the fort itself stood under
water, and spies brought word that the English Indians were
purposing to profit by the high water and make an attack by
the way of the river on the French settlement.   They had
already made an attack on the Tohomes and Mobile villages,
but had been driven back.

   Removal of the Fort.—In this extremity a council of
officers decided, for better protection, to concentrate forces
and means and bring the two posts closer together by removing the fort colony nearer to Massacre Island.   A new
fort was built nearer the mouth of the river and the garrison
removed to it, the colonists following and settling around ; but
very much discouraged at the loss and trouble of the change.

   During the summer months, in order to spare his store of
provisions, Bienville allowed his unmarried men of good
character to live among the neighboring Indian tribes.   It
was a privilege they eagerly sought, and one which made
rare returns of frolic and pleasure, particularly when the
visit was to the gentle Natchez or to the Colapissas living
on the shores of Lake Pontchartrain.   The days were filled
with long fishing and hunting excursions with all their whole-
some and exciting adventures, the nights with jollity and fun
with the young folks around the camp fires, under the green
leaves.   Once a violinist was taken along, and the pretty Indian girls were taught to dance the stately gavotte and cotil-
lon, and to sing the sprightly French songs, the woods peal-
ing with merriment.   It was not always easy for the Frenchmen
to return at Bienville's summons, and the Indians were as
sorry as they over the parting.*   The good fellowship which

---

* A young ship carpenter, named Pennicaut, one of Bienville's followers who obtained this privilege summer after summer, has written a most charming description
of his adventures among the Indians.

resulted from this friendly commingling of his men with the
natives, and his stern punishment of any offence of his men
against hospitality, was one of the reasons of Bienville's good
reputation among the Indians and of his safety among them.
For almost at any time, had they wished it, they could have
combined and swept him and his colony out of existence.

QUESTIONS.

Give an account of Bienville's charge. Bienville's life and character.
Fort St. Louis de la Mobile. Spaniards at Pensacola. Indian troubles.
Epidemic. Dissensions. Charges against Bienville. Why was Bien-
ville dismissed? By whom succeeded? What instructions were given
De Muys and d'Artaguette? What of the investigation into Bien-
ville's conduct?

CHAPTER XI.

LOUISIANA CHARTERED.

Crozat's Charter. 1712.—The reason why Pontchartrain
did not send relief to the colony was that the financial condition of France was extremely depressed. The many wars and
extravagant expenditures of the court during the long reign
of Louis XIV* had brought the country almost to bankruptcy. All the executive branches of the government suffered for want of money. Public expenses were lowered in
every way, and France's great glory and pride, her colonial
establishments, were cut down with a mere pittance. As for
Louisiana and the mouth of the Mississippi, Pontchartrain
saw that he must abandon them, unless he could find some
one who would assist him in the responsibility of providing
for their needs.

After two years' negotiation the Sieur Antoine de Crozat,
a capitalist and favorite of the court, was induced to become

---

* Louis XIV, called the "Grand Monarque," gave his name to the 17th century in
France. He reigned seventy-two years; died in 1715, and was succeeded by his
great-grandson, Louis XV. The Duke of Orleans, nephew of Louis XIV, was regent during the minority of Louis XV.

the chartered owner of the colony for fifteen years, for what profit he could draw out of the monopoly of its trade.

Lamothe Cadillac. 1710.—Lamothe Cadillac was named governor. One of the most prominent French pioneers in America for twenty years; indefatigable, shrewd and clever, he would have been an excellent governor but for his obstinate adherence to his own opinions and opposition to the opinions of others.

Bienville again petitioned to be allowed to return to France, or to his old position in the navy. But his wisdom in managing the Indians made his presence a necessity in the colony. Pontchartrain ordered him to remain, and assigned him to the command of the Mississippi, with headquarters at Natchez, where a fort was to be built (called Rosalie, after the Countess of Pontchartrain).

Bienville, who. with his brothers, Canadian friends and kinsmen, had been supreme for so long a time in the colony, did not welcome the new governor put over them in a kindly spirit. Cadillac, on his side, was resentful, arbitrary and domineering to the Canadians.

It was not long before the settlement was in a state of petty warfare, worse even than in the time of De la Salle and De la Vente. Cadillac stood at the head of one cabal, Bienville at the head of the other, and the aggressive enmity of both fell short only of personal conflict.

Crozat, to make sure of Cadillac's zeal, gave him an interest in his trading profit. But the efforts to develop a lucrative trade in the colony were a dismal failure. St. Denis was sent to Mexico with packs of goods; ships were loaded for the Central American ports; trading posts and magazines were established at Natchez, and at all the principal stations along the river.* To force the colonists to buy of him, no vessels

* Under St. Denis a trading post was established on Red river, on the site of the present town of Natchitoches. St. Denis explored Red river much further and advanced on a tour of exploration as far as Rio Bravo del Norte, to observe the movements of the Spaniards, to see whether they had advanced over that river into Louisiana. He found that they had formed a settlement on the western side of the

or goods but those of Crozat were allowed to enter the province. Prices were put up to suit Crozat's desires. And as much as possible, all the expenses of the colony were paid in merchandise at these exorbitant prices. The inhabitants were forbidden selling anything out of the province, and prohibited even from owning a sea-going vessel. The peltry of the Canadian trappers was bought at the lowest of prices, which, as there was no competition, were fixed by Crozat's commissioners; and he obliged them to receive pay in his merchandise also at his own valuation.

Under the circumstances it is not surprising that huge stores of goods rotted in the various warehouses before finding a purchaser. As for the commerce with Mexico and the Spanish posts upon which Crozat's greatest expectation had been based, they were destroyed by recent prohibitive measures of Spain against French trade.*

In the Crozat charter the king had agreed to provide for the garrison as usual. But neither pay nor uniforms arrived for the soldiers, who, naked and destitute, and not able to buy except from Crozat's stores, began to desert to the English in Canada. To the sum of discord and distress and desertion came threatened Indian troubles.

First War of the Natchez. 1716.—In January, 1716, news came to Mobile that the Natchez† were raising the hatchet against the French. They had pillaged Crozat's

---

Bravo and erected a fort called Presidio of St. John the Baptist; no settlement had been made by them east of that river, but they claimed jurisdiction to that river under the name of province of "Texas," signifying friends, because the Indians were friendly.

About the same time a small settlement and trading post was established on the Yazou, on Sicily Island and high up on the Ouachita (Monroe). Charleville, one of Crozat's traders, penetrated into the Schawanese tribes, then known as the Chouanoes, as far as the Cumberland river. His store was situated on a mound near the present site of Nashville. The same year also French posts and missions were established upon the upper tributaries of the Sabine, also a little settlement was made thirty miles west of the present Nacogdoches.

*According to a clause in the treaty of Utrecht (which ended the War of the Succession), Spain closed her American ports to French goods, and gave trading privileges to England.

† The reason of the outbreak seemed to be the neglect of Cadillac, in a voyage ⟩ and down the river, refusing or slighting the offered calumet of the Natchez. he Natchez suspiciously concluded that war was intended and struck the first ow.

storehouse, killed his commissioners, and were putting to death all Frenchmen caught traveling up and down the river. Nothing could be more disastrous to the colony. There was no nation so important to it as the Natchez, none with whom it was so necessary to keep on good terms. But since they were in revolt it was vital to subjugate them promptly and in an impressive manner.

The difference between Crozat and Bienville had deterred the latter hitherto from taking up his position at the projected fort. Now he hastened in every possible manner to get to it at once. But he could obtain from Cadillac only a force of forty-nine men. With these he started, and by April arrived at the village of the Tunicas, about fifty miles below the Natchez.

As he had not force enough to war, he saw himself obliged to gain his point by subtlety. He learned that the Natchez had assassinated another Frenchman coming down the river from the Illinois, and were lying in wait at the same place for fifteen more who were expected. He was warned, also, by the French missionary against the Tunicas, who had received presents to kill him. Concealing his anxiety at this last information, and his knowledge of the state of affairs among the Natchez, he assembled the Tunica warriors and gave out to them that his mission was to make a trading establishment among the Natchez, but as his men were very fatigued with the voyage, he was going to camp on an island a third of a league below, to rest for some time, and that they would do him a favor by sending some of their tribe to announce his arrival to the Natchez.

This was done at once. He proceeded to the island, where he immediately erected an intrenchment and the necessary shelters for his men. A few days later three Natchez arrived, sent by their chief to present the calumet to Bienville. He waved it aside, saying that they could get some of his soldiers to smoke it, but that for himself, being a great chief

of the French, he would only smoke a calumet presented by
a Sun chief.   The next day the three warriors returned.
Bienville sent with them a young Frenchman, who spoke
their language perfectly, to whom he explained everything to
say to the chiefs, and all the answers necessary to induce
them to come to the island.   The same day he sent one of
his bravest and most adroit Canadians in a pirogue, to slip
by the Natchez during the night and hasten up the river to
warn the fifteen men coming down from the Illinois.   He
gave him, to place in different points of the river, a dozen
great sheets of parchment on which was written in large
characters: " The .Natchez have declared war against the
French, and M. de Bienville is camped at the Tunicas."

In about a week there were seen approaching the island
four pirogues, in each of which were four men erect, chanting the calumet, and three sitting under parasols, with twelve
swimmers round about.   It was the Natchez Suns coming
to fall into the trap prepared for them.

Bienville ordered one-half of his men not to show themselves, but to keep under arms near by.   The other half
were to stand unarmed around his tent, and when the boats
landed were to take the arms of the savages as they stepped
ashore ; and he charged them only to let the eight chiefs he
named enter his tent; the rest were to remain seated at the
door.   The eight chiefs entered, holding their calumet,
which they presented to Bienville.   He pushed it aside with
contempt and asked them what satisfaction they were going to
give him for the five Frenchmen that they had assassinated.
They hung their heads without answering, at which Bienville made a sign to have them seized and conducted to
the prison he had prepared for them.   They were put in
irons.   In the evening bread and meat were presented to
them.   They refused to eat.   All sang their death song.
The next morning he persuaded them to send one of their
number to the village for the heads of the assassins.   Five

days later the little Sun returned, fetching three heads.
Only two were identified as belonging to the guilty parties.
Bienville threw the rejected head at the feet of the Suns
and reproached them for sacrificing an innocent man. The
chiefs confessed that the head was that of a warrior who
had taken no part in the killing of the Frenchmen, but that
being the brother of one of the murderers who had escaped, he
had been put to death in his place. Bienville kept his Natchez
visitors prisoners a month while awaiting the capture of the
third criminal. The great Sun fell ill. His irons were removed, and he was taken into Bienville's tent, and treated
with great kindness.

The river began to rise and the water stood over the island;
the tents had to be raised on scaffoldings. As many of his
men fell ill, Bienville concluded to make terms without waiting further. The Natchez agreed to put the escaped assassin
to death when they found him, and consented to Bienville's
executing two of the warriors captured in the Sun's party, as
it had been proved that they had a hand in the killing. They
pledged themselves also to furnish timber and assist in building the fort for the French at their landing, and henceforth
to observe a loyal peace with them. They were released and
restored to their villages.

Fort Rosalie. 1716.—In the course of the month a solid,
handsome fort was constructed according to agreement.
Bienville put his lieutenant, De Pailloux, in command and
returned to Mobile.

Cadillac Recalled. 1716.—On his arrival in Mobile,
Bienville found that Cadillac had been recalled, and he put
in command until the arrival of the new governor, De l'Epinay.

De l'Epinay. 1717.—De l'Epinay was an old lieutenant
of marine who had seen considerable service in Canada.
Crozat not only gave to him, as to Cadillac, an interest in the
profit of his charter, but agreed to pay him two thousand

livres a year additional, if, as the governor, he would strictly
and severely execute the ordinance protecting his monopoly
of trade.

De l'Epinay was accompanied by a new commissary, Hubert.   On the vessel that brought them came also a band of
emigrants and three companies of soldiers.   Bienville was
maintained in his same position, and received as recognition
of his past services the Cross of St. Louis.   But his disappointment at not succeeding Cadillac was great.   He thought
that his services entitled him to the first place in the colony,
and he resented the belittling of himself and his Canadian
fellow pioneers in favor of strangers to Louisiana.

The secret dissatisfaction soon broke out into open contest.
Hubert, the new commissary, sided with De l'Epinay, and
the usual accusations were banded from one side to the other.
De l'Epinay was charged with tyrannical conduct, scandal-
ous morals, withholding the presents sent to the Indians for
himself, and illicit trading.   Bienville was accused of being
a paid pensioner of the Spanish government.   It was a libel
which he never forgot nor forgave.

Crozat Gives up His Charter. 1717.—Crozat, finding out
at last there was no trade to be had with Spanish ports, and
not enough in the colony in spite of all his protection to pay
him for his expenditures, prayed the king to be relieved of
his charter.   His prayer was granted; and Louisiana and
Canada, by another charter, was made over for twenty-five
years to a company called the Company of the West and of
the Indies.   The president of the company was the famous
John Law.*

---

* John Law, a Scotchman, was one of the most celebrated financiers who ever
lived.   A friend and protege of the regent, Duke of Orleans, he was allowed to apply his theories to the amelioration of the national debt of France.   He opened a
bank called the Bank of France, which operated most successfully in re-establish-
ing credit and reducing the interest on the debt.   By degrees Law, extending his
schemes, took into it the entire colonial interests of France in one comprehensive
company, the stock of which, under his manipulations, rose to a fabulous height;
fall again to the lowest depths.   The Company of the Mississippi, as it came to be
'led, met at first with a most glittering success, and its failure involved the bank-
'tcy of Law and the greatest ruin in France.   In Louisiana it was, on the whole,

Give an account of the Crozat charter. Disputes between Bienville and Cadillac. Cadillac's efforts to secure trade. St. Denis' explorations (see note). First war of the Natchez. Terms of peace. Building of Fort Rosalie. Who succeeded Cadillac? Who was De l' Epinay? Who was John Law?

CHAPTER XII.

THE COMPANY OF THE WEST.

The Company of the West by its charter acquired for twenty-five years the exclusive monopoly of the trade of Louisiana, with the absolute ownership of any mines that might be discovered in the country, the title to any lands they improved, and the right of granting concessions to its stockholders, upon condition of settlement and improvement. They were given all the forts, magazines, guns, ammunition, vessels, provisions, etc., in the colony, with all the merchandise surrendered by Crozat. They were empowered to raise troops, fit out ships of war, cast cannon, make war or peace with the Indians, and nominate governors and officers (to be commissioned, however, by the king). On its side, the company obligated itself to build churches, provide clergymen, and to bring into the colony during the term of its charter six thousand whites and three thousand blacks. The first directors of the company, six in number, were to be named by the king; afterwards they were to be elected every three years by the stockholders.*

The Superior Council. 1719.—During the Crozat charter, 1712, a council, called the Superior Council, was ap-

___

most beneficial in developing the colony. The title by which it is now known, the Mississippi Bubble, records the verdict passed upon it by posterity. Law tell like his stock, from vast wealth to utter worthlessness. He ended his days a poverty-stricken, homeless adventurer.

*The first directors of the company named by the regent were: Law, director general of the Bank of France; Diron d' Artaguette (former royal commissary), receiver general of the finances of Auch; Duché, receiver general of the finances of La Rochelle; Moreau, deputy of commerce of St. Malo; Piou, deputy of commerce of Nantes; Castaigne and Mouchard, merchants of La Rochelle.

pointed for three years, to administer justice in civil and
criminal cases. It was composed of five members—the governor, the royal commissary, the commander of the royal
troops, who elected the other two members, and an attorney
general, clerk, etc.

The term of this first board having expired, a new one*
was appointed, composed of the directors of the company
presided over by the governor, with the director general of
the company as senior counsellor. But, although he had the
seat of honor at the board, the governor had no more power
than his one vote entitled him to, and he was in reality subor-
dinate to the senior counsellor, who performed the functions
of president of the tribunal, counting the votes, pronouncing
judgments, affixing seals, etc.

Inferior Councils.—Hitherto this council was the sole tribunal of the colony, but the increasing extension of population demanded that tribunals should be stationed in several
parts of the province. The directors of the company and the
agents, with two to four of the most notable of the inhabitants of any neighborhood, were, therefore, constituted into
such inferior tribunals. Their judgments were appealable to
the Superior Council.

Bienville Governor. 1718.—The new company applied
all the stimulus of capital and determination to the development of their enterprise.

They recalled De l'Epinay, and gave the government to
Bienville (with the title of Commandant General for the
King), as to the one man qualified by experience and ability
to carry out their expectations. The appointment was backed
by three ships loaded with abundant supplies of money,
provisions, merchandise and a full corp of directors, under

---

*The first Superior Council under the Company of the West was composed of
lenville, commandant general ; Hubert, senior counsellor ; Boisbriant and Chat-
.ugue, king's lieutenants ; l'Archambault, Villardo and Legas, puisne counsel-
rs ; Cartier de Baume was the attorney general, and Cuture the clerk.

a director general,* and more than seven hundred emigrants.

A large and capable corps of engineers was sent out under the Chevalier Leblond de la Tour, a knight of St. Louis, to superintend the construction of the necessary public works.

Bienville went to action with an energy which showed that he considered the expectations of the company of easy fulfilment with the means at his disposal.

To make sure of his western boundaries against the Spaniards, he sent Chateaugnay to take possession and build a fort at La Salle's old site on the coast of Texas. De la Harpe, with fifty emigrants, was sent to establish a post on Red river among the Caddodaquious. The newly arrived engineers were ordered to examine and report upon the depth of water at the mouth of the Mississippi, with a view to securing a good channel into it.

NEW ORLEANS, 1718.

New Orleans. 1718.—He himself, with a party of workmen, set out to accomplish a design which had lain near his heart ever since the days of his command at Fort Maurepas. This was to found a city on the banks of the Mississippi;

---

* Among the first arrivals, in August, 1718, was the first historian of Louisiana, Le Page du Pratz. He came with a force of ten men, and selected a tract of land near the new city. Du Pratz relates the anchoring of his ship in the open road before Dauphin Island; the chanting of the Te Deum for the safe voyage, the landing of the passengers and their effects, etc. On the island he was lodged and fed by a friend, an old ship captain who treated him to the most wonderful good cheer, the fish particularly eliciting glowing praise.

for he was convinced that a city thus situated would one day
be one of the trading centres of the continent. He had
chosen the spot years before, and had even settled some Canadians there to prove its fertility and height above overflow.
It was a ridge of high land near the bank of the Mississippi,
about one hundred and fifty miles from its mouth; commu-
nicating with Lake Pontchartrain in the rear by a small
bayou (afterwards named Bayou St. John). He named the
place after the Duke of Orleans, regent of France, the patron
of Law and the Company of the West.

Colonization. 1718.—Over in France the Mississippi
Company continued parceling out its capital of land in large
concessions to its shareholders, who sent over emigrants by
the ship load to take possession. The Yazou* district,
Natchez, Natchitoches, Pointe Coupee, Baton Rouge, Manchac, Houma, Tchoupitoulas (jnst above the site of the new
city), Cannes Brulées, Bay of St. Louis, Pascagoula, all
were made over to noble or millionaire families. Law himself secured a tract of four miles square on the Arkansas, to
which he shipped Protestant Swiss and German emigrants.

The small establishments of Mobile and Dauphin Island
staggered under the sudden increase of population put upon
them. According to the terms of the Mississippi Company,
free lodging, food and transportation were guaranteed to the
colonists. As the concessions were scattered all over the lower
Mississippi valley, boats and carts had to be made to convey
the emigrants. The overworked carpenters did what they
could, but delays were unavoidable, and while the emigrants
were waiting for the means of transportation they were

---

* A company headed by Leblanc, secretary of state, the Comte de Bienville, and
the Marquis de Assleck, took possession of the Yazous. Concessions at Natchez
were made to the Commissioner Hubert, and to a company of St. Malo merchants.
Natchitoch s was conceded to Bernard de la Harpe, the compiler of "Journal
Historiques;" Tunicas to St Reme; Pointe Coupee to De Meuse; the present site
of Baton Rouge to Diron d'Artaguette; the bank of the Mississippi opposite
Manchac to Paris Duvernay; the Tchoupitoulas lands to De Muys; that of the
Oumas to Marquis d'Artagnac; the bank opposite to De Guiche, De la Houssaie and
De la Houpe; Bay St. Louis to Madame de Mezieres; and Pascagoula to Madame
de Chaumont.

forced to eat the provisions sent to feed them in their new homes, and spend the money they had brought to furnish them. No lodgings being provided, they were forced to sleep under any shelter they could find. In the summer months this produced great distress and sickness, particularly among the women and children.

Capture of Pensacola. 1719.—But the colony was to receive an interruption, and an interruption of the pleasantest kind to the Canadian governor and his soldiers.

In April, 1719, Bienville's brother and nephew, the two De Serignys,* sailed into the harbor of Dauphin Island, bringing the news of war between France and Spain. This was the opportunity for which the French had been waiting for twenty years, to capture Pensacola. Bienville summoned a council of war, and it was decided to attack the Spaniards at once, before they heard the news and had time to put themselves in a state of defence.

As soon as his cargoes were discharged De Serigny sailed there with his ships, the Marechal de Villars and the Philippe, followed by the Count de Toulouse, which happened to be in port. They carried one hundred and fifty soldiers. Bienville sailed in a sloop with eighty men. With a fair wind they made a good run to Isle Ste. Rosa, the outpost of the Spaniards. Anchoring as close to land as possible, the troops disembarked unperceived, and soon mastered the small garrison stationed there. Putting their prisoners in irons and dressing in their uniforms they easily deceived and captured the detail, who came out next morning to relieve guard. Embarking then in the Spanish boat, they crossed the bay, entered the fort, surprised the sentinels on duty, and captured the whole place—soldiers, magazine, storehouse and the commandant, who was still in bed. Chateaugnay was

---

* De Serigny, the brother, was charged with the commission to examine and sound the coast of Louisiana. His maps form the beginning of the scientific cartography of the Mississippi Delta.

put in command, and the Spanish garrison shipped for Havana on the Comte de Toulouse. The governor of Havana received the French officers in charge most ceremoniously, thanking them for the politeness of their visit; but no sooner were the prisoners in his hands than he seized them with their ship, placed the soldiers in irons and put the entire crew, officers and all, in prison. He then equipped the French vessel with a Spanish crew and Spanish soldiers, and sent them with his squadron to retake Pensacola. The Spanish vessels drew up behind the Isle Ste. Rosa. The French vessels, flying the French colors, boldly entered the channel. Scarcely was anchor dropped, however, when the French flag was lowered, the Spanish run up, and three cannon shots fired. At the signal the rest of the squadron made its appearance, twelve sail in all. The next day eighteen hundred men were landed and began the assault, which soon reduced the fort. Chateaugnay was sent to rejoin his compatriots in Havana. The Spanish commander then sailed over to Mobile and summoned Serigny, who was in command, to surrender. Serigny, surrounded by his soldiers, Canadians, and savages in all their war paint, received the messenger and told him that the Spaniards could come when they pleased, they would find the French ready to receive them. And in truth the French made so gallant a show that the Spaniards did not venture to land, nor even come within gunshot of the French batteries. One of their vessels, entering the bay, captured some flat-boats of provisions and ravaged the plantations along the shore. Fortunately, that night Bienville was sending a reinforcement of Indians to his brother. These fell upon the marauders. Very few escaped.

The sight of a squadron of French war ships in the gulf hastened the departure of the Spanish fleet. With this strong reinforcement, Bienville and Serigny shortly afterwards sailed again to Pensacola and captured it a second time, and destroyed its fortifications.

After this sprightly episode, the colony returned to its former routine of life.

Inflation. 1719.—Emigrants continued to arrive by the hundred, two hundred, four hundred at a time. Ignorant of all life except that of the small peasant of France, dazed from the long voyage, weak from sea-sickness, a more helpless mass of people never landed in a new country. And no emigrants ever landed in a more unfavorable spot than Dauphin Island. Put ashore with their scanty effects, they were forced to wait weeks for the means of transportation to their concessions; without shelter, with insufficient food, unable to find work or gain anything by cultivating the arid soil, tortured and blinded by the dazzling white sand, under the rays of a tropical sun, exposed to the infection of the ships from the West Indian Islands, always waiting and hoping and being disappointed, it is easy to believe that most of the unfortunate creatures died on the spot of their misery. The directors of the company, more and more helpless before the increasing difficulties of the situation, and more and more unable to meet the demands upon them, were panic stricken at the crisis which they saw impending. They could think of no remedy but a change of base.

Bienville exerted himself in vain in favor of New Orleans. The emigrants, he maintained, could be landed there and easily distributed to their concessions, or find self-support in cultivating the rich alluvial soil. He was outvoted at the council, which decided in favor of the old capital, Biloxi.

Biloxi. 1720.—The move was effected with all haste, and at great expense to the company and colony; and in a short time Fort St. Louis de la Mobile was only a garrison post, and Dauphin Island a way station for incoming and outgoing ships. But, as Bienville had maintained, there was no change from the removal except to still greater financial loss and human misery. The emigrants continued to increase in numbers and their quality decreased. Formerly small bodies of con-

victs were sent to Louisiana to work out their sentences there in
clearing and developing the land. Now the company, to keep
up by flattering numbers its enterprise in the eyes of the shareholders, began to send as emigrants any material they could
get, even by force or fraud.   Prisons, reformatories, asylums
and hospitals were raided, and the inmates shipped to the
Mississippi.   Kidnappers in the streets of Paris and other
large cities of France drove a thriving trade by furnishing
emigrants at so much a head.   And to add to the dark picture, slave ships brought their wretched, reeking African
cargoes, and dumped them, like so much ballast, on the
sands of Biloxi.   The result can be imagined.   Crime and
outrage could not be prevented.   The famine became so
great that more than five hundred died of hunger.   Fish and
oysters were all the food that the starving creatures could
find, and to get them they had to wade out in water up to
their waists.   Their dead bodies were found in heaps around
piles of oyster shells.

New Biloxi.—A drunken, sleeping sergeant, by letting his
lighted pipe fall in his tent, started a fire which consumed
Biloxi to the ground.   A council of all the colonial officers
was held, and another transference of headquarters was decided upon.   Bienville again made an effort in favor of New
Orleans, and was again outvoted, on the pretext that there
was not enough water at the mouth of the Mississippi to permit the entrance of loaded vessels.   The point of land opposite Deer Island, called thenceforth New Biloxi, was chosen
for the seat of government, and orders for its establishment
carried into effect at once.   A fort and extensive buildings
were put up on the mainland, and a hospital on the island.

Bienville met the denial of the possibility of loaded vessels
entering the mouth of the Mississippi by the proposition to
send the "Dromadaire," a vessel of the company, through
it as a test.   One of the directors opposed this violently on
the strength of a certificate from the captain of the "Drom-

adaire," that his vessel could not get through the mouth of the river. Bienville then declared that he would send the vessel through on his own responsibility; the director warned him that if he did so he would be held liable for damages. Bienville, shortly afterwards, did in fact carry the "Drom-adaire" triumphantly through the passes.

Pauger, De la Tour's assistant, was dispatched to the passes to make maps of them and a report to send to France, to prove Bienville's theory, that the Mississippi was navigable for large vessels and that New Orleans must be the capital of the province. Pauger* went also with a force of convicts to lay out New Orleans as a regular city. He accomplished the task satisfactorily; clearing the neglected space, aligning streets, assigning allotments, and making a plan of the whole, containing the names of the owners of the allotments.

The Mississippi Bubble. 1721.—Just at the time the news of Law's failure and flight, and collapse of the Mississippi scheme, reached the colony. All enterprise and hope were for a moment paralyzed, and a financial panic seemed inevitable. But ships, emigrants, soldiers and merchandise continued to arrive as before, and it soon became evident that whatever the amount of bankruptcy caused in France to the stockholders and investors in the Mississippi scheme, Louisiana was not going to be given up as a bad debt.

In France the board of directors to whom had been confided the liquidation of the company made known their determination not to abandon the enterprise by sending out new directors and two officials, Messrs. Daunoy and De la Chaise, to examine into the late accounts.

The statements published by the Company of the West proved that during the term of its charter it had transported to Louisiana 7020 persons, among these 600 negroes. The

---

* Pauger's map of New Orleans is the earliest we have.

expenditures had been enormous; those of the last year alone
having risen to 474,274 livres.

QUESTIONS.

Give an account of the Company of the West? The judicial administration of the colony? What of New Orleans? Give an account
of the capture of Pensacola and following circumstances? What of
the inflation of 1719? The sufferings of emigrants? Move to Biloxi?
Scenes there? New Biloxi? How did Bienville exert himself in favor
of New Orleans? What of the passage of the "Dromadaire" through
the mouth of the Mississippi? What was the effect of the breaking
of the Mississippi Bubble in Louisiana? How many persons had the
Company of the West brought into Louisiana?

----- •◆• -----

CHAPTER XIII.

NEW ORLEANS.

New Orleans, Capital of the Colony. 1722.—Bienville's
reiterated letters on the subject, with Pauger's map and reports, at last convinced the Louisiana administrators in
France, and the long desired authorization was received to
remove the capital of the colony to New Orleans.

Centralization.—From this moment Louisiana ceased to
be a mere colonial experiment, and began to be self sustain-
ing from its own efforts. The work of transference was
begun without delay and was prosecuted with vigor. In
June, 1722, De la Tour and Pauger lead the way, by sailing in a loaded vessel through the mouth of the river. As
soon as word was brought back that they had passed the bar,
other boats followed with men, building materials, ammunition and provisions.

Under De la Tour's supervision, the city took form and
shape. A church and houses were built, levees thrown up,

ditches made, and a great canal dug in the rear for drainage; a cemetery located, and a quay constructed protected with palisades. Bienville arrived and took up his residence there in August. To Pauger was assigned a post at the Balize.* With fifty workmen and a dredge boat, he performed marvels in an incredibly short time. Besides keeping a pass open, he built out of the drift caught from the river, lodgings, storehouses, boats, a smithy, and a chapel with a belfry that could serve for a light-house, while his gardens furnished the gladdest of welcomes both to the eye and heart of the weary incoming sea traveler.

Beginnings of New Orleans.—New Orleans, however, had no more fortunate beginnings than Mobile or Biloxi. In the midst of the building and transportation the September storm came on, with a hitherto unexperienced violence. For five days the furious hurricane raging from east to west, swept land and sea. The ripened crops of rice, corn, and beans on the river bank were utterly destroyed, the houses and buildings of the planters blown down. In New Orleans the church and most of the new edifices were demolished, and three vessels wrecked in the river. At Biloxi, the magazine with all the stores, and a ship with its cargo of ammunition and food were ruined; almost all of the boats, sloops and pirogues were lost, and two ships rendered totally unfit for service. For a week the greatest apprehensions were felt on account of the three ships anchored at Ship Island and for a ship on its way to the mouth of the river loaded with pine timber for a storehouse, which had cost the company over a hundred thousand livres. All of them arrived in course of time at New Orleans, passing with facility over the bar. Another crop of rice sprouted from the seeds scattered by the storm—a proof of the fertility of the land—which came as a great consolation to the colonists; but the destruction of

---

* Balize means buoy.

other food which could not be replaced brought upon them the affliction of a famine.

To complete the sum of disasters, fevers broke out with great mortality, and the indomitable Bienville himself fell ill, and for a time his life was despaired of. But the city grew despite it all, and became, as it was destined to become, the centre of the colony, attracting inhabitants from all quarters.

After the bankruptcy of Law, his concessions upon the Arkansas became entirely neglected. Most of his colonists, seeing themselves abandoned by him, moved down to New Orleans, in hopes of finding a passage back to their native country. The council, not willing to lose them, gave them land on both banks of the river, about twenty miles above the city. It is still called from them the " Cote des Allemands " (divided between the parishes St. Charles and St. John the Baptist). The industrious Germans took to garden culture and soon supplied the markets of New Orleans with vegetables. Every Saturday their little fleet was seen descending the river loaded with their fresh verdant produce.

Restoration of Pensacola to the Spaniards.—The termination of the war with Spain, and a double marriage alliance between the two crowns, made the retention of Pensacola by France an impossibility. It was formally surrendered by Bienville in the beginning of the year 1723.

Second Natchez War. 1723.—The disaffected Natchez tribes had gradually recovered from the crushing punishment inflicted upon them and again influenced by either the English or by the Chickasaws, allies of the English, had commenced their depredations and ambushed assaults upon the French—attempts which had grown in boldness until fears were entertained for the safety of the post. After the usual routine of pacificatory measures—summoning the chiefs to him, haranguing them, giving presents to them, Bienville saw himself forced to an attitude more intelligible to the savage mind.

In October, 1723, he landed there with a small army of seven
hundred men—regulars, volunteers and Indians. To give the
villagers no time to rally or fortify, he began his march against
them the morning after arrival. "Stung Serpent," a noted
Natchez chief, still loyal to the French, hurried to Fort
Rosalie, where the commandant slept, and confessed that the
people of the White Apple, Jenzenaque and Gray Village
were in a state of insurrection, and obtained from Bienville
the promise that vengeance should strike only the three guilty
villages. It was on All Saints' Day that the army, with all
precautions for their surprise, filed through the narrow paths
of the forest surrounding the doomed White Apple village.
They came to a mud cabin, before which were three squaws
pounding corn. The women ran in and closed the door after
them. Two or three warriors inside made a defence, but
they were expeditiously killed and scalped and the women
made prisoners. With the exception of some individual exploits by Canadian and Indian scouts, this was the only warlike achievement of the French in the campaign. The White
Apple village was found deserted; it was burned and the
army returned to St. Catherine's Concession, whence they
had set out in the morning.

A few days later, Bienville led his army against the Gray
village, with the same results. The village and temple were
burned. From a captured squaw it was learned that the Indians were awaiting the French at the Jenzenaque village, a
half league away. On this the army was wheeled about, and a
Tunica chief leading the way, marched toward the enemy. A
strong cabin was discovered on a height, the fifes struck up,
and the army forming into a square advanced. This cabin,
like the others, was found empty. The Tunica chief, taking a
turn around the height, perceived below him one of the
enemy's chiefs, a Little Sun, or rather they both at the same
time saw one another; aimed and fired. The Tunica chief
stretched his enemy dead on the spot, but fell himself danger-

ously wounded at the instant. The army then again returned
to St. Catherine. Bienville summoned Stung Serpent to him
and they agreed upon a peace; but the Natchez, not the
French, were felt to have been victorious in the skirmish.

Bienville Recalled. 1724.—There had been no more
harmony between Bienville and the Directors General Hubert
and Duvergier than between him and the Governors Cadillac
and De l'Epinay. And, as in the former cases, discords
took the shape of charges and accusations. The suspicion
caused by the old stories of De la Salle and De la Vente
had never wholly died out, and every dissatisfied official returning to France revived them by their versions of new
tyrannies and flagrant peculations.

Hubert and Duvergier took to France their accusations in
written documents with notarial signatures and attestation.
These produced prompt effect in official headquarters. A
letter from the king directed Bienville to sail to France immediately and answer for himself.

Black Code. 1724.—To provide the security and protection of the law to the growing number of negro slaves im-
ported into the colony, Bienville published his celebrated
Code for the Blacks, or "Code Noir," taken from the regulations compiled by the jurists of Louis XIV for the island
of St. Domingo. It was the last public ordinance to which
he affixed * his name before returning to France. After his
departure the Superior Council investigated the charges made
by Hubert and Duvergier. They reported that they found
them to be only the calumny of the malicious. The notary
who had signed them had his commission revoked and was
himself condemned as a libeler.

---

*Also signed by De la Chaise, Fazende, Brusle, Perry, members of the Superior
Council. De la Chaise had succeeded to Duvergier as Commissary General of the
colony. The following is the list of captains commanding in Louisiana, with the
date of their commissions: 1714, Marigny de Mandeville; 1717, De la Tour, D'Artaguette; 1719, Du Tisne, Lamarque; 1720, Leblanc, Desliettes, Marchand de Cour-
celles, Renault d'Hauterive and Pradel.

The year following, rumors being rife in the colony that the Indians were rejoicing over the recall of Bienville, and that his reappearance in the colony would be the signal for hostilities from them, De Noyan, Bienville's nephew, made a request to the Superior Council that the Natchez, Houmas, Tunicas and other tribes might give voice to their sentiments and refute so grievous a calumny against his uncle. The Superior Council acceding, these nations made their declarations that they all regretted Bienville.

Bienville was, nevertheless, destituted, and in his ruin involved his family and friends. Chateaugnay was relieved of his rank, the two De Noyans were broken and sent to France.

Boisbriant was recalled to give an account of his conduct. Pauger, Perry, Perrault, as members of the council, were censured; the two latter were sent to France. Fazende, also dismissed, was allowed to remain in the colony. In short, for the first time since its colonization, Louisiana was to own in its government neither member nor friend of the family of its founders.

Arrived in France, Bienville presented his justification to the minister, the memoir* of the services that had filled his life; since a mere stripling he had followed his brother Iber-

---

* The following is an extract from his memoir:
   "It is not without trouble I arrived at being absolute master of so many nations
" of such barbarous tempers and such different characters, almost every one of
" which has a particular language. One can conjecture how many difficulties I
" encountered and what risks I ran to lay the foundations of the colony and
" maintain it to the present time. Necessity, it is said, renders us industrious; I ex-
" perienced that it also renders us intrepid in danger, and makes us perform, so
" to speak, the impossible in the different conjunctures in which one finds oneself
" in an unknown world with such a small force. I first applied myself to putting
" myself in a position to govern by myself without the aid of an interpreter. I
" applied myself to the language which appeared to me to be the dominant one
" among the savages, and of which the knowledge would facilitate me in learning
" the others in the end. I was fortunate enough from the first years to gain their
" confidence and their friendship. I studied to know well their customs so as to be
" able to retain them in peace with one another; so that for the twenty-seven years
" during which I had the honor of commanding in the province, I was the arbiter
" of their differences. I always governed these nations, born in independence, so
" to speak, despotically; and I pushed my authority to the deposing of chiefs.
   " The Sieur de Bienville dares say that the establishment of the colony is due
" to the constancy with which he has attached himself to it for twenty-seven years
" without going out of it since he made the discovery of it with his brother Iber-
" ville."

ville in quest of the country for the government of which he was now, a middle-aged man, called to account.

Give an account of the removal of capital to New Orleans. What of the beginning of the city? What of the Germans belonging to Law's concession? When was Pensacola restored to the Spanish? Give an account of the Natchez war. The recall of Bienville. The Black Code. What of the investigation into his conduct by the Superior Council? What of Bienville in France?

CHAPTER XIV.

NATCHEZ MASSACRE.

Perier Governor. 1725.—Bienville's successor, Perier, arrived and took up his abode in the capital, where, for a time, all went well in the march of improvement.

Ursuline Sisters.—A great event in the community was the arrival of six Ursuline Sisters to found a convent for the education of the young girls of the colony, and to serve in the hospital. While their convent was being built, they took up their residence in Bienville's* old hotel.

The Jesuits, who came over at the same time as the Ursulines, were given a tract of land immediately above the the city, in what was long known as the faubourg St. Mary. They had a house and chapel built and laid out their ground in a plantation for Myrtle wax† trees.

---

*Situated in the space now bounded by Chartres, Decatur, Bienville and Cust-omhouse streets. One of the nuns thus describes it in a letter to her father: "The " finest house in the town. It is a two-story building with an attic . . . with six " doors in the first story. In all the stories there are large windows, but with no " glass. The frames are closed with very thin linen, admitting of as much light as " glass."

† Wax was an important and valuable article of trade at a time when candles were the principal means of illumination.

City in 1725.—The government house had been built on the land next to the Jesuits. In the centre of the city stood the Cathedral; facing it was the Place d'Armes, on each side of which were the barracks. A house for the sessions of the Superior Councils and a jail were built on the square immediately above the Cathedral. A levee ran in front of the city, and a wide ditch for drainage on Bourbon street. Each lot was at first surrounded with a small ditch, in addition to the larger ditches around the squares, but these in course of time were filled. On the plantations the culture of indigo had been added to that of tobacco and rice; the fig tree was introduced from Provence, and the orange from St. Domingo.

To provide wives for the bachelors, numbers of young girls were again brought into the colony. They were poor, but of good character and honest family. Each of them was supplied with a small box, called in French "cassette," containing clothing, which gave the girls the name of filles a la cassette. They remained in charge of the nuns until married.

Natchez Massacre. 1727.—After Bienville's last treaty with them the Natchez seemed determined to remain on good terms with the French, but the systematic tyranny and injustice of Chepart, the officer in command of Fort Rosalie, infuriated the tribes into such hatred that they inflicted a blow which made the colony reel, and appalled the home government. The crowning outrage of Chepart was most wanton. Looking for a suitable tract of land for a plantation, he cast his eyes upon the charmingly situated White Apple village, and determined to possess it. He sent for the Sun of the village and ordered him and his tribe to vacate it. The Sun replied that the ancestors of his tribe had possessed the village as many years as there were hairs in his war lock, and it was only right that he and his descendants should still live in it. But the French commander, refusing to listen to reason or remonstrance, fixed the day for evacuation. The Sun assembled the council of his village and made a speech in which he exposed the rapacity and tyranny of the French and urged the tribe to make a stand against it.

Village by village was aroused, and the different Suns adopted the determination to strike one bloody blow, and free themselves forever of the burthensome yoke upon them. Emissaries were sent to the adjoining tribes. Packages containing an equal number of sticks were prepared and sent to every village, with directions to take out a stick every day after the new moon. The attack was to be made on the day on which the last stick was taken out.

Great care was taken to keep the design from the women. One of the female Suns, however, had her suspicion aroused, and extracted the secret from her son. The bundle of sticks for her village had been deposited in the temple, the keeper of which was to take out a stick daily and burn it in the sacred fire. The princess, by reason of her rank, had access to the temple at all times. She found an opportunity to take one or two sticks from the bundle and threw them into the fire; this destroyed the count and prevented unanimity of action. It is said that she even gave notice of the massacre to one of the officers of the garrison; but her warning was unheeded.

The fatal day arrived. By daylight the Natchez, in small groups, strolled into Fort Rosalie and the establishment adjoining until they outnumbered the whites. Pretending that they were going on a hunt, they borrowed guns and offered to buy powder and shot. At 9 o'clock the signal was given. Each Indian fell on his man. By noon two hundred were killed, and ninety-two women and fifty-five children and all the negroes were made prisoners. Chepart was among the first slain. During the massacre the great Sun, with apparent unconcern, smoked his pipe in the government warehouse. His men brought in to him the heads of the officers

placing that of Chepart in the centre and the others around
When the Sun was informed that not a white man was left
alive, except a carpenter and tailor specially reserved from
the massacre, he gave the command to pillage. Every build-·
ing was sacked and the spoils divided. Two soldiers, who
were accidentally in the woods, escaped and carried the
news to Perier, in New Orleans.

The colony trembled from limit to limit. New Orleans
was given over to panic. Every settlement of Indians, however small, became an object of dread. There was an insignificant and peaceful group of Chouachas living above the
city. Perier sent a band of negroes from the neighboring
plantation and had them ruthlessly destroyed—men, women
and children.

Ships were sent to France for troops. Couriers were despatched to the Illinois, Red river and Mobile countries,
warning the white men there. Emissaries were also sent
among the Yazous to hold them true to France.

The Choctaws were the first in the field. Seven hundred
of them, under the Canadian Le Sueur, fell upon the Natchez
while they were still in the midst of their feasting and rejoicing, killed sixty of their warriors, and rescued fifty-nine
women and children, and one hundred slaves who had been
taken prisoners. It was February before the troops from
New Orleans, fourteen hundred men, under Loubois, arrived. The Natchez, in the meantime, had fortified themselves in the White Apple village in two strong houses, Fort
Flour, and the well named by the French, Fort Valor. Their
defence was splendid. The French opened siege with all the
science of continental warfare—sappers, miners, cannon;
but from the first they were hopelessly overmatched in every
soldierly qualification by their savage foes.

The honors of the campaign rested with the Choctaws.
They at least had the merit of terminating it. Waiting in
vain for the French to make a promised breach in one of the

forts, and seeing one day thirty Frenchmen running from the
trench before a sortie of the Natchez, the Choctaws opened
a parley with Fort Flour. Alabamma Mingo, one of their
most famous chiefs, made a speech to the obstinate foes, in
which he convinced them that although the French could not
fight them the Choctaws were sufficient in numbers and possessed patience enough to blockade them and force them into surrender through starvation. The Natchez agreed to deliver to the Choctaws the remainder of their women,
children and negro prisoners, if the French would evacuate
their position and with their guns retire to the banks of the
river. This was executed. Two nights after the Natchez
secretly made their escape from their forts, eluding all pursuit of the French. With their allies, the Yazous, some of
them sought refuge with the Chickasaws. The others, crossing the Mississippi, made their way westward through forest
and swamp to an imposing mound, in the present parish of
Catahoula, just above the juncture of Little river with the
Ouachita. Here they remained until tidings reached them
of a great armament of white men and Indians led by Perier
close upon them. They withdrew to a far stronger military
position, to a thirty-foot bluff on the eastern end of a plateau,
known now as Sicily Island, situated at the southwest extremity of a small lake (Lake Lovelace). There they in-
trenched themselves. It took Perier nine months with
twenty different scouting parties to locate them.

Last Stand of the Natchez. 1731.—In the middle of the
summer the reinforcements from France arrived—eight hundred French soldiers and Swiss mercenaries. This, with
what he could raise from among the colonists and his Indian
allies, enabled Perier to garrison all his settlements and lead
a thousand men against his enemies.

In the beginning of the year 1731 he ascended the Mississippi to the mouth of the Red river, where all of his
forces were to assemble. Proceeding through Red river to

Black river and up the Ouachita, he reached the lair, in
which the Natchez stood like beasts at bay. As before,
the Natchez held their own gallantly, until they brought
about a parley. Perier refused to treat with any but chiefs.
Two Suns and the great warrior who had defended Fort
Flour presented themselves. They were treacherously made
prisoners. Perier then demanded the surrender of all French
prisoners; this was acceded to. During the night the warrior from Fort Flour made his escape; the two Suns, not so
fortunate, were discovered and held. Perier then offered to
spare the lives of all the Natchez men, women and children
who delivered themselves up to him. The next day four
hundred women and children and forty-five men left the
Natchez fortifications and ranged themselves inside those of
the French; but they came in such small groups that the
whole day was consumed in the surrender. Seventy still
remained in their fort, asking a delay until the morrow. It
was raining in torrents. Between the water under foot and
the water overhead, not being able to take them, Perier was
forced to consent. At 9 o'clock at night the weather cleared,
and the French could approach the Natchez forts. They
were found deserted! Again the great fighting bulk of the
nation, under the leadership of the redoubtable warrior of
Fort Flour, had given the slip to their captors. The stronghold was destroyed and two prisoners taken were scalped and
burned. Perier returned to New Orleans with his trophies
of women and children, the two Suns and forty men, all of
whom he sold into slavery in St. Domingo.

Escaped Natchez.—The number of Natchez Indians
who escaped during the siege and capitulation was three
hundred. They spread themselves over the Red river country, savagely attacking the Natchitoches fort under St. Denis.
Beaten back, they took possession of a deserted Natchitoches
village, from which they were driven out by St. Denis, after
an obstinate fight. They then sought refuge with the Chicka-

saws, who from the first had offered their villages and strongholds to them.

Give an account of the city in 1725. What product had been added
to agriculture? Give an account of the Natchez massacre. The effect
on the colony. Describe the expedition against them. What of the
treaty? Describe the last stand of the Natchez. What became of
those who were taken prisoners? Those who escaped?

————•◆•————

CHAPTER XV.

LOUISIANA A ROYAL PROVINCE. 1731.

With the peace, prosperity and life of the colony threatened
by an Indian war, the administrators in France could not
hope to carry on its development with any profit. They
therefore remitted their charter to the king, and Louisiana
once more came back into the wardship of the royal government. The colonists themselves, shaken by past events, lost
confidence in the men over them. The commandants of the
different posts who had served under Bienville's long administration, wrote to the Minister of the Marine representing
his merits over those of any man who had ever governed in
the colony. Pontchartrain himself must have felt the force
of their arguments if not of his experience with Bienville.
Perier was recalled, and the Canadian, relieved of his dis-
grace, reinstated.

Bienville Governor. 1733.—Stopping at St. Domingo
on his way to Louisiana, Bienville had an interview with his
old friends, the unfortunate Natchez who had been sold into
slavery. They assured him that they had only been driven
into revolt by the hard treatment they had received from the
French officers at Fort Rosalie, and that they bitterly regretted the sad termination of their long alliance with the

French. The governor was much impressed with their changed fate and the wretchedness of their demeanor.

Arrived in New Orleans, Bienville took up. his residence in his former hotel and addressed himself to his old routine of governing.

War With the Chickasaws. 1736.—The first and most important claim upon his attention was naturally the Natchez question. He could arrive at no accurate estimate of the number of them still at large. But, through his Indian allies, he knew that there were three bands of them; one on the Ouachita, one on the Yazou and one with the Chickasaws.

French security demanded that these last should be proceeded against in an exemplary manner. In case the Chickasaws could not be forced or bribed to give them up, they must be included in the war also. The Choctaws were his main reliance. Strong and powerful, their rivalry of the Chickasaws had kept them in a state of well disciplined warfare. But Bienville found that during Perier's unskilful administration a division had crept into the Choctaw nation. That English traders and emissaries, with liberal display of promises and presents, had secured a considerable party among them favorable to the English. While he prepared his armament against the Chickasaws he addressed himself to healing this division. He sent his Canadians among them again. Under their instigations many of the Choctaw villages rose and killed the English staying there, and were fired into keeping a succession of war parties in the field against the Chickasaws, burning their corn fields, waylaying their hunting parties, and harassing them greatly. The same tactics were employed to induce the Indians along the Mississippi, to strike down from the north against the Chickasaws, who, between two fires, kept close in their territory, appealing for help to the English.

Bienville's plan of campaign was one in which he thought he had secured every possible means for success. It was to

penetrate by the Tombigbee river into the Chickasaw country, where he was to be joined by d'Artaguette (a young
brother of Diron), commandant at the Illinois, with a force
of three hundred good men.   Orders were sent to d'Artaguette fixing the place of meeting on the Tombigbee, four
days' journey from the Chickasaws' villages; the time, between the 10th and 15th of March.

Bienville, the better to further his preparations, took up
his position during the summer in Mobile, where, in a grand
council, he exposed his plans to the Choctaw chiefs, and secured their willing co-operation in them.   But the means of
transportation, to be furnished by the middle of October, were
not ready by the middle of January.   A courier was despatched to D'Artaguette, putting off his march until the
middle of April.

Finally, all was ready and a grand start made on the 1st
of April.   The armament made a fine show on the Mobile,
rowing up the river in the early morning sunlight; thirty
pirogues followed by thirty flat-boats loaded with five hundred soldiers, without counting the brilliant staff of officers
and company of forty-five blacks commanded by free negroes.

It took twenty-three days to get to the place of meeting on
the Tombigbee.   No trace of D'Artaguette was to be seen.
The Choctaw chiefs arrived, however, and promised to meet
the French, with all their warriors, in fourteen days, at the
little creek, Ottibia, that separated the Choctaw and Chickasaw territories.   They arrived promptly at the time and
place shortly after the French.

After throwing up a fortification to protect their boats and
provisions, and leaving a small garrison behind them, the
army set out on the march to the Chickasaw country.   It was
a hard march, through deep ravines filled with water waist
high, and across thick-grown canebrakes.   But after this they
came to a beautiful country easy of travel.   Camp was pitched
about six miles from the Chickasaw villages.   The great chief

of the Choctaws asked Bienville which village he intended
attacking first. Bienville told him the Natchez, as they were
the authors of the war. The great chief then explained that
the first village was the nearest Chickasaw village to the
Choctaws, and did them most harm, and that he would like
to attack that first, particularly as it was filled with provisions which the Choctaws needed. Hardly doubting but that
the Choctaws would return home after taking this first village, their habit being to fly after they had struck a blow,
Bienville persuaded them to attack the Natchez village first,
promising to return and take the other one afterwards. The
Choctaws appeared satisfied, and their guides, leading the
army as if to conduct it to the point agreed upon, came to a
small prairie, where were three little villages placed trian-
gularly on the crest of a ridge, at the foot of which flowed
a brook almost dry. This little prairie was only separated
by a small forest from the large prairie where lay most of the
Chickasaw villages. Bienville defiled his army the length
of the woods that skirted the prairie, and stopped on a slight
eminence, where a halt was made for dinner. It was just
past mid-day.

The Choctaws, who had gained their point by a ruse and
were before the village they desired, hastened to complete
the trick by bringing on the action. With war cries and
yells, they began skirmishing around the village, and drew
its fires upon the French. The French officers then joined
their demands to the Choctaws that this village should be
at once taken. Pressed on all sides, Bienville ordered
the attack. A company of grenadiers—a detachment from
the French and Swiss troops—and forty-five volunteers under
De Noyan, were commanded to lead it.

From the height where the French were, four or five Eng-
lishmen could be seen bustling around among the excited
Chickasaws, and over one village floated the English
flag. The French battalion moved out of the woods,

crossed the brook, and began to ascend the ridge. A murderous fire poured upon them simultaneously from the
three villages. One of the negro mantelet bearers in front
was killed. The rest threw down their mantelets and fled.
The column of grenadiers, attaining the summit of the ridge
and the entrance to the village, met the full fire of the hidden batteries * about them. Two or three cabins were taken
and burned; but when it came to crossing, under fire, the
open space between these and the next, the Chevalier De
Noyan, looking about him, saw only a few officers, a rem-
nant of grenadiers, and about a dozen volunteers. The other
soldiers, hopeless at fighting an unseen enemy, were seeking
shelter from the range of their loopholes behind the captured
cabins, and refused to be driven out by their sergeants.
Almost all the officers were killed or disabled. De Noyan
and four officers fell wounded at the same moment. In vain
he sent his aid to rally the soldiers; the killing of the aid
among them only added to their panic. He finally got a
message to Bienville that unless assistance were sent, or a
retreat sounded, not an officer would be left alive. There was
also a sudden alarm in the camp that a reinforcement from
the Chickasaws of the great prairie was approaching. Bienville ordered the retreat, sending a company to protect it and
fetch off the wounded. The officers, massed together, were
found still fighting and holding their own. The Choctaws
were under cover of the hill; they had lost twenty-two men,
which discouraged and disgusted them not a little.

The night was passed in felling trees and making hasty defences against surprise, but the Chickasaws held themselves
silent and secure in their strongholds. Bienville dared not

* Bienville thus describes the Chickasaw stronghold: "After having surrounded
" their cabins with several rows of great stockades filled with earth, they hollow out
" the inside until they can let themselves down into it shoulder deep, and shoot
" through loopholes almost level with the ground; but they obtain still more ad-
" vantage from the natural situation of their cabins, which are placed so that their
" fires cross, than from all the arts of fortifying that the English can suggest. The
" coverings of the cabins are a thatching of wood and mud, proof against fire-arrows
" and grenades; nothing but bombs could damage them."

renew the attack the next morning. Litters were made for
the wounded, and the humiliated French colors led the way
back to the Ottibia and embarked. The water was now so
low that in many places a passage had to be cut for the
boats. The Tombigbee was slowly reached, and finally the
Mobile. From the Tohomes Bienville heard the first news
of the full extent of his disaster:

The young commandant, d'Artaguette, had set out from
the Illinois at the date first named, with one hundred and
forty white men and two hundred and sixty Iroquois, Arkansas, Miamis and Illinois. Arrived at the place of meeting,
his scouts could discover no signs or traces of Bienville's
army. The next day, the courier who had been sent to the
Illinois appeared with Bienville's letter and change of plan.
D'Artaguette called his officers and Indian chiefs together in
a council of war. They advised striking a blow immediately. Pushing forward their march they arrived within a
mile of the great Chickasaw prairie. It was Palm Sunday.
The army left their baggage under a guard of thirty men
and confidently took the road to the village. It was the road
to certain death to all but two of them. Hardly had the attack
on the village begun, when D'Artaguette saw a troop of
from four to five hundred savages issue from behind the
neighboring hill, and bear down upon him with such rapidity
aud force that the Miamis and Illinois Indians, the greater
part of his army, took to flight. He turned to gain the road
to his baggage, to save or at least blow up his powder.
Fighting desperately, step by step, he, his officers, men, and
the Iroquois and Arkansas who stood by him, struggled a
short space. Then the savages overwhelmed them. Nineteen were taken alive, among them D'Artaguette, wounded
in three places, and Father Senac, a Jesuit priest.

An Avoyelle woman slave, who escaped from the Chickasaws to the Alabamas some time afterwards, related the fate
of the prisoners. Two were put aside to exchange for a

Chickasaw warrior in the hands of the French. The remaining were divided into two lots and burned in two huge fires prepared by the Chickasaw women. All died heroically, one Frenchman singing his death song to the last like an Indian brave.

Bienville never recovered from the pain and humiliation of this double defeat, and Diron D'Artaguette, maddened with grief at the loss of his young brother, changed from a trusty friend into a carping enemy of the governor.

Chickasaw War.—Bienville returned to New Orleans, inflexibly determined to retrieve himself by another expedition against the Natchez—an expedition which must not only be a brilliant success, but a brilliant triumph.

He wrote to France for artillery and bombs and soldiers, and to the governor of Canada for a reinforcement of volunteers. He sent engineers to explore the best routes to the Chickasaws by the Mobile and Mississippi rivers, and he kept his coureurs de bois diligently employed in maintaining the French sentiment among his Indian allies.

On the reports of the engineers the route by the Mississippi and Yazou rivers was selected, and the years 1738–1739 were consumed in building a fort and depots for provisions, at the mouth of the St. Francis river and another, Fort Assumption, on the opposite side of the Mississippi, at the mouth the Margot river, the meeting place for the whole army.

Two hundred horses were sent from New Orleans for transportation of the provisions which were to be drawn from the abundant fields of the west. Beeves and oxen were ordered from the Natchitoches district. In the summer of 1739, the assistance demanded from the home government arrived—arms, ammunition, provisions, with seven hundred soldiers—bombardiers, cannoneers, miners—under the Sieur de Noailles D'Aime, who was put in command of all the troops.

But the new soldiers, on their arrival, suffered so severely from scurvy and fever that less than half were able to go on duty. Shipped from New Orleans as fast as possible, great numbers of them died on the way up the river. Bienville himself landed at Fort Assumption in November, with his colonial troops and Indians. He found the reinforcements from Canada and the Illinois waiting. They raised his army to the respectable strength of twelve hundred white men and two thousand four hundred savages. But it was one thing to get an army to the fort on the Margot, and another to get it into the Chickasaw country. The continual rains and the overflow made the routes laid out by the engineers impracticable for the heavy wagons and artillery, while the bottom lands could only be crossed by boats or bridges. More than one-half of the live stock from Natchitoches perished in the woods before reaching the Arkansas. Three months passed and the situation did not improve. Without a road to the Chickasaws and without the means of transportation, the French army on the Mississippi saw itself threatened with a more inglorious fate than befell the one on the Tombigbee; and the safety of the Chickasaws was more brilliantly proved than ever. A council of war was held to decide how to end the situation in the manner least mortifying to the French.

The Chickasaws, on their side, were not indifferent to the tremendous preparations made against them. From the first they had dropped all around the neighborhood of the French camp, calumets and symbols of peace. On these hints, disdained at first, the French were now glad to act. But some warlike demonstration was necessary to satisfy the Indians, so five hundred of them, with one hundred Canadians, were permitted to go against the Chickasaw villages. With no hamperings but their light savage accoutrements, they made their way through the forest with ease and celerity. But the Chickasaws, thoroughly warned and on their guard, held themselves close in their strongholds, from which no demon-

strations could entice them, save once or twice when they
came out for a brief moment to display a white flag. After
some days of skirmishing, negotiations were opened, and
the Chickasaw chiefs persuaded to go to the French camp
and ask for peace. They were cautioned, however, that they
would not get it unless they consented to deliver up their
Natchez refugees. The cunning savages, prepared for this
condition, declared that although they had bound and im-
prisoned their Natchez guests, in order to surrender them to
the French, unfortunately some of their young men had released them and all had escaped to the Cherokees except three.

Under the circumstances, peace was soon agreed upon.
The Chickasaws made no further excuse for or explanation of
the escape of the Natchez; and again the French were forced
to submit to having them slip through their fingers. Bienville destroyed his buildings and returned with his army to
New Orleans.

There, oppressed with his sense of failure, and feeling his
old reputation to be no longer the same in the colony, he
wrote to the Minister of Marine, asking to be relieved of his
office.

1741.—While awaiting the minister's answer he applied
himself with his characteristic care and solicitude to the
needs of the colony. He vainly tried to get from the king
the establishment of a college in New Orleans for the education of boys; and also some relief for the suffering caused
by the depreciation of paper money,* epidemic, overflows
and short crops.

---

* The financial affairs of the colony had been necessarily carried on largely
with paper money. During the period of settlement royal warrants on the
treasury in payment of salaries were used; during the Crozat charter, checks
upon him had passed into current use. The card money of Canada, a most fluc-
tuating medium, had always been in circulation, and finally the Company of the
West had made an issue of paper for the payment of its debts. All these different
issues appearing, and being retired, added to the arbitrary fixing of prices in the
colony, and consequent speculation of money lenders, had produced financial chaos.
Now, an edict of the royal government, withdrawing at short notice the paper
of the Mississippi Company from circulation, threatened utter collapse and ruin.

A Charity Hospital. 1739.—An humble sailor, Jean
Louis, dying in 1739, left his savings to found a hospital
where the poor could be tended for charity. Bienville applied the legacy, as directed; bought a suitable piece of
property, provided the beds and proper furniture, with medical and nursing attendance, and so inaugurated the first
charity hospital in the city.*

The Minister of Marine granted Bienville's resignation and
named the Marquis de Vaudreuil to succeed him. Pending
the arrival of his successor Bienville endeavoured to arrange
the affairs of the Indians, so that his absence from the colony
would not injure it. He convened the prominent chiefs of
the Alabama country at Mobile, made them presents, and
had them sign treaties, which would pave the way for their
good understanding with his successor. He left Louisiana
forever on the 10th of May 1743. He came into the colony
a youth, full of hope and courage; he left it a prematurely
aged man, worn with care, anxiety and disappointment. He
had given forty-five years of unremitting toil to the task left
him by Iberville.

QUESTIONS.

How did Louisiana once more become a royal province? Give an
account of Bienville's interview with the Natchez at St. Domingo.
What did he find out about the escaped Natchez? Of the division
among the Choctaws? Of his tactics against the Chickasaws? Give
an account of his expedition into the Chickasaw country; his defeat
and the fate of D'Artaguette. How did Bienville prepare for his next
expedition? Give an account of it. What did his sense of failure
force him to do? What of his solicitation for the colony? Of the
first charity hospital in New Orleans? Who was Bienville's successor? When did Bienville leave the colony forever?

* It may be considered the parent of the present noble institution which commands the admiration not only of the State, but of the whole South.

CHAPTER XVI.

The Marquis de Vaudreuil, Governor. 1743-1753.
The Marquis de Vaudreuil was a Canadian and a son of a
former governor of Canada. He came to Louisiana to find
it suffering its penalty as a royal province of France.

War * had been relighted in Europe between France and
England, and in America the colonies of the two rival powers, always glad of an excuse, sprang also eagerly to arms,
and from Canada to New Orleans the rifle and the tomahawk
were kept on the alert. The Chickasaws, who from the first
had only made a pretence of observing the recent treaty, rose
against the French more vindictively than ever. Traveling
along the Mississippi became a perilous adventure, and
life in the Mississippi settlements most insecure. Even the
environs of New Orleans were not safe. The German
coast was surprised and pillaged, many of its farmers killed,
and its women and children taken prisoners, and everywhere in the French lines sudden alarms would send the
colonists, fleeing in terror-stricken bands, to the city or
nearest garrison post. At Mobile the panic became so extreme that Vaudreuil had to remain there with troops for
awhile to restore calm. Reinforcements arriving from
France, he was able to station garrisons at the various threatened points. To protect the city from an attack by the English, he erected batteries on each bank of the river at English
Turn. He also led an army against the Chickasaws, but he
was no more successful than his predecessors had been. The
savages, resorting to their former triumphant tactics, shut
themselves in their forts and defied him and his army.

More alarming to the colonists than the hostilities of the
Chickasaws, even, was the increasing division among the

---

*Called the war of the Austrian Succession, 1740, over the succession of Maria
Theresa, of Austria, to the throne of her father.

Choctaws, who now, instead of using their strength in defending the French against the English, were consuming it in domestic strife and civil warfare.

In 1751 the mother country sent her last ship load of emigrants to her daughter colony, and her last donation of marriageable girls, sixty in number, to be wives for deserving bachelors.

To encourage agriculture, the king promised to buy all the tobacco raised in the colony.

Sugar Cane.—Besides tobacco and indigo another commodity had been added to the agricultural products and profits of the soil.   The Jesuits of Hispaniola obtaining permission to send sugar cane and some negroes acquainted with its culture to their brethren in Louisiana, these put a portion of their plantation in it.

Levees.—As the settlements above and below the city were now in a flourishing state of cultivation, the question of levees began to be an important one.   De Vaudreuil issued the first levee ordinance in the State, requiring the inhabitants to keep up the levees before their property, on pain of having it confiscated.   He also issued the first police regulations in the city of New Orleans, restricting the number of drinking saloons, the sale of liquors, and adjusting the civic relations of negroes.

In 1753 the Marquis de Vaudreuil was promoted to the governorship of Canada and left Louisiana.[*]

M. de Kerlerec was appointed to succeed him.

De Kerlerec.   1753-1763.—De Kerlerec was an officer of the royal navy, in which he had served for twenty-five years.

---

[*] During the last year of De Vaudreuil's government the following incident occurred which has been made the subject of a drama by a French officer, Le Blanc de Villeneuve, stationed in the colony at the time.
  A Choctaw and a Collapissa had a quarrel, in which the latter killed the former and fled to New Orleans.   The relatives of the Choctaw came to the city to demand the Collapissa from de Vaudreuil.   The Marquis, after trying in vain to pacify the Choctaws, was obliged to order the arrest of the murderer; but he made his escape. His father went to the Choctaws and offered his life in atonement for the crime of his son.   They accepted.   The old man stretched himself on the trunk of a fallen tree, and a Choctaw at one stroke cut his head from his body.

Like his predecessor, he was to conduct his administration under the shadow of war.

Seven Years' War. 1757-1763.—It was no mere question of succession to distant thrones that was this time to wet the soil of America with the blood of her colonists. The dispute was native to the country and one which had been growing since its first settlement. The time had come when it had to be decided to which of the European powers America was to belong; whether its future development was to be according to the religion and thought of the Anglo-Saxon or of the Latin race; whether the Lilies of France or the Cross of England should recede.

The rival colonists had clashed over every boundary line, and fought over every advanced post in the continent. As we have seen, the policy of France was to unite Canada and New Orleans by a chain of fortified posts, which should insure her the possession of the great waterways of the continent, and crowd England between the Alleghanies and the Atlantic coast. Midway between Canada and Louisiana lay the valley of the Ohio. Should the English gain possession of it, they would cut in two the French line of fortifications and sever the territory of Louisiana. The English had already sent out from Virginia and established trading posts along the branches of the Ohio, and their traders were deftly winning the Indians into allies. The French, quicker in action than their rivals, descending through Lake Erie, drove the English away and built three forts to guard their position. One of them, Fort Duquesne,*

---

* An interesting episode connects Louisiana with Fort Duquesne. George Washington, then a colonel in the British army, was sent by Governor Dinwiddie, of Virginia, against the fort. On the route he heard of a French detachment coming to surprise him. He manœuvred to surprise it, and in the engagement Jumonville, the ensign in command, was killed. Jumonville de Villiers (the ancestor of one of our distinguished creole families), the brother of the ensign, obtained permission of Kerlerec to leave his station at Fort Chartres and go to avenge his brother's death. He hastened to Fort Duquesne with a large force of Indians and soldiers. Washington, with his men, lay entrenched in a rude fortification called Fort Necessity, not far from the scene of his first engagement. Jumonville attacked him, and, after a sharp fight, had the honor of forcing the future "Father of his country" into surrender.

on the forks of the Monongahela and the Alleghany rivers (site of the present city of Pittsburg), commanding the key of the situation, became the first objective point in the momentous conflict.

Although the seat of war was in the far north, Louisiana suffered her measure of damage from it. Her ships of supplies from France and the islands were intercepted and captured by vigilant British privateers. Her commerce was crippled and almost destroyed. The home government, burthened with the expenses and necessities of the war in Canada, could neither renew the supplies nor protect the commerce. The yearly tribute of presents to the various Indian tribes had to be suspended, and this sent the discontented warriors into trading and treating with the English. The poorly clad, poorly nourished and ill paid soldiers also deserted in large numbers from their different garrisons to the ever convenient English.*

Kerlerec put the colony into the best state of defence possible with his inadequate means. His only reliance was upon the Swiss mercenaries, and these he distributed among the untrustworthy French soldiers in the different posts throughout the Mississippi and Alabama country.

City Defences.—A fortification consisting of a palisade wall was made around the city. The batteries at English Turn were repaired and resupplied, and a vessel was stationed at the mouth of the river, to be sunk in the pass in case of emergency.

From time to time the news of the fortunes of the distant hostilities drifted into the colony. Early in 1759 there came floating down the river boats containing the garrison and officers of Fort Duquesne, which, after much gallant fight-

*In the summer of 1754, four of the soldiers of the garrison of Cat Island rose and murdered their officer, who ill treated them. They tried to escape to Georgia, but a party of Choctaws sent after them captured them. One killed himself. The rest were brought to New Orleans. Two were broken on the wheel; the other, belonging to a Swiss company, was, according to the law of Swiss troops, nailed into a coffin, which was sawed in two through the middle.

ing on both sides, was evacuated and abandoned by the French.   The news of the fall of Quebec and Montreal followed in due time, and eventually that of the complete triumph of the English over the French.   The Lilies of France had been beaten out of her northern possessions by the Cross of England.

Treaty of Paris. 1763.—By this treaty between England, France and Spain, France signed her defeat and made over to Great Britain all her territory on the North American continent, east of the Mississippi, with the exception of New Orleans, and the adjacent district called the Island of Orleans, lying between Manchac and the Lakes.

Spain received back Havana, which had been captured by the English, but paid for it by the cession of Florida, and all her possessions east of the Mississippi.

Louisiana Ceded to Spain.—On the same day, the 10th of February, by a secret treaty, France voluntarily divesting herself of the last vestige of the princely legacy left her by Marquette, Joliet, La Salle and Iberville, secretly ceded to Spain the one remaining bit of territory she still possessed in America: New Orleans, the mouth of the Mississippi, and all her lands lying to the west of the Mississsppi.

During Kerlerec's administration, discord both civil and ecclesiastical was rife in the city.   Violent quarrels broke out between the Capuchin priests, who had titular spiritual charge of the colony, and the Jesuits, who, though only tolerated as visitors, had managed to gain a large following, to the weakening of the influence of the Capuchins.   The Superior Council was invoked by the Capuchins to interfere and prohibit this usurpation, as they called it, of the Jesuits.

A still more violent quarrel broke out between the governor and the royal commissary, Rochemore.   On charges of the latter, an investigation was ordered into Kerlerec's administration.   The report being against him, Kerlerec was recalled to France and thrown into the Bastile.

A stride in advance in the sugar culture has to be chron-
icled during this administration. The experiment of the
Jesuits having proved successful, the Sieur Dubreuil put his
whole plantation in cane, and erected a mill and made an
experiment at boiling the juice.*

Abadie Governor. 1763.—The chief magistracy of the
province was vested in M. d'Abadie, under the title of
Director General. The military force was reduced to three
hundred men, under the orders of Aubry, as senior captain.
The cession being, however, still a secret, Louisiana appeared as before, a French province to her colonies and the
country at large.

British Take Possession.—The Spaniards retired from
Florida; and from post after post in the Illinois, Alabama
and Mississippi regions, the French flag and garrison were
withdrawn, to be replaced by the British. French and Spanish names were changed for English ones: Fort St. George
at Pensacola; Fort Charlotte at Mobile; Fort Panmure at
Natchez, etc. The transfer of authorities was made amicably and expeditiously. The Indian allies of the French made
here and there a few attempts at guerilla warfare against
their new masters; but the French interposing peaceably,
most of them ended by following the French flag in its retreat and settling around New Orleans.

In a few months English vessels traveling up and down
the Mississippi became a familiar sight. They became also
a welcome one, for, fetching in articles of commerce of which
the colonists had been so long deprived by the war, they acquired a thriving though illicit trade all along the coast.
Tying their boats to a tree a short distance above New Orleans, they attracted customers even from the city.†

* The sugar was so badly made, however, that it leaked out of the hogshead on
its way to France; and the ship was so lightened that it came near upsetting.
† As it was under the pretext of going to Manchac, where they were building a
fort—Fort Bate—that the English vessels traveled up the river, the place where they
tied up for the contraband trade was called "Little Manchac." "I am going to
Little Manchac" was the current expression for a shopping excursion to this con-

Jesuits Expelled. 1763.—In obedience to the decree of Pope Clement XIII, expelling the Jesuits from the dominions of the kings of France, Spain and Naples, Abadie was forced to expel them from Louisiana. All their property, including their fine plantation, was sold at auction, and the Fathers made to leave the colony in which, in truth, they had done all to benefit and nothing to injure.

Cession to Spain Made Known. 1764.—In the month of October, 1764, Governor Abadie received from his sovereign, Louis XV, the communication which made him acquainted with the cession of Louisiana to Charles III, King of Spain. He was ordered to remit the government to the officer or envoy sent by the King of Spain to receive it, evacuate the territory and retire to France with all his officers and all the soldiers who did not wish to engage in the service of Spain.

The publication of this communication threw the colony into the greatest grief and consternation. They had been forced to submit to the triumph of the English flag, and the loss to England of all the magnificent country bought with two centuries of their blood and labor; but that was according to the fortunes of war. Now they were called upon to yield the one last corner of the continent over which the French flag floated and see themselves and the great mouth of the Mississippi tossed like a trifle to a nation who had never lifted a finger for them, a nation too insignificant as a foe to be much esteemed as a friend.

M. d'Abadie died in 1765, and thus could not carry out his instructions. The government was put in to the hands of Aubry, the commander of the royal troops.

The Acadians. 1765*—Before the feelings of the colonists had time to calm, there arrived in their midst a band of

traband depot. D'Abadie, seeing the necessities of the colonists, closed his eyes to the custom.

* Acadia, or Nova Scotia, as it is now called, had been conquered from France by the English, and transferred to the British crown, by the treaty of Utrecht, in 1713. It was stipulated that those of the French who chose to remain in the country as subjects to the King of England should enjoy free exercise of their reli-

compatriots whose unhappy fate seemed to foretell their own. On the open levee, in front of New Orleans, the pilgrims from Acadia landed and told their sad story—a story which has found worthy immortality in verse† Their country also had been ceded away; their homes, their churches, their allegiance.

The citizens greeted them with tender and generous hospitality, furnishing them food, clothing, lodging and sympathy. Aubry gave them land, settling them on the river bank above the German coast, at what is still known as the Acadian coast; also in the Attakapas and Opelousas districts, where their descendants live to this day; a worthy, industrious and frugal population, retaining, even in the wealth and official distinction that many have attained, the primitive faith and simplicity of their early history.

QUESTIONS.

Who was the Marquis de Vaudreuil? What of the war declared in Europe? Give account of colony and city under De Vaudreuil? Who succeeded to De Vaudreuil? Give an account of the Seven Years' War. Kerlerec's defences. The treaty of Paris. British possession of the country. Expulsion of the Jesuits When was the cession to Spain made known? What of its effect on the colony? Who succeeded to Abadie? Who were the Acadians?

gion; the rest were allowed to remove within a year. Very few withdrew Bleak and bare as their country was, they loved it with all the blind devotion of the simple, ignorant peasant. But it was years before they could bring themselves to take the oath of allegiance demanded by the English. They hoped against hope, that something would come to pass to prevent their utter disseverment from their nation and church. The English accused the Roman priests of fomenting discord, and they suspected the Acadians of inviting Indian inroads. A new and still more binding oath was drawn up, but its imposition on the Acadians was a task fraught with pain and trouble. For fifty years the process of reconstruction was maintained by the British and resisted by the Acadian. It was then determined by the conquerors that all who refused to take the oath should be exported from the country The whole number removed was over six thousand. Their deserted dwellings and buildings were burned. The wretched people, distributed among the British colonies from Massachusetts to Georgia, among a people speaking a different language and professing a different religion, had a sad lot. After hardships and vicissitudes of all kinds many of them wandered back to Canada, and many banded together to journey to Louisiana, where they might once again rest under the flag of their mother country, hear the language of their ancestors, and pray at the altars to which they were accustomed.
† Evangeline, Longfellow.

CHAPTER XVII.

RESISTANCE TO SPANISH DOMINATION.

The Louisianans were not to be ceded away from their country and flag without a protest. Public sentiment ripened into action. Each parish throughout the colony was requested to send delegates to a meeting to be held in New Orleans. The parishes responding with their best and most notable citizens, a large and impressive assembly met. The attorney general, Lafreniere, opened proceedings with an energetic and eloquent speech, proposing a resolution in which the colonists of Louisiana *en masse* supplicated the King of France not to sever them from their country * The resolution passed unanimously, and Jean Milhet, one of the richest and most influential merchants of New Orleans, was deputed to carry it to France and lay it at the foot of the throne.

Milhet departed on the first vessel. In Paris he sought out Bienville, now a white-haired patriarch eighty-six years of age. Together, they went with the memorial to the Prime Minister, De Choiseul, whom they asked to present them to the king. But as De Choiseul had been the counsellor of the cession of Louisiana, he was not in the mind to further any remonstrance against it. He received the deputies with civility and listened to them with patience, but he so artfully thwarted their designs that Milhet was never able to present his paper.

Over a year passed after the official news of the cession and the meeting; Milhet did not return from France, and no Spanish envoy presented himself to take possession of the

* The following are the names of those who were foremost in the first political convention held in Louisiana: Lafreniere, Doucet, St. Lette Pin, Villeré, the chevalier d'Arensbourg, Jean Milhet, Joseph Milhet, St. Maxent, De la Chaise, Marquis, Garic, Masson, Masange, Poupet, Noyon, Boisblanc, Grandmaison, allande, Lesassier, Braud (royal printer) Kernion, Carrere, Dessales, etc.

colony. To all appearances either the King of Spain or the King of France was hesitating about it. The colonists therefore rebounded from their first feeling to hope and courage.

Ulloa. 1766.—Suddenly the bright horizon darkened. A letter came to the Superior Council in July, 1766, from Don Antonio de Ulloa, announcing his arrival in Havana on his way to take possession of Louisiana, of which he had been appointed governor. He did not reach the colony, however, until the following spring. He was accompanied by two companies of infantry, a commissary of war, De Loyola; an intendant, Navarro; and a royal comptroller, Gayarre. They met a respectful but cold reception from the citizens.

Requested by the Superior Council to present his credentials, Ulloa refused, saying that he did not wish to take possession until the arrival of the rest of the Spanish troops, adding that he had nothing to do with the Superior Council, which was a civil tribunal, and that in taking possession he only recognized Aubry as competent to treat with him.

The colonists fell again into despair over their situation. Instead of mitigating it by his personal influence, Ulloa only rendered it worse, and the prospect of submission to him became unendurable. Although a distinguished man of science and letters, he was most unattractive and impolitic. Cold, haughty, reserved and dictatorial, he was in every respect a painful contrast to the people whom he was sent to govern; and, restricting his intercourse entirely to the military governor, Aubry, he ignored the colonists in a manner most exasperating to the independent, free-spoken creoles.

He offered to take the French soldiers into the service of Spain, but they refused to change their allegiance. The Spanish soldiers were lodged, therefore, apart from them, and Aubry was forced to garrison the city with his troops and still to act the part of governor. In reality he was only the mouthpiece and deputy of Ulloa, who assumed surreptitiously all the rights of his unacknowledged official position.

He had a census of the inhabitants taken, made a tour of inspection of the different military establishments in the province, and as Aubry had received no money from France to pay French soldiers or to carry on the government, he advanced him the funds to do so. He issued various ordinances and decrees, one of them forbidding trading vessels entering the port without previously submitting to him the estimate and price of their cargoes, and restricting all trade to six Spanish ports and to vessels commanded by Spaniards. Vessels sailing to or from Louisiana were even prohibited from entering any Spanish port in America, except in case of distress, and then had to submit to strict examination and heavy charges.

What the people of Louisiana most dreaded in the transfer to Spain was the application to them of the narrow-minded, arbitrary decrees of trade of the Spanish colonies, which would ruin their commerce to the profit of the commerce of Spanish ports. This decree of Ulloa was the realization of their worst fears. Commercial ruin stared them in the face.

The merchants, in a body, presented a petition* to the Superior Council, signed by names that are still distinguished in Louisiana, begging a suspension of the decree until they could be heard on the subject. The ship captains also presented a similar petition.

Ulloa meanwhile descended the river to the Balize, and remained there seven months, awaiting the arrival of the wealthy lady from Peru whom he was to marry. Aubry made peri-

---

* The merchants who signed the petition against the decree to the Superior Council, were: Joseph Milhet, Rose, Cantrelle D. Braud, J. Mercier, L. Ducrest, Petit, Duforest, Toutant Beauregard, L. Boisdore, B. Duplessis, Bracquier, P. O. Caresse, J. Vienne. P. Segond, Voix, Durel, Blache, M. Poupet Jr., Poupet, Estebe. Rodrigue, J. Sauvestre, G. Gardelle, Ducarpe, F. Durand, J. and N. Boudet, Rivoire, Macuenara, F. Denis, J. Arnoult, A. Renard, P, Senilh, A. Bodaille, Laulhe, Dubourg, Festas, Frigiere, Ranson, Fournier, St. Pe, Detour, Villefranche Salomon, Delassize Blaignat, Langlois, Fortier, Lafitte, Henard, Estady, Astier, Brunet, Bienvenue, Sarpy, Doraison, Cavelier, Papion, Gaurrege. Revoil, Guezille, Juignan, St. Anne, Moullineau, P. Hery, A. Ollivier, Broussard, Dumas, Grueuiard, Chateau, Simon, Hugues, Sarrou, Raguet, Nicolet, Brion, Betremleux, Blanin, Dutertre, Bijon, D'hubeck, Dralde, Bonnemaison, Joli, Forstal, L'Enfant.

odical visits to him; during one of which he made a private
act of possession in favor of Ulloa and had the French flag
replaced by that of Spain. Relieved from the presence of
Ulloa and still awaiting the result of Milhet's mission the
colonists began again to indulge their patriotic dreams.

Milhet returned from France; instead of the good news
expected, he brought the report of total failure. Indignation succeeded to disappointment. Throwing off all
concealment, the colonists voiced their hatred of Spain and
Ulloa, and their loathing of the yoke about to be put upon
them. Calm was completely destroyed. From one end of
the colony to the other the wildest excitement prevailed.
Meetings were held in which heated addresses increased still
more the violence of feeling. Finally the country was again
invited to send delegates to another grand meeting to be held
in the capital.

As before, Lafreniere took an important part and made
an impassioned speech. He was ably sustained by the two
brothers Milhet, and by Doucet, a lawyer lately arrived
from France. The proceedings terminated by an address to
the Superior Council, calling upon it to declare Ulloa refractory and usurpatory, for having raised the Spanish flag
in several places in the colony without having exhibited and
registered his authority at the Superior Council or in such a
manner that the citizens could see them; for having on his
own private authority and without reason detained captains
and their ships in port; for having put French citizens under
arrest on board the Spanish frigate; and for having held councils with Spanish officers in which decrees of arrest had been
rendered against French citizens; the citizens therefore
prayed the Superior Council to order Ulloa out of the colony.
The paper was signed by five hundred and fifty respectable
names. It was ordered printed by the royal commissary and
circulated in every parish. After the address was read to the
council and handed to a committee for consideration, the

attorney general * submitted a brief in which the duties of
councils and parliaments to the people were explained and
the legal points bearing upon the competency of the Royal
Superior Council to act in the premises exposed.

On the 29th of October the petition was taken up by the
council, and after some debate a decree was passed ordering Ulloa to produce his powers from the King of Spain, if he
had any, that they might be recorded on its minutes or to
depart within a month. Ulloa accepted the last alternative,
and on the following afternoon embarked with all his household on a frigate then at the levee. Aubry with a detail of
soldiers escorting him and leaving a guard on the vessel.

Expulsion of Ulloa.—At daylight the next morning a
crowd of revelers, who had passed the night at a wedding
feast, appeared on the levee shouting, and singing patriotic
songs. The frigate, containing the hated Spaniard and his
equally hated wife, lay before them in the gray dawn. They
could not resist the temptation; one of them cut its ropes,
and with delight the crowd watched the vessel move from its
moorings, yield to the current and drift away from the city.

A few days afterwards a memorial or manifesto, explain-
ing and justifying the expulsion, was printed and dissemi-
nated. The Superior Council despatched one of its members,
Mr. Lesassier, with a copy of the decree and an explanatory
letter to the Minister of Foreign Affairs in France. The
citizens sent another address to the king voicing their sentiments against Ulloa, and praying to be allowed to remain
Frenchmen, and Aubry, who had protested against the expulsion, also wrote his account of the affair, reiterating what

---

* Lafreniere in his speech referred to the successful opposition of the British
American colonies to the Stamp Act, and drew the attention of the council to the
noble conduct of the people of Burgundy in 1526, when summoned by Launoy, the
viceroy of Naples, to recognize as their sovereign the emperor Charles V, to whom
Francis II had ceded the province by the treaty of Madrid. The States and courts
of justice being convened to deliberate on the emperor's message, they unanimously answered that the province was a part of the French monarchy and that the
king had not the power of alienating it. The nobles resolutely declared that if
the king abandoned them they would resort to arms and the last drop of their blood
would be spilt in defence of their country.

he had written shortly after the arrival of Ulloa, that notwithstanding the Spaniard's reputation in all the academies of
Europe, he was not the proper man to govern the colony,
not having the qualities requisite to command Frenchmen.
Instead of gaining the hearts of the people, he had done
everything to alienate them. He seemed to despise the
colony and particularly the Superior Council, and by his in-
discreet conduct had rendered the Spanish domination
dreaded, uttering threats which menaced a horrible tyranny
in the future. Aubry also described the great distress financial and commercial, since the advent of Ulloa, the depression
of all values and the decrease of population.

Ulloa from Havana sent to his goverernment a report
of the insult to his king and to himself. He passed in review by name the men who had taken a prominent part in
the rebellion, as he called it. He described them as extravagant and overwhelmed with debts and only seeking in revolution an escape from their responsibilities. All, he said,
were children of Canadians, who had come to Louisiana
axe on shoulder, to live by the work of their hands.

The momentary calm that follows the storm fell over
Louisiana and the Louisianians. During the interval between
the sending of their communication to their government in
France and getting an answer, there was much discussion
and speculation about future events. There was some
thought of casting off all monarchical allegiance, and erecting Louisiana into a republic, to be placed under the protection of England. An emissary was sent to the English governor at Pensacola to know what support could be gained
from Florida in this event. The English official returned an
unfavorable answer, and, it is said, transmitted the message
he had received to Aubry, who, in his turn, delivered it to the
Spanish government.

O'Reilly. 1769.—Like a thunderclap, six months afterwards, came the announcement from the commandant at Balize

of the arrival of Count O'Reilly, lieutenant general of the
armies of Spain, with a formidable number of ships and
troops.   The news was enough to chill the colonists with fear.
The pitiless, bloody record of Spain as an avenger in the past
arose before them, with the vision of their own defenceless
position.   The leaders of the Spanish opposition hastened to
Aubry, in despair at what they had brought upon the colony.
The French general reassured them.   As no blood had been
shed in the expulsion of Ulloa, he thought that a prompt submission would be accepted as sufficient atonement for the
past.   He sent an officer to tranquilize the inhabitants along
the coast and warn them to keep quiet.

That evening a Spanish officer arrived with dispatches from
O'Reilly, stating that he had come to take possession of the
country for the King of Spain and would exhibit his credentials at his first interview with Aubry.   The next day Aubry
assembled the citizens and made them an address announcing
the arrival of the Spanish envoy; counseling submission and
obedience, and taking upon himself to assure them that if
they followed his advice they could have full confidence in
the clemency of the King of Spain.

Lafreniere, with the two Milhets and Marquis, offered to
go personally to O'Reilly to present their submission and the
submission of the citizens.   Aubry gave them a letter of introduction, and O'Reilly received them courteously.   Lafreniere introduced himself and companions as delegates
from the people, charged to make profession of submission
and respect to the King of Spain.   Throwing the blame of
what had occurred on the illegal conduct of Ulloa, he protested that the credentials which O'Reilly brought were
more authoritative to the colony than the army under his
command; but the colony implored his benevolence for such
privileges of time as would be needed by those who should
wish to emigrate from it.   O'Reilly responded kindly that
was not possible for him to come to any decision until he

had examined all the facts of the case on the spot; that the colonists could be assured that no one loved to do good more than he, and that it would plunge him into despair to cause the smallest injury to any one. He begged the colonists to be tranquil, and trust to his good sentiments toward them. He mentioned the word sedition; Marquis interrupted him and explained that that word was not applicable to the colonists. O'Reilly kept the party to dinner, treated them with all courtesy, and sent them away full of hope in regard to the past. Their report of the interview calmed the agitation in the city, which sank into much needed repose and peace.

QUESTIONS.

Give an account of opposition to Spanish domination. Arrival of Ulloa. Refusal to exhibit his credentials. Expulsion. Their communication to the home government. Further proceedings of the colonists. O'Reilly's arrival.

SPANISH DOMINATION.

CHAPTER XVIII.

O'REILLY TAKES POSSESSION.

On the night of August 17, 1769, the Spanish frigate, followed by twenty-three other vessels, sailed up the river and anchored in front of the city.

At mid-day of the 18th Aubry had the general alarm beaten. The troops and militia marched out and formed, facing the vessels, on one side of the Place d'Armes. General O'Reilly landed, and three thousand soldiers filing after him formed on the other three sides of the open space.

O'Reilly, advancing to Aubry, presented his credentials from the King of Spain and his orders to receive the province. The papers were read aloud to the assembled citizens. Aubry made a proclamation relieving the colonists from their allegiance to France, and delivered the keys of the city to O'Reilly. The vessels discharged their guns, the soldiers fired salvos of musketry and shouted. The Spanish flag was raised on all public buildings, the French flag lowered. Spanish guards relieved the French guards. A Te Deum was then celebrated at the church, and the ceremonies terminated by a grand parade of the Spanish military, who, with their discipline and finished equipments, presented a truly awe-inspiring appearance to the colonists.

O'Reilly took up his residence in one of the handsomest houses in the city and assumed a mode of life more regal and

O'REILLY.

stately than the people had ever seen from their governors. In the largest apartment of his hotel a kind of throne was placed under a canopy, and here, like a mimic king, he gave audiences and held receptions. The colonists, faithful to their professions, came in numbers to pay their respects. They were accompanied by their wives and daughters, who, with their personal attractiveness and handsome toilettes, endeavored to throw the graceful charm of society over the grim and sombre state of a military ceremony.

The Spaniard maintained a graciousness of demeanor which exceeded even the most sanguine expectations. He had written, however, privately to Aubry, demanding full and entire information respecting the expulsion of Ulloa, with the literal citation of all orders, protestations, and pub-

lic and private documents relating thereto, and particularly
the names of the persons who wrote and published the
decree of the council ordering the expulsion and the manifesto succeeding it.

Aubry, accepting the role of informer, furnished not only
all that was officially required, but such gratuitous personal
evidence as would make him agreeable to the Spaniards.
Masan, Chevalier of St. Louis; Foucault, the commissary;
Marquis, ex-captain of a Swiss company; the two De
Noyans, nephews of Bienville; and Villeré, were named as
the richest and most distinguished citizens who had taken
part in the Spanish expulsion. All the documents with signatures attached, and the manifesto with Braud's stamp as
printer, were put into O'Reilly's hands.

Upon different pretexts, O'Reilly secured the attendance
of Lafreniere, the two De Noyans, the Milhets and Boisblanc on the same day at his levee. He received them with
more than his usual courtesy, and suavely begged them to
pass into the next room with him. They, unhesitatingly
complying, walked into the apartment, to be surrounded
by Spanish grenadiers with fixed bayonets. Then throwing off his mask, O'Reilly denounced his guests as rebels to
the King of Spain, informing them that they were prisoners
of state and their property and fortunes confiscated. The
gentlemen, then under strong guard, were conveyed to the
places which had been selected for their imprisonment; some
to the barracks, some to the frigate in the river, and some
to their houses, where a guard was stationed.

Villeré, who had been marked also for arrest, was on his
plantation on the German coast. On the news of O'Reilly's
arrival he had intended to put himself and family under the
protection of the British flag at Manchac, when he received a
letter from Aubry assuring him that he had nothing to appre-
hend, and advising him, on the contrary, to come to the city.
As flight seemed to imply a consciousness of guilt, this advice

was more congenial to Villeré's character. He set out at
once for New Orleans. At the city gate he was stopped and
carried a prisoner aboard the frigate. Madame Villeré,
hearing of her husband's arrest, hastened also to the city, and
taking a boat had herself rowed to the frigate. She was
ordered away. Villeré, hearing the supplicating voice of his
wife, made an effort to get on deck to see her. The sentinel
opposed him. There was a struggle, and the gallant creole
fell, transfixed with a bayonet. He died shortly afterwards.

Trial of the Patriots.—O'Reilly confided the trial of the
prisoners to his own officials, who made all the examina-
tions, records of testimony, etc., necessary for a prosecution
for treason according to Spanish criminal law.

Foucault pleaded that as he was royal commissary of the
King of France, he was accountable only to him. The plea
was sustained. Braud pleaded that he had only printed the
manifesto on order of Foucault, which, as royal printer of
Louisiana, he was bound to respect. He was released The
other prisoners confined their defence to a denial of the jurisdiction of the tribunal before which they were arraigned.
They claimed that the offences with which they were charged
took place while the flag of France was waving over them
and the laws of that kingdom were still in force in the colony,
and that as the people of Louisiana could not wear the yoke of
two kings at once, they could not at the same time, offend
against the laws of two kingdoms. O'Reilly had decided
from the first, for an example, to proceed with the utmost
rigor of the law against six of the prisoners, and as the law
authorized a less severe punishment than death unless the
charge was proved by two witnesses, the trial in reality was
merely to separate those who were to lose life and property
from those who were to lose liberty and property, and as
there was no defence made, the accusation meant condem-
nation. The sentence condemned Nicolas Chauvin De
afreniere, Jean Baptiste, Bienville, De Noyan, Pierre

Caresse, Pierre Marquis and Joseph Milhet to death. They were to be conducted to the place of execution on asses, with ropes around their necks; to be hung, and to remain hanging until O'Reilly ordered otherwise. Warning was issued against any one's rescuing the bodies or in any way frustrating the execution of the sentence on pain of death. As Villere had already met his punishment, all that Spannish authority could do was to condemn his memory as infamous. Petit was sentenced to prison for life; Masan and Doucet for ten, and Boisblanc, Milhet and Poupet for six years. All copies of the manifesto and all papers relating to the event were to be burned in the public place by the hangman.

Execution of the Sentence. September 28, 1769.— As there was no hangman * in the colony, O'Reilly was prevailed upon to commute the sentence to death by shooting. On the morning of the fatal day the guards were doubled at every gate and station of the city. All the troops were put under arms and were kept prepared for action along the levee and on the public square. Those of the citizens who could, fled into the country. Doors and windows were barred; all sign and sound of life suppressed. At 3 o'clock the patriots were led out of their prison to the square in front of the barracks. They were tied to stakes and received their death with the calm firmness of the innocent and of the brave.

O'Reilly Governor. 1769.—In the cession of the colony, Louis XV had expressed the hope that justice should be administered according to the accustomed laws, forms and

---

* The historian Dumont relates: "As at one time there was no executioner in the colony and no one who would take the exercise of the office, and as every well organized government needed an official executioner, it was decided to give the charge to a negro, named Jeannot, belonging to the Company of the Indies. He was summoned and told what was intended. He tried to get out of it, although the office would have given him his freedom. But he saw that there was no escape, that he would be forced into it: 'Very well,' he said, 'wait a moment.' He hastened to his cabin, seized a hatchet, laid his arm on a block of wood, and cut off his hand. Returning he showed his bloody stump to the commissioners."

usages of France. O'Reilly, in his policy of reconstruction. heeded no such desire. A proclamation in November announced to the colonists that all hitherto existing forms of government were abolished and that Louisiana was to be placed under the same regulations that reigned in other Spanish colonies. For the Superior Council, a cabildo was substituted, composed of six regidores, two alcades, an attorney general, syndic and clerk, over all of which the Spanish governor was to preside. The Spanish language was ordered to be employed by all public officers; and the colony was to be made as much as possible by superior force, Spanish at least in appearance.

During the winter the governor made a tour of inspection of the settlements along the river coasts. The most notable planters were invited to meet him; but he received only a dignified and cold submission from them. Some of the French soldiers enlisted in the Spanish service. Many were discharged and received grants of land; those who wished to remain in the French service were offered free passage to St. Domingo or France. Aubry sailed with those who returned to France. His vessel reached the continent in safety, but foundered in the river Garonne. Aubry perished, with nearly all on board.

Large numbers of merchants and mechanics of New Orleans, having no taste for the sample of government they had seen, emigrated to St. Domingo. Many of the most prosperous planters followed them. The movement, indeed, became so great that O'Reilly, to check it, withheld passports from the applicants.

O'Reilly, himself, took his departure from the colony during the summer, leaving behind him a reputation which has become immortalized in Louisiana in the sobriquet of "Bloody O'Reilly."

He appointed as successor one of his colonels, Don Luis de Unzaga.

Unzaga Governor. 1770-1777.—Unzaga's appointment was confirmed by the court of Spain. His mild and easy administration relieved the colonists from the gloom into which the horrible rigor of O'Reilly had plunged them. He married the daughter of a prominent creole of the province, and some of his officers following his example, good will was not long in being established between the two nations. But the colony was nothing more than a royal apanage. The narrow-minded commercial policy of Spain which the New Orleans merchants had dreaded was applied rigorously, and produced the effect they had predicted, by killing all enterprise. The only trade carried on was still by the alert English in contraband. Besides large warehouses in Manchac, Baton Rouge and Natchez, and their vessels of goods moored at Little Manchac, they now had two large boats, with their cabins fitted out like stores, which they kept traveling up and down the river, stopping at the call of any planter. Unzaga closed his eyes at the infraction of the law, without which he knew it would be impossible for the colony to subsist.*

War of Independence. 1775.—In the British colonies resistance to the arbitrary taxation of the home government had culminated in the memorable war which was to result in the independence of America and the federation of the United States. During the desperate struggle that ensued after the battle of Lexington, the need of supplies by way of the Mississippi brought American merchants and emissaries to New Orleans, where, with Unzaga's connivance, they established commercial connections to buy arms and ammunition to ship to the colonial forces.

---

* It was during Unzaga's administration that the celebrated religious war between the French and Spanish Capuchins took place; from the Spanish father, Cirilo, attempting to substitute the grim fanaticism of Spanish practices for the pastoral government of the French father, Dagobert, an episode much celebrated in local fiction and poetry, and one which has elevated the French Capuchin, good Father Dagobert, into the ecclesiastical hero of the place. Unzaga acted during the troublous discussion with the toleration and equity which eminently distinguished him in all his administrative difficulties.

Unzaga Appointed Captain General of Caraccas, was succeeded by Don Bernardo Galvez.

Don Bernardo Galvez. 1783-1785.—Galvez was a brilliant young officer of twenty-two, the colonel of the Spanish regiment of Louisiana and powerfully connected; his father being viceroy of Mexico and his uncle secretary of state and president of the Council of the Indies, an office second in authority only to the king.

Galvez, like Unzaga, did all in his power to render his nation and his government acceptable to the colonists. He opened his administration by mitigating the strict decrees against

BERNARDO DE GALVEZ.

trade, and French vessels were once more permitted to land at New Orleans. Competing with the English, they soon succeeded to their monopoly, and enterprise and activity revived among the creole merchants and planters, who were further encouraged by the offer of the Spanish government to buy in future all the tobacco raised in the colony. In the city, assistance was furnished more and more openly to the warring American colonies. Not only were regular shipments of supplies made to Virginia and Pennsylvania, but emissaries passing backward and forward in their effort to stir up a revolt also in the Floridas made it a stopping place and rendezvous. An American in Philadelphia even fitted out there an expedition into the British territory, which captured the fort at Manchac and ravaged the plantations as far as Natchez.

War.—It could not be expected that France should remain neutral in the conflict between the Americans and her old foe.

From private encouragement and assistance she passed to open recognition of the independence of the revolted colonies and to a treaty of alliance with them. England responded by hostilities against France. Spain offered her mediation for a general peace based on the separation of the colonies from the mother country. England, haughtily refusing, Spain determined to take a hand herself in the quarrel, by declaring war against England. It was the opportunity above all others desired by Louisiana's young martial governor.

Capture of British Forts.—Raising a volunteer corps among the Americans in the city, the colonial militia, people of color, and Indians, Galvez mustered a force of about fourteen hundred men. Marching up the river he captured Fort Bute; forced Baton Rouge to capitulate, and in her capitulation to include Fort Panmure at Natchez, and three other small garrisons in the neighborhood.

Mobile Captured. 1780.—Returning to New Orleans, he immediately commenced preparations for an expedition against Mobile, and sailed from the Balize with over two thousand men. In the gulf he was overtaken by a storm, which came near wrecking the whole expedition. They succeeded, however, in reaching Mobile river, where, in spite of the confusion and demoralization of his army, Galvez marched to Fort Charlotte and forced its surrender.

Expedition Against Pensacola. 1781.—The conquest of Pensacola was next determined on, but this place was too well fortified to hope for the easy triumphs of the past. Galvez sent to Cuba for troops. The captain general promised but did not send them. Galvez then sailed there in person and obtained them. Crossing the gulf, however, he encountered a terrible hurricane; many of his transports foundered, the rest were dispersed. He put back to Havana, collected and refitted a new armament and sailed for Pensacola with a ship of the line, two frigates, several transports and fourteen hundred men, with full equipment of artillery.

He landed on the island of St. Rosa in March, and erected a battery to protect his ships while crossing the bar. But when the attempt was made the commodore's ship got aground and he refused to proceed. Galvez had the channel sounded, and found water enough for his largest vessels, but the Spanish officers still refused to risk the royal fleet, in a channel they did not know, under fire of a formidable fort. Galvez then decided to carry through his own colonial gunboats and thus force the Spanish commodore into following his example. Towards noon he went aboard, ordered the penant at the mainmast, saĺutes fired and sails set. The fort commenced a brisk cannonade, but his boats sailed triumphantly through it, and Galvez landed on the island of St. Rosa, amid the acclamations of his men. The rest of the fleet crossed the bar next day with like success.

Attack.—After some parley, with a view of excluding the town of Pensacola and its inhabitants from exposure to the fortunes of war, the English commander withdrew with all his forces into the fort. The Spaniards threw up their earth works on both sides the British walls and stationed their batteries. From these and from the fleet in front a tremendous fire was poured into the fort. Again and again the men were driven from their guns, but the Spaniards gained no decided advantage. On the contrary, the British erected a battery whose heavy guns soon silenced the Spanish ships and drove them to the other side of the bay. After a month's siege an accident turned the uncertain victory to the account of Galvez. The powder magazine in one of the advanced redoubts took fire from a shell and blew up, opening a passage to him. He had barely taken possession of it when the British displayed a white flag. A capitulation was agreed upon by which the whole province of West Florida was surrendered to Spain. The garrison was allowed the honors of war and transportation into the English dominions.

The brilliant services of Galvez were rewarded with the

Cross of the Royal Order of Charles III, the title of Count, promotion to Lieutenant General in the army, and Captain General of Florida and Louisiana. He sailed shortly afterwards to Havana, to take command of the Spanish forces in a combined French and Spanish attack on Jamaica,. leaving the government of Louisiana during his absence to Don Estevan Miro, colonel of the Spanish regiment of Louisiana.

Peace of Paris. American Independence, 1783.—The great and glorious struggle of the Americans drew to an end. Great Britain was forced to acknowledge their independence. The peace was signed in Paris, January 20, 1783.

By a following treaty Spain retained her conquests of Florida, and the line between her territory and that of the United States was fixed at a point in the Mississippi river; latitude, 32 deg. north, extending to the middle of the Apalachicola river, following it to its junction with Flint river, thence to the St. Mary's and down its middle to the Atlantic ocean. Navigation of the Mississippi, from its source to its mouth, was declared free to the subjects of Great Britain and citizens of the United States.

The new lines were, however, not fixed before they were called into dispute. The State of Georgia claimed a large territory inside the Spanish boundary, and sent commissioners to New Orleans, demanding its surrender. The question referred to the court of Spain reopened negotiations between the two countries, which lasted several years. And the navigation of the Mississippi, declared free on paper, was practically closed by the Spanish imposition of oppressive taxes and duties.

1784.—During their short and brilliant war against their English neighbors, the Louisianians suffered great agricultural and commercial depression. The paper money fell to half its value; crop after crop failed. The sorely needed

peace did little to mitigate the crisis. For two years succes-
sively hurricanes had swept the country bare of vegetation
and buildings; and the waters of the gulf, driven inland in a
great tidal wave, had submerged land and stock. In addition,
there were the usual overflows from the river, and a rainy
summer following brought an epidemic of fever. The necessaries of life rose to an extreme height and want and suffering wrung bitter complaints from the inhabitants. The
winter that succeeded was unknown in severity in all previous experience. White frosts appeared in September. By
November the cold was intense. In February the whole
width of the river in front of New Orleans was so filled
with blocks of ice that for five days all communication between the two banks was interrupted.

Early in 1785 Galvez was appointed viceroy of Mexico,
to succeed his deceased father, and Miro became governor
of Louisiana.

QUESTIONS.

Give an account of O'Reilly in New Orleans. Arrest of the patriots. Their trial and execution. Spanish reconstruction in Louisiana. Unzaga's administration. Administration of Galvez. Capture
of the British possessions. Give account of the Peace of Paris—the
boundaries it fixed and the provision regarding the Mississippi river.

———•◆•———

CHAPTER XIX.

Governor Miro. 1785-1791.—Miro continued the wise
policy of his predecessors, exerting himself to obtain from
the Court of Madrid as much extension of commercial privileges as possible, foreseeing that in commerce lay the very
life of the colony. He was fully impressed with the importance of the Mississippi as the artery of trade of the country.

"As many as forty vessels at a time," he wrote to the home government, " could be seen on its waters."*

The natural, and in that ante-railroad period the only outlet for the produce of the Middle, or, as they were then called, the Western States, the river was indeed asserting its importance in a manner that both governments were forced to consider. After the War of Independence there poured down upon its currents one continuous line of flat-boats laden to the edge with the produce of the rich soil from above. These cargoes found ready sale, and were soon the main source of food supplies to the city. The flat-boats, after being unloaded, were broken up and sold for timber. But the sturdy flatboatmen from Ohio and Kentucky, on their return, had always a long list of seizures, confiscations, imprisonments, and vexatious interferences of all kinds by the Spanish authorities, to report, and the people of the States, strong and bold in their new liberty, were not of the kind tamely to brook such treatment. They considered that the Mississippi river belonged to the people of the Mississippi valley, and they were determined to have the use of it to its mouth. Among the violent, invasion of Louisiana and forcible seizure of New Orleans were talked about. The more peaceable applied to Congress to obtain from Spain by negotiation the full observance of the last treaty.

Miro, alive to the critical temper of Americans and to the defenceless condition of the colony, redoubled his vigilance and relaxed the restrictions upon the river trade. To fill up the country, he encouraged emigation from the West into the Spanish possessions on the Mississippi, and another large number of Acadian families coming into the colony, he settled them in the neighborhood of their compatriots on.

*One of the first acts of Miro's administration was the building of a hospital for lepers in New Orleans on what was long called "la terre aux lepreux," or lepers' land, situated on Metairie Ridge. Ulloa had attempted to confine some of the lepers at Balize, but the public discontent caused him to desist.

both sides of the Mississippi and in the Attakapas* district.
To increase Spanish population, the Spanish government had in this, and also during the previous administration, transported to Louisiana a number of families from
the Canary Islands.†   These were settled, some at Terre-
aux-boeufs; some at Bayou Manchac, where they formed a
village called Galvezton; and some at Venezuela, on Bayou
Lafourche.

The English inhabitants of the Natchez district were encouraged to remain and take the oath of allegiance to Spain;
they were forbidden, however, the public exercise of their
worship, and the king sent out, at his own expense, Irish
priests to convert them to the Roman Church.

At the same time, Miro spared no means to conciliate the
Indians, and he succeeded in drawing to New Orleans
thirty-six of the most influential Chickasaw and Choctaw
chiefs, gave them rich presents, harangued and feasted
them.

1787.—General Wilkinson, a distinguished officer in the
War of Independence, became a prominent figure in the
crisis.   He conceived the plan of relieving the strained condition by establishing such relations between the people of
the interior and the Spaniards as would be profitable to both.
He came to New Orleans and made the acquaintance of
Miro, who, fearful at every rise of the river of an invasion
from the indignant Americans to the north, eagerly welcomed any arrangement by which such a possibility might
be avoided.   He even flattered himself that Wilkinson's
friendship and the necessity of the Mississippi to the Middle
States, properly handled, might result in their secession from
the Union, and the erection of a friendly republic under the

---

*In the beginning of 1787 the districts of Opelousas and Attakapas, which so far
had been under one officer, were divided into two separate commands. Nicholas
Forstal was appointed commander of the Opelousas district, and the Chevalier de
Clouet, who had before presided over both, was left in charge of the Attakapas.
†Called to this day " Islingues," from islenos, islanders.

dependence of Spain, between the Spanish and the United States boundaries.

New Orleans. 1788.—In the capital life was changing from the rude simplicity of the early Canadian days to the tone and fashion of European cities, of which the foreign officers and their families set the standard. Handsome residences of brick and stucco with hand-wrought iron gates and balconies, and spacious court yards, began to replace the low, tile-covered cottages of the first settlers. But the march of improvement was arrested by a most disastrous occurrence.

On Good Friday, 1788, the house of one of the Spanish officials caught fire from the lights on the altar of the domestic chapel. The flames spread until the entire city seemed doomed; eight hundred and fifty-six houses, the Cathedral, Convent of the Capuchins, Town Hall, the arsenal and all its contents, were consumed. Nothing could exceed the scene of ruin and desolation that ensued. New and handsomer buildings, however, were soon being built on the old sites, and Don Andres Almonaster,* a rich and influential citizen, commenced his generosities to the city by replacing the burned schoolhouse, and laying the foundation of a new and handsome cathedral.

In the beginning of 1789 Louisiana learned that Charles III was dead, and that Charles IV, his son, succeeded him. But the new king was more intensely Spanish than the last, as the colony soon perceived.

Inquisition.—The Spanish Capuchin priest, Antonio de Sedella, who had lately arrived, was commissioned to introduce the Inquisition into the city. He made his preparations with the utmost secresy and caution, and notified the gov-

---

*Don Andres Almonastor y Roxas was a native of Andalusia. He was a Knight of the Royal Order of Charles III, colonel of the militia, alderman and royal lieutenant of the corporation, founder and donor of the cathedral, the court house, of the Hospital of St. Charles and of its church; also of the hospital for lepers and of the convent and school of the Ursulines. He died in 1798, and was buried in the cathedral, in which perpetual masses are celebrated for his soul.

ernor that he might soon, at some late hour at night, find it necessary to require guards to assist him.

Miro did not hesitate to risk his own authority to prevent an establishment, the idea of which made him shudder. The night following the Capuchin's notification, when the representative of the Inquisition was quietly sleeping, he was aroused by a heavy knocking; opening the door, he saw an officer and a file of grenadiers. Thinking they had come in answer to his letter, he said: " My friends, I thank you and " his excellency for the readiness of this compliance with my " request. But I have now no need for your services, and " you shall be warned in time when you are wanted. Retire " with the blessing of God."*

Great was his stupefaction when he was told that he was under arrest. "What," exclaimed he, "Will you dare lay your hands on a Commissioner of the Inquisition!" "I dare obey orders," replied the undaunted officer; and the Reverend Father Antonio de Sedilla was instantly carried on board of a vessel which sailed the next day for Cadiz.†

Goddess of Liberty. 1791.—Tender of the political as well as religious condition of the people, the King of Spain prohibited the introduction into the colony of any boxes, clocks, or other objects stamped with the figure of the American goddess of liberty.

French Revolution. 1791.—It was a time indeed to fear the spread of ideas of liberty. The heroic stand of the United States against England, and the independence and freedom thereby gained, had fired the long discontented French people into a revolt against their monarchy.

The revolution which broke out with such deplorable violence in France was followed in the French colonies with even more bloody exhibitions. In St. Domingo the negroes,

---

* Gayarre, Spanish domination.
† A few years later Pere Antoine returned and lived and worked in the city til 1837. He made himself so beloved by the people that his memory is still erished by both Protestants and Catholics.

not satisfied with the freedom granted them, resolved to rule supreme. A general massacre of the whites was plotted and carried out with revolting cruelty. Those who could escape fled to neighboring countries; many came to Louisiana. Among the refugees were a company of French comedians. They opened a theatre in New Orleans, originating the regular French dramatic performances which have still continued in the city.

Miro was permitted to retire from Louisiana and return to Spain in 1791. He had endeared himself to the colonists by his kind manners and fine moral qualities and had done much to reconcile them with the Spanish Domination.*

Carondelet. 1792-1797.—Francois Louis Hector Baron de Carondelet, like his predecessors, was a colonel in the royal army. He was a native of Flanders, and at the time

of his appointment was governor of San Salvador in Guatemala. He is described as a short, plump gentleman, somewhat choleric in disposition, but not lacking in good nature.

As Miro had done, Carondelet tolerated the open disregard of the duties imposed upon the Mississippi trade, and New Orleans was permitted to stride forward to the commercial position which her geo-

BARON CARONDELET.

graphical situation warranted. Numbers of Philadelphia merchants established branch houses in the city, and Americans began to crowd in to fill the lucrative positions daily offering. But as before, whenever prosperity seemed most assured, events in Europe disturbed it.

* Miro had a census of the population taken in 1789, with the following result: Total, 31,433, showing a doubling of the population since 1769. The slaves and whites were about equally divided; the free colored amounted to 1100; the number of Acadians to 1587.

News arrived that the French Republic had been proclaimed, and Louis XVI beheaded; and with it came the declaration of war by Spain against France.

The Spanish reconstruction had never gone to the hearts of the Louisianians, they still were Frenchmen, had never ceased to speak their own language, nor to long for an opportunity to return to their own nationality, and they had been French Republicans in spirit ever since Louis XV had thrown them off and abandoned them to the vengeance of O'Reilly. They saw now a chance for changing their government for one animated by the freedom and progressive spirit of the United States, but French in language and nationality. One hundred and fifty of them boldly signed a petition addressed to the new republic, praying to be placed under the protection of France. At the theatre in New Orleans, the new French patriotic hymn, the Marseillaise, was demanded from the orchestra, and in all drinking saloons stirring revolutionary songs were sung.

Carondelet had another paper signed, in which other colonists pledged themselves to the King of Spain, and to the present government of Louisiana. The orchestra at the theatre was forbidden to play martial or revolutionary music, and revolutionary songs were prohibited on the streets and in the drinking saloons, and six of the most violent partisans of the Republic were shipped away to Havana. The fortifications of the city were strengthened and repaired; the governor himself going on horseback every morning regularly to superintend the work. Fort St. Charles was built immediately above the city, and another fort, St. Louis, immediately below. In front of the principal streets was placed a strong battery, which commanded the river and crossed its fire with that of the forts. In the rear of the city were three other forts: Burgundy, St. Ferdinand and St. Joseph. They were maller than those in front, and connected with a ditch forty eet wide and seven deep. With the earth taken out of the ditch, a parapet, three feet high had been made protected by a palisade twelve feet high. The two batteries at English Turn were abandoned. A large fort (St. Philip) was built at Plaquemine Turn and a smaller one placed on the opposite side of the river. The militia was drilled and disciplined.

These measures had their effect on the colonists immediately under the power of Spain, but the agitation outside continued unabated. A society of French Republicans in Philadelphia circulated an address in Louisiana, calling upon their brethren, in the name of Liberty, Equality and

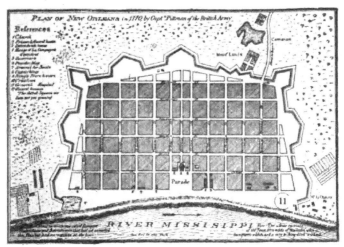

CITY OF NEW ORLEANS IN 1770.

Fraternity, to strike a blow against the Spanish despotism which enslaved them and join the nations of the free; promising that down the waters of the Ohio would soon come abundant help of men and money. The French minister to the United States turned his efforts to getting up an expedition composed of Frenchmen and Americans, which he pro-

posed to lead himself into Louisiana. Profiting by the prejudice against the Spaniards, he gathered a large band on the
borders of Georgia and even gained a strong party of Indian
warriors to join the movement. August de la Chaise, a native Louisianian (grandson of the royal commissary of 1723),
was sent to Kentucky to recruit invaders there, who were to
descend to New Orleans by way of the Ohio and Mississippi.

The authorities of the United States, however, firmly in-
terfered to prevent this violation of international treaty, and
the governor of Georgia issued a proclamation against the
proposed use of his territory. De la Chaise, disappointed in
his hopes, dispersed his force of two thousand men and retired to France.

Treaty of Madrid. 1795.—Finally the long pending
negotiations between the United States and Spain drew to a
close. The boundary line was changed to the 31st deg.
north latitude, running eastward to the Chattahoochie and
thence out on the former line to the ocean. The free navigation of the Mississippi was again stipulated and permission given to the people of the United States to use New
Orleans for three years as a place of deposit for their produce
and merchandise and to export the same free of all duty; the
term of three years to be extended at its expiration or another
place of deposit designated on the island of Orleans.

Making of Sugar by Etienne de Bore.*—M. de Boré
had settled on a plantation six miles above New Orleans, on
the same side of the river, and, like most of the planters in
Louisiana, had devoted himself to the cultivation of indigo.
Huricanes and overflows, however, had much diminished his
fortune, and in addition an insect had appeared, which attack-

---

* Etienne de Boré came of distinguished Norman family. He was born in 1740
in the Illinois, but was taken at an early age to France. After the completion of
his education he entered the Royal Mousquetaire or troops of the King's house-
old. After his marriage he returned to Louisiana and engaged in planting. M.
　Boré was the grandfather of Louisiana's distinguished historian, Charles
ιyarré.

ing the indigo plant, soon left it nothing but a bare stem. Ruin stared him and the other planters in the face. The manufacture of sugar had been abandoned since 1766, as impossible in the climate, and only a few now planted cane, to be sold as a delicacy in the market or boiled into sugar or made into a kind of rum called tafia. Boré determined to risk

what was left of his fortune by one more attempt at sugar making. His wife, and his friends also remonstrated with him. He nevertheless purchased seed cane, planted and got ready for grinding and boiling. On the day when the rolling was to begin a large number of neighbors and friends assembled in and about the sugar house, watching with anxiety the success or failure of the experiment.

ETIENNE DE BORE.

" Would the syrup granulate?" " Would it make sugar or not?" The moment came. The sugar boiler tested again and again. " It granulates!" he called out, " It granulates!" " It granulates!" the crowd in the sugar house repeated. The cry was caught up outside and flew from mouth to mouth to the city.*

But the sugar planters were then confronted by what seemed another and more horrible ruin—an insurrection of the negroes. The news of the St. Domingo revolution had penetrated to the large slave population of Louisiana. What had been accomplished there, it was thought, might be accomplished here. A conspiracy was formed at Pointe Coupee on the plantation of Julian Poydras, one of the wealthiest planters of Louisiana, then traveling in the United States.

*Gayarré, Spanish Domination.

The plot spread throughout the parish and a day was fixed for the general massacre of the whites. A disagreement as to the hour produced a quarrel among the leaders which led to the betrayal of the plot and arrest of the ringleaders. The negroes rose to the rescue, but were repulsed, and the ringleaders were tried, condemned and hung as a warning at various points on the river bank.

In 1795 another conflagration almost consumed New Orleans, causing even greater financial loss than the previous one. Only two stores in the whole city escaped, but fortunately the new cathedral, just completed by Don Andres de Almonaster, was spared. In order the better to avoid such calamities in the future, Carondelet recommended that premiums be granted to those in New Orleans who should rebuild with terraced or tiled instead of shingle roofs.

It was also during this year, 1795, that the first regular newspaper made its appearance in the city. It was called Le Moniteur de la Louisiane.

Carondelet completed his extensive works in the city by digging the Canal Carondelet, which connected the city with Bayou St. John, giving access to boats from the lake. The convict labor and details of slaves contributed by the planters were employed at it. As affording drainage for the city and bringing into it wood and small products from the lands across the lakes, the canal has more than justified the Baron's high expectation of it. In 1796 he also gave the city regular police protection and established eighty lamps for the lighting of it.

The revolution in France turned at this period a tide of emigration into Louisiana most acceptable to the Spanish authorities. It was composed of French royalists flying from the new Republic. Among the most conspicuous were the Marquis de Maison Rouge, the Baron de Bastrop and M. de Lassus de St. Vrain. They proposed plans for the removal of a large number of their countrymen and large tracts of land were granted them on the banks of the Ouachita.*

Appointed to a command in Quito, Carondelet left New Orleans in the autumn of 1797. He was succeeded by Gayoso de Lemos.

Gayoso de Lemos Governor. 1797-1799.—De Lemos governed for two years.

During his intrigues to detach the Western States from the Union, Carondelet had delayed, through various pretexts, the giving up of the forts Panmure and Walnut Hills, held by Spain within the boundaries of the United States. Now that all hopes of such a secession from the United States was ended by the firm allegiance of the Western people, Gayoso evacuated the territory.† General Wilkinson arrived with federal troops and took up his headquarters at Loftus' Height (Roche a Davion). Don Jose Vidal assumed command of the Spanish fort at Natchez.

The three years fixed by the Treaty of Madrid elapsed and a royal order was issued, prohibiting New Orleans as a place of deposit and designating no other place in its stead. When this became known in the Western States, it caused the most intense indignation and an expedition against New Orleans was openly advocated. President Adams, obliged by popular opinion to make some demonstration, ordered three regiments of the regular army to concentrate on the Ohio till further orders. Twelve additional regiments were ordered by Congress to be raised and other preparations were made which seemed to indicate an immediate campaign against Louisiana.

In the midst of the excitement Gayoso died suddenly, and Don Francisco Bouligny, colonel of the regiment of Louisiana, assumed his office.

---

* These grants were made on certain conditions which were never complied with and a full title was never vested.
† By act of Congress, the land ceded was organized into the Territory of Mississippi.

Casa Calvo. 1799-1801.—The Captain General of Cuba sent over the Marquis de Casa Calvo to be temporary governor in the colony.

The government of the United States, instead of proceeding to armed means for the protection of the rights of her citizens, arrested warlike preparations and reopened negotiations with Spain. The acquisition of New Orleans was the only sure guarantee of a final solution of the matter. While the negotiations for it were pending, the King of Spain revoked the decree against trade and restored to the people of the United States a place of deposit in New Orleans.

Salcedo Governor. 1801-1803.—Don Juan Manuel de Salcedo, brigadier general in the armies of Spain, arrived in Louisiana to relieve Caso Calvo. One of his first measures was to send arms and equipments to the militia of the Natchitoches district, in order that they might make a stand against an American inroad threatened in that quarter. At the same time, his intendant, the Comptroller of Customs, Morales, issued a decree forbidding the granting of any land to a citizen of the United States, and again suspended, by proclamation, the right of deposit in New Orleans. The news of it almost produced a revolt among the Western people; they rose and for the last time demanded redress from Congress. "The Mississippi is ours," they said, "by the law of nature. Our rivers swell its volume and flow with it to the Gulf of Mexico. Its mouth is the only issue which nature has given to our waters, and we wish to use it for our vessels. No power in the world should deprive us of our rights. If our liberty in this matter is disputed, nothing shall prevent our taking possession of the capital, and when we are once masters of it we shall know how to maintain ourselves there. If Congress refuses us effectual protection we will adopt the measures which our safety requires, even if they endanger

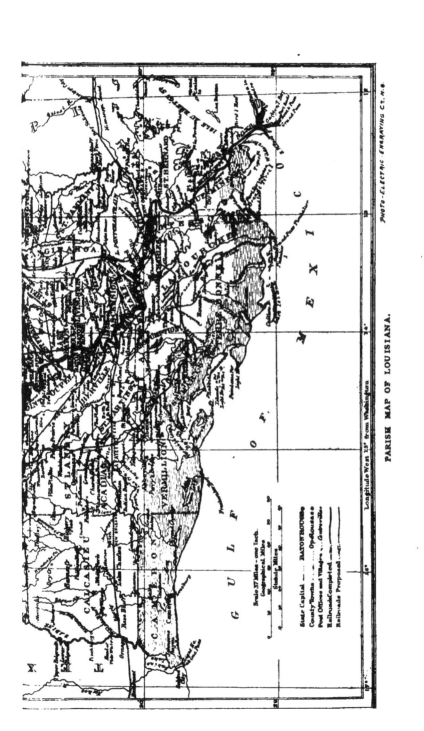

PARISH MAP OF LOUISIANA.

Longitude West 13° from Washington

PHOTO-ELECTRIC ENGRAVING CO. N.Y.

the peace of the Union and our connection with the other States. No protection, no allegiance." *

QUESTIONS.

Give an account of Miro's administration. Of the importance of the Mississippi to the Middle States. Restrictive duties of the Spanish authorities. Effect on the Western people. Inquisition in New Orleans. French Revolution. Carondelet's administration. Treaty of Madrid. Making of sugar. Administration of Gayoso. Casa Calvo. Salcedo. Last demand of Western people for free navigation of the Mississippi river.

———•◦•———

FROM COLONY TO STATE.

CHAPTER XX.

THE THREE POWERS.

The first years of this century witnessed some very important events in the history of Louisiana. By these events the whole current of affairs was changed. The great territory that then bore the name of Louisiana was brought from under the Spanish domination and joined to the American Union. It must be noticed, however, that the interests of the Louisianians themselves were not at all consulted. Their country was simply a valuable piece of property; two other nations, we shall see, sold it for as high a price as they could obtain, and in the end the Americans carried off the prize. It was a splendid bargain for the United States, and the inhabitants of the purchased territory soon found that under the free American Government a glorious future was opened before them.

* Quoted by Gayarré from Marbois' History of Louisiana,

Let us trace the history of these important events.

Napoleon's Bargain with Spain.—In the year 1800, Napoleon Bonaparte, who was then at the head of the French government with the title of First Consul, determined to induce Spain to give back Louisiana to France. It was his intention to establish once more the power of France in America, and to use Louisiana as a point from which he could attack the possessions of the English, with whom he was constantly at war.

When he proposed to the King of Spain that the province should be ceded back to France, His Catholic Majesty,* who had not found Louisiana a very profitable possession, and who feared that the grasping Americans might one day take it from him, listened very favorably to Napoleon's proposition. He finally declared that he would give up the province, if Napoleon would make over to the Duke of Parma, who belonged to the royal house of Spain, that part of Italy which was called the Duchy of Tuscany. Napoleon promised to comply with this condition, and October 1, 1800, a secret treaty was signed at St. Ildefonso, of which the third article was as follows: "His Catholic Majesty promises and binds himself "to give back to the French Republic, six months after the "conditions in regard to Louis, Duke of Parma, have been "executed, the colony of Louisiana, with the same boundaries "which it had when it was owned by France, and which it "should have according to the treaties made more recently "between Spain and other States."

Thus Spain thought she had placed between the Americans and her Mexican possessions a power friendly to herself; if she had dreamed that Napoleon would in a few years sell the colony to her American rival, it would never have passed out of her hands.

For more than a year Napoleon kept his bargain with Spain a profound secret. His minister was the famous Tal-

---

* This was the official title of the King of Spain.

leyrand, who was very skilful in concealing what he knew and
in baffling all inquiries. Napoleon had very good reasons for
pretending that France did not own Louisiana. England had
a powerful fleet, which was always sailing along the English
Channel and watching the movements of French vessels. If
it were known that Louisiana belonged to France, England
might easily send this fleet across the Atlantic, seize the colony, and extend her dominion from Canada to the Gulf of
Mexico. If she made the attempt, Napoleon, who was then
carrying on extensive wars in Europe, was not at that moment able to prevent her.

Jefferson's Purchase.—In the meantime the Spanish
governor, Salcedo, still remained in Louisiana, and his intendant, Morales, ventured to deny to the Western people the
right of deposit at New Orleans. We saw in our last chap-
ter how boldly the people of Kentucky protested against this
action. If the American Government had refused to listen
to their complaints, they would doubtless have attacked
the Spaniards and tried to seize New Orleans. But Thomas
Jefferson, who was then President of the United States, appreciated the grievances of which the Kentuckians complained, and resolved to do all that he could to remove them.

As soon as it was finally known that Louisiana had been
ceded by Spain to France, he sent over James Monroe (afterwards President of the United States), to join Robert R.
Livingston, United States Minister at Paris, and he instructed
these two representatives to negotiate with Napoleon for the
purchase of New Orleans and the right of way to the Gulf.
But as Napoleon saw that it would not be in his power to
hold Louisiana against the English, he very shrewdly determined to sell the whole country to the United States. He
would thus prevent England from seizing it; he would at
the same time make friends of the Americans; and he would
himself obtain a handsome sum to carry on the war against
the English. Accordingly, therefore, he opened negotiations

with the American agents to find out how much they would give, not for New Orleans alone, but for the whole of Louisiana. After long discussions with a French Commissioner named Barbé-Marbois, Monroe and Livingston agreed upon the sum of eighty million francs (about fifteen million dollars) as the price that America should pay. The treaty of sale was signed at Paris April 30, 1803.

Napoleon was highly pleased with the result. " This accession of territory," he said, " strengthens forever the power of the United States. I have given England a maritime rival which will sooner or later humble her pride." His prediction was fulfilled in the war of 1812-15, when the American vessels won many victories over the English.

In the United States, Jefferson's purchase was disapproved of by some people, but the joy of the Western States carried everything before it. The result was that in 1804 Jefferson was re-elected President.

Spain, very naturally, showed some indignation at Napoleon's bold stroke, and maintained that he had agreed not to yield Louisiana to any other nation. But this agreement was never proved, and Jefferson refused to consider the Spanish protest. It was then feared that Spain would try to prevent the transfer of the colony; but she afterwards withdrew her protest, " as a proof of her friendship for the United States."

Laussat in Louisiana.—We must now return to the events in Louisiana. On March 26, 1803, M. Laussat, the Commissioner sent over by Napoleon to receive Louisiana from the Spaniards, arrived at New Orleans. As the treaty of sale with the United States was not signed till a month later, Laussat did not suspect that after he had taken possession of the colony, he would be ordered to transfer it to another government.

He was received with proper honors by the Spanish governor, Salcedo, and soon after issued an address, in which he

told the Louisianians that the transfer of their country to
Spain in 1763 had beeen the act of a weak and corrupt government, but that the great and magnanimous Napoleon, as
soon as his victories had given him the power, had hastened
to restore Louisiana to the care of France.   Laussat did not
know that at this very time Napoleon was bargaining to
sell Louisiana to the United States at the highest possible
price.

Laussat received two addresses in answer to his own.   The
first was from the planters of Louisiana; it was signed by
Manuel Andry, Noel Peret, Foucher, and many others.   They
expressed the joy they felt in becoming citizens of France;
but they declared that they had no cause to complain of their
treatment at the hands of the Spanish governors, with the single exception of the cruel Irishman, O'Reilly.   "Let the
"Spaniards, they added, "have the undisturbed enjoyment
" of all the property they own on this soil, and let us share
" with them like brothers the blessings of our new position."
The second address, signed by well known citizens of New
Orleans, such as De Boré, Fortier, Labatut, and De Buys,
expressed exactly the same sentiments.   Thus the Louisianians, for the most part, were delighted to be transferred to
France; but many of them, says Marbois, feared that Napoleon might set free all of the slaves in Louisiana, as he had
done in St. Domingo, and that the terrible events which had
taken place on that island might be repeated in their own
country.   This dread of the First Consul's policy was enough
to lessen their joy in acknowledging the government of
France.

Laussat, who had formed great plans for building roads
and bridges in the colony, and otherwise increasing its prosperity, soon began to hear rumors that Louisiana had been
ceded to the American Government.   Several months, however, passed before orders finally reached him that he was to
receive Louisiana from the Spanish governor, and then hold

himself ready to transfer it to the young American Republic.

France Takes Possession.—On the 30th of November, 1803, Laussat proceeded to the City Hall (the old Cabildo),

CABILDO (SUPREME COURT BUILDING).

where he met Governor Salcedo and Casa Calvo, who had been appointed to transfer Louisiana to France. The three gentlemen solemnly took their seats in the council chamber. After the necessary documents had been read, the keys of the city were handed over to the representatives of France, and Casa Calvo announced that all Louisianians who did not wish to withdraw from the colony and live elsewhere under the Spanish rule were released from their oath of fidelity to His Catholic Majesty. The three representatives then walked out on the gallery facing the old Place d'Armes (now Jackson Square). In the centre of the square the flag of Spain was proudly waving. Since the arrival of O'Reilly, thirty-four years before, the people of Louisiana had lived under this banner. It now descended from its staff amid salutes of artillery and the flag of France rose in its place. Before many days had passed the French flag was to be replaced by the " Stars and Stripes." As this fact was already known, the ceremony that had just taken place was not regarded by the populace with any great enthusiasm, though with the fondness for display which has always distinguished New Orleans, an immense crowd had assembled to witness it.

When the ceremony was over Laussat issued a proclamation to the people of Louisiana, which in beautiful and appropriate words told them of the new destiny that had been prepared for them by Napoleon's treaty with America. He told them that according to this treaty they would in a short time enjoy all the rights and privileges possessed by the citizens of the United States. He then prophesied that the Mississippi would soon be covered with a thousand ships from all nations. "May a Louisianian and a Frenchman," he concluded, "never meet upon any spot of the earth without feeling tenderly drawn to each other, and without saluting each other with the title of brother!"

The old Spanish council was abolished, and in its stead Laussat appointed a regular city government. Etienne de Boré, the rich and successful sugar planter, was chosen mayor, while the council was composed of the following distinguished citizens: Villeré, Jones, Fortier, Donaldson, Faurie, Allard, Tureaud, and Watkins. Derbigny was the secretary, and Labatut the treasurer. As Laussat had no troops to protect New Orleans when the Spanish garrison withdrew, a number of young Creoles and Americans formed themselves into a company and offered their services to guard the city. New Orleans was patrolled by these young men till the arrival of the United States Commissioners, who were to receive Louisiana for the American Government.

Rivalry of Laussat and Casa Calvo.—In the meantime there was a great deal of rivalry between Laussat and the Marquis of Casa Calvo, each trying to outdo the other in a series of magnificent dinner parties, given to the chief inhabitants of the colony. It was the French Republic vying with the Spanish Monarchy. Each representative wished to prove how much affection his country felt for the Louisianians. In a history of Louisiana, by a French traveller named Robin, who attended some of these banquets, there is an interesting description of the guests, and from it we translate the following: "The ladies of the colony appear at these " fetes with an elegance which is truly astonishing; the prin- " cipal cities of France can offer nothing more brilliant. " These ladies are generally tall and dignified. The white- " ness of their complexion is set off by light robes orna- " mented with flowers and embroidery; so that one of these " fetes is like a scene in fairyland. Sometimes as many as " four hundred guests are grouped around the tables at sup- " per. What a pity," he continues, " that a taste for such " pleasures should spread in a new country, which has so " much need to practise economy!"

QUESTIONS.

Who was Napoleon? What bargain did he make? Give an account of Jefferson's purchase. Who was Laussat? How was his address to the people received? Describe the act of taking possession. Describe the banquets of that day.

CHAPTER XXI.

UNDER THE AMERICAN FLAG.

The American Government Takes Possession.—On the 17th of December, 1803, Wm. C. C. Claiborne, Governor of Mississippi, accompanied by General Wilkinson, arrived at New Orleans to take possession of Louisiana in the name of the American Government. The 20th instant was chosen as the day of the cession. That day, for the third time in the memory of a generation then living, the people of Louisiana, without their feelings being consulted, were transferred from one government to another. The Commissioners met Laussat at the Cabildo. The keys of the city, held by France for twenty days, were now presented to Governor Claiborne, and as the " Stars and Stripes" ran up to the head of the flag staff, loud huzzas filled the air. These came, it is said, from a group of Americans. The rest of the population, who felt that the change of government was not an act of their free will, showed no enthusiasm. As soon as he had received the keys Governor Claiborne arose and addressed the people. He congratulated them on becoming citizens of the United States, and praised the government which he represented.

GOVERNOR CLAIBORNE.

Limits of Louisiana. 1803.—Thus it was that the United States came into possession of the great province of Louisiana. What were the limits of this new purchase? They embraced more than one million square miles and more than ninety thousand inhabitants. The boundaries were about as follows: On the north, the lower limit of Canada; on the south, the Gulf of Mexico; on the east, the Mississippi river and a line drawn through Bayou Manchac and the lakes to

JEFFERSON'S PURCHASE.

the sea; and on the west, the Rocky Mountains and an irregular line running from these mountains to the mouth of the Sabine river.

Under the same purchase the United States claimed also a part of Oregon and that portion of Florida west of the Perdido river. These claims were not settled till some years later.

Division of Louisiana.—On March 26, 1804, the Congress of the United States passed an act for the government of the great territory purchased by Jefferson. This territory was thereby divided into two parts: first, all that portion north of the 33d degree of latitude (the present northern boundary of Louisiana) was to be called the District of Louana. The name was afterward changed to the Territory Louisiana, and then to the Territory of Missouri; hence at part of Louisiana will no longer concern us in this his-

tory. Secondly, "All that portion of the country ceded by
" France to the United States which lies south of the Missis-
" sippi Territory, and of an east and west line to commence
" on the Mississippi river at the 33d degree of latitude, and
" extending to the western boundary of the said cession, shall
" constitute a territory of the United States under the name
" of the Territory of Orleans." We shall see that eight
years later the Territory of Orleans became the present State
of Louisiana.

This new territory was to be under a governor and a legislative council, both to be appointed by the President of the
United States. The introduction of slaves from Africa was
forbidden, and as the inhabitants thought the negroes necessary for the cultivation of their plantations, this measure·
caused great dissatisfaction.

Claiborne Made Governor.—On Friday, October 5, 1804,
Claiborne * was sworn into office as governor of the new Territory of Orleans. He had just suffered a great domestic
affliction in the death of his wife and child ; and in his opening address he touched the hearts of his audience by declaring that the only happiness left to him would consist in trying to govern wisely those who had been put under his
charge.

Legislative Council.—To assist Claiborne in the govern-
ment of the Territory, the following council was appointed:
Julien Poydras, Morgan, Bellechasse, Watkins, de Boré,
Dow, Coutrelle, Clark, Roman (of Attakapas), Jones, De
Buys, Kenner, and Wikoff (of Opelousas). The first judges
appointed were Dominick A. Hall, district judge of the
United States, with E. Kirby and J. B. Prevost, judges of the
Superior Court.

---

* Wm. Charles Cole Claiborne was sprung from an old Virginia family. In 1793
he had moved to East Tennessee, where he held high offices. He was chosen
judge of the Supreme Court and member of Congress. In 1801 he was appointed,
by Jefferson, governor of the Mississippi Territory, which position he occupied
until he was sent to Louisiana by the same President.

Discontent of the Louisianians.—Thus the new government had been organized, but there was still a great deal of
dissatisfaction among the inhabitants.   To forbid the impor-
tation of slaves was a great grievance, but a more serious one
was that the legislative council was not elected by the people,
as in the other Territories of the United States.   The new
Governor, moreover, it was declared, was ignorant of the
manners and customs of the people over whom he was placed,
and even spoke the French language very imperfectly.   The
discontent reached such a point that four members of the
council resigned, and Claiborne had to appoint others in their
places.

Before this, however, a committee of three—Destrehan,
Derbigny, and Sauvé—had been sent to Washington with a
memorial, asking that the Territory of Orleans should be
admitted into the Union as a State, and that the slave trade
should be continued.   These requests were not granted; but
Congress passed a bill allowing the Louisianians to elect a
territorial legislature of twenty-five members; and this legislature was permitted to send on to the President the names
of ten individuals, from whom he should choose a legislative
council or senate of five members.   It was further declared
that the Territory of Orleans should be admitted as a State
as soon as the population amounted to 60,000.

Something had been gained, but neither the native Louisianians nor the American settlers were satisfied.   Was there
any excuse for such treatment of the Louisianians by the
Congress of the United States?   Had the American Government not promised that the inhabitants of the Territory
should be admitted as soon as possible to the enjoyment of
all the rights and privileges possessed by the citizens of the
United States?   Why then should the Territory of Orleans
not be formed into a State, and the inhabitants permitted to
choose their own governor and elect their own judges?   Such
were the bitter questions asked by the Louisianians.   The

only answer of Congress was that the number of inhabitants in the Territory was only forty thousand, and that the great majority were Frenchmen and Spaniards, who were not yet acquainted with the laws and Constitution of the United States; hence it would be wise for Orleans to serve its apprenticeship as a Territory before being admitted into the Union as a "sovereign State."

This answer did not satisfy the Louisianians, and the old newspapers of New Orleans are filled with anonymous letters criticising very sharply the American Government and its representative, Governor Claiborne. The latter had become unpopular because he vetoed several bills passed by the legislature.*

Other Causes of Discontent.—From one of Claiborne's letters we learn that the trial by jury, to which the Louisianians had not been accustomed under the Spanish Government, and which was now introduced, was at first very unpopular. Moreover, a number of lawyers crowded into the Territory, and, by investigation of the titles to lands, and by sharp practice, succeeded in amassing large fortunes and gaining the hatred of the people.† Last, but not least, the introduction of the English language into the courts of justice was a serious cause of discontent. "These courts," says Judge Martin, "had interpreters of the French, Span- "ish, and English languages. They translated the evidence, "and the charge of the judge when necessary, but not the "argument of the lawyers. The cause was opened in the "English language, and the jurymen who did not under- "stand English were then allowed to withdraw to the gal- "lery. The argument of the defence being in French, these "were then brought back; and the rest of the jury, if they "were Americans and did not understand French, were al-

---

* It was not possible under the territorial government to pass a bill over the governor's veto by a two-thirds vote of the legislature.
† Gayarré.

"lowed to withdraw in their turn. All went together into
"the jury room—each declaring that the argument to which
"he had listened was the best—and they finally agreed on a
"verdict in the best manner they could." To add to the
confusion in the courts, the Territory of Orleans was governed partly by a set of laws drawn up in imitation of the
Code of Napoleon,* and partly by the old Spanish laws,
which very few lawyers understood.

Governor Claiborne, who appreciated the feelings of the
people, and hoped that in time these feelings would change
for the better, bore all the attacks upon himself with patience,
and tried in every honorable way to draw over to his side
those that opposed him. He nobly declared that the newspapers could not injure him as long as he did his duty, and
that he believed the freedom of the press should be maintained, even if injustice were sometimes the result. By his
simplicity and his pleasant manners, Claiborne soon made
many friends for himself. At first he seems to have dis-
trusted the old inhabitants of Louisiana, and to have believed that in case of war they would prefer the government of France to that of the United States; but gradually
his opinion changed, and he declared that the great majority
would, under all circumstances, be loyal to the American
Government. In the war of 1812 the conduct of the Creoles
proved that he was right.

QUESTIONS.

Why was Claiborne sent to Louisiana? What was the extent of
Louisiana? How was Louisiana divided? Who was made governor?
Why were the people of Louisiana discontented with the new gov-
ernment? Why did the United States decline to make Louisiana a
State? Describe the courts of justice. Show the limits of Louisiana
on map of 1810, and on large map of the State.

---

* This Code was drawn up in France by order of Napoleon; it was based on
the Roman law. It is still the foundation of our civil law in Louisiana.

CHAPTER XXII.

DESCRIPTION OF LOWER LOUISIANA AT TIME OF CESSION.

New Orleans in 1803.—The little city already had over 8000 inhabitants. They were, for the most part, French and Spanish Creoles, but the Spaniards had intermarried with the French, and the language of the latter was generally spoken. The number of the Americans was increasing daily, and many refugees from the island of St. Domingo sought a home in Louisiana. Houses were being built with great rapidity. Those along the river bank were the most attrac· tive. In a desirable street the best stores rented at eighty dollars a month.*

The streets at that time, even the principal ones, were almost impassable. There was no paving as yet, and the vehicles in rainy weather sank to their hubs. A street was generally called by the name of the principal inhabitant, as the proper designations were to be found only in the city archives. As soon, however, as the Americans took possession, there was a change for the better. The streets were raised and kept cleaner. Already the city was very prosperous. The Mississippi was crowded with barges bringing down the products of the rich countries above, and the merchants of New Orleans were growing wealthy. As yet there was no Carnival in the winter season, but splendid entertainments were numerous, and the different classes of society were devoted to gayety.

The Parishes.—When Claiborne became governor of the Territory of Orleans, his legislative council divided it into twelve settlements, which at first were called *counties*. These were the counties of Orleans, German Coast, Acadia, La-

---

* The increase in the value of property at the present day is shown by the fact that a fine store now rents at over five hundred dollars a month.

fourche, Iberville, Pointe Coupée, Concordia, Attakapas, Opelousas, Rapides, Natchitoches, and Ouachita. The limits of these divisions were not clearly fixed, and the divisions themselves differed very much in size and population. Some were three hundred miles in extent, and others only forty-five; some contained ten times as many inhabitants as others. Finally, by an act of the legislature, approved March 31, 1807, the Territory of Orleans was divided into nineteen districts, to which the name of " parishes " was given, from the fact that the old Spanish division for religious purposes was used as the basis in fixing the boundaries.* In no other State of the Union are the counties so named. Since that time it has been found convenient, as the population increased, to divide still further the larger parishes, and they now number fifty-nine.†

Robin, who visited many of the Louisiana parishes in the early part of the century, gives us some idea of the inhabitants and their manner of life. If a traveler ascended the river to Pointe Coupée, he saw along the banks rich plantations, pretty houses, and numerous settlements. In the Parish of St. Charles a large number of Germans had settled as far back as the time of John Law and his " Mississippi Bubble." They had always been industrious, and many of them were now rich. Owning few slaves they frequently worked their own plantations, and from their gardens New Orleans was supplied with every kind of vegetable. Sixty miles above the city began the " Acadian Coast," where the wanderers from Nova Scotia had settled more than forty years before. In the early days they had been largely supported by supplies from the Government;

---

* Hence the names of the Saints in the designation of the old parishes.
† The 19 parishes of 1807 were: 1. City of New Orleans, 2. St. Bernard, 3. St. Charles, 4. St. John the Baptist, 5. Plaquemines, 6. St. James, 7. Ascension, 8. Assumption, 9. Interior Parish of Lafourche, 10. Iberville, 11. W. Baton Rouge, 12. Pointe Coupée, 13. Concordia, 14. Ouachita, 15. Rapides, 16. Avoyelles, 17. Natchitoches 18. St. Landry, 19. Attakapas, called Parish of St. Martin. Four more parishes were added from West Florida at a later period.

but at this epoch they were very prosperous. They raised rice and corn, and they owned immense herds of cattle. Their lives were very simple, but they were as fond of dancing parties as they are at the present day.

At Pointe Coupée, where Julien Poydras owned a large plantation, there were many old and aristocratic French settlers. They lived in great luxury, surrounded by large numbers of slaves, who did all the work. There were hardly any taverns along the banks of the river. Indeed, they were unnecessary, for a traveler was welcomed wherever he went; and Louisianians were as famous for their hospitality in those days as they are at the end of the nineteenth century.

After passing Pointe Coupée, houses became much scarcer, and as one ascended the river, one saw only small settlements here and there, which were protected from the Indians by forts. Above Baton Rouge, on the east bank of the river, the inhabitants were, for the most part, Americans. These supplied their French friends across the river with slaves and all kinds of provisions. Some of them had passed over to the west bank and settled the Red river district. In the prairies below the mouth of Red river, on Bayous Lafourche, Plaquemines, Atchafalaya, and Teche, there were, says Dr. Monette, numerous French settlements. In St. Bernard parish * and on the Amite river there were many Spaniards, who had come over from the Canary Islands during the Spanish domination. These were the Isleños or "Islanders."

Traffic on the Mississippi.—All kinds of craft plied on the river, from the cumbersome flat-boat to the swiftly gliding pirogue. When they reached New Orleans the flat-boats were broken up and the timber sold, it being almost impossible to haul them back against the current. In ascending the stream other boats made use of sails, oars, and sometimes of a rope dragged along the levees. The traveler making a trip

* Named in honor of Bernardo de Galvez, the Spanish governor.

up the river usually engaged some Canadians or Indians as oarsmen. What a difference between this method of travel and a trip on one of our magnificent steamboats at the present day!

Chief Products of the Territory in 1803.—The products of Louisiana at that period seem very insignificant when compared with those of our time. For instance, there were seventy-five sugar houses in the Territory, and the whole yield was only five million pounds, which is equaled by a single plantation of to-day. The one sugar refinery of which the Territory boasted produced only 200,000 pounds a year, and as the process of refining was not well understood, the sugar was poor. In his history, Judge Martin tells us that only 20,000 bales of cotton were raised,* and that there were only 5000 casks of molasses. The prairies of Opelousas and Attakapas, however, were covered with great herds of cattle, and furnished New Orleans with more fresh meat than could be consumed.

Domestic manufactures hardly existed at this period. The Acadians wove their homespun cloth as they do to-day, but slavery was unfavorable to the rise of factories. The slaves, though skilful enough in the cotton fields, seemed entirely unsuited for the cotton factory.

-Indians.—In 1803 there were still a number of scattered Indian tribes in Louisiana. On Bayou Vermilion, for instance, there was a village of Attakapas (man-eaters—so called because they were once cannibals). On the Ouachita and Red river were found the Caddos and the Choctaws, the former tribe still having a force of five hundred warriors. The Indians, however, seem to have given very little trouble to the whites, who traded with them for skins and other fruits of the chase. In fact, the savages were dependent upon the whites for the powder and ball they used in their hunting

---

* The sugar crop of 1891 was 492,000,000 pounds, and the cotton crop of Louisiana averages about half a million bales,

expeditions, and they gradually lost their hatred of the "pale-faces." It must not be supposed, however, that they had been civilized by their intercourse with the white men. Catholic missionaries from the earliest times had attempted to convert them to Christianity, and change their savage disposition, but they had met with very little success. The Indians, from their manner of life and their traditions, were neither willing nor able to accept the laws of civilization. They possessed, however, many fine qualities, and the story of their gradual disappearance in Louisiana has a pathetic interest. The Indian women who to-day sell sassafras and herbs in the French market are descended from the once dreaded tribe of Choctaws; while those on the Teche, who make the wonderful baskets, are all that are left of the Attakapas.*

QUESTIONS.

Tell something about New Orleans in 1803. Why are the counties in Louisiana called *parishes?* Describe the German, Acadian, and French settlements along the Mississippi. Who are the "Islanders?" How was the Mississippi navigated before the day of steamboats? What were the chief products of Louisiana? Was there any manufacturing? Who were the Attakapas? The Choctaws?

CHAPTER XXIII.

TROUBLOUS TIMES.

Aaron Burr.—One of the most remarkable men in the early part of this century was Aaron Burr. In 1800 he was elected Vice President of the United States, and while holding this office he fought a duel with the famous statesman

---

* A great deal was done for the Indians around New Orleans by the poet-priest, Father Rouquette, who devoted his life to this work. He died in 1887.

Alexander Hamilton, in which the latter was killed. Some time after this Burr made a journey through what was then called the Western Country. His manners were very attractive, and he made many friends among the prominent men of the time. To some of these he seems to have confided his reasons for traveling in the West, but the exact purpose of his journey has never been discovered. Burr purchased 300,000 acres of land on the Red river, and he afterwards declared that his only intention was to settle this vast plantation. But when, in 1806, his secret agents were to be found in Louisiana and Kentucky, it began to be whispered around that Burr was a daring conspirator. His design, according to some, was to invade Mexico and make himself master of that country. Others declared that he intended to separate the Southern and Western Country from the Union, and, seizing New Orleans, make this city the capital of a new Union.

General Wilkinson, who was commander of the United States troops in the South, threw New Orleans into a state of defence, and arrested by military orders several of Burr's agents, who were stirring up trouble in the city. All of this caused the greatest excitement in New Orleans. Troops patrolled the streets, and Wilkinson felt justified in suspending the writ of *habeas corpus*—that is, he arrested suspicious persons and refused to surrender some of them when he was ordered by the courts to do so. This high-handed conduct stirred up a violent opposition to him, for the people thought that the laws were sufficient to protect the city.

In the meantime, however, Thomas Jefferson, President of the United States, having been informed of Burr's strange conduct, had issued a proclamation against him, and in 1807, while Burr was passing through the Mississippi Territory, with one hundred men in his train, he was discovered. He gave himself up, but afterwards escaped. A reward of two thousand dollars having been offered for his arrest, he was captured and sent on to Richmond for trial. No act of treason, however, could be proved against him, and he was released. All the excitement that he had caused was soon at an end.

College and Schools.—As early as the year 1805 a college was opened to students in New Orleans. It was situated near the corner of Hospital and St. Claude streets, and was called the College of Orleans. For twenty years it offered courses of instruction to the young men of that day. One of the most distinguished of its students was the Honorable Charles Gayarré, the historian of Louisiana.*

Some years later, at the suggestion of Governor Claiborne, public schools were established in the different parishes, but so little money was given for their support that, except in the parish of Pointe Coupée, they did not flourish. There were, however, a number of private schools in New Orleans, which were well attended. It was not till a good many years later that the importance of popular education was more fully recognized, and larger appropriations were made for the public schools.

Revolt of the Baton Rouge District.—All West Florida—that is, the district north of Lake Pontchartrain, east of the Mississippi, south of the 31st degree of latitude, and west of the Perdido river †—was claimed by the United States as part of the Louisiana Purchase. But Spain refused to give up this district, declaring that she had never yielded it to France, and that therefore France could not have sold it to the United States. Hence Spanish garrisons were still kept at Baton Rouge and Mobile. The inhabitants of the Baton Rouge district were largely Americans, who had come from Mississippi and Ohio. They disliked the government of Spain, and, as early as 1805, they had tried to seize the fort at Baton Rouge and expel the Spaniards; but the

* Alcée Fortier, in "Memoirs of Louisiana."
† The Perdido is the present western boundary of Florida.

garrison was on the alert, and the attempt failed. In the year 1810, however, the inhabitants determined to make another attempt. One hundred and twenty men were collected, and, under Captain Thomas and Captain Depassau, they marched upon Baton Rouge. The Spanish garrison consisted of one hundred and fifty men. The Americans attacked with great spirit, and the Spanish commander, Colonel de Grandpré, was shot down at the head of his soldiers. The garrison, seeing that they had lost their leader, surrendered, and were allowed to retire to Pensacola.

The Americans then held a convention at Baton Rouge, in which they declared the whole territory of West Florida to be " a free and independent State." At their request the President of the United States took the new State under his protection. That portion of it, however, which lay east of Pearl river, was left in the power of Spain until 1813, while the Baton Rouge district, as we shall see, was added to Louisiana. Its inhabitants, by a daring feat of arms, had won their independence, but they were well satisfied to have their destiny joined to that of Louisiana.

Slave Insurrection.—The year 1811 was long remembered on account of a dangerous uprising of the negroes in the parish of St. John. Five hundred of them formed a plot among themselves to march upon New Orleans, burning the plantation houses on their way and forcing all the slaves they met to join them. They provided themselves with weapons, and as they proceeded down the banks of the Mississippi with flags flying and drums beating, they chanted wild songs that filled with dread the hearts of the unprotected planters. A number of white people were put to death, but the great majority were warned in time, and fled to places of safety. As soon as the news reached New Orleans, the militia and the United States troops, under General Wade Hampton, were ordered out, and when they met the blacks, the latter were soon dispersed. Many of the ringleaders were condemned to death, and their heads placed on lofty poles along the Mississippi—a dreadful warning to those who might attempt the same thing in the future. It is said that old negroes still living in Louisiana tell the story of this slave insurrection as they heard it from their fathers.

QUESTIONS.

Who was Aaron Burr? Why was he arrested? What was the first college in Louisiana? Describe the revolt of the Baton Rouge district. Slave insurrection.

————•◆•————

CHAPTER XXIV.

LOUISIANA ADMITTED AS A STATE.

Before Congress.—The same year (1811) permission was received from the Congress of the United States to call a convention in the Territory of Orleans for the purpose of drawing up a constitution. The Territory, which now had more than seventy-five thousand inhabitants, was at last to be admitted into the Union as the State of Louisiana. This permission, however, had not been obtained without some difficulty. When the question of admission was brought before Congress, it provoked nearly as much discussion as it had in former years. Many members declared that the Territory of Orleans was almost a foreign country, and should not enjoy the same privileges as the original thirteen colonies. The inhabitants, it was said, were largely Spaniards and Frenchmen, and if they were permitted to send representatives to Congress, these representatives would interfere with the rights of the Atlantic States. There could be no sympathy, it was declared, between the people of Louisiana and the inhabitants of the North and the East. Josiah Quincy, of Massachusetts, went so far as to say that if Louisiana were admitted into the Union the rest of the States would be justified in withdrawing from that Union, "amicably if they could, violently if they must."

The Convention.—In spite, however, of this bold language, the bill passed, and the constitutional convention met at New Orleans, November 4, 1811. Members came from the whole Territory of Orleans, but not from the Baton Rouge district; for this district had not yet been added by Act of Congress.

The president of the convention was Julien Poydras, the rich planter of Pointe Coupée. By the 22d of January, 1812, the new constitution had been prepared, and being duly forwarded to Washington, it received the approval of Congress. Under this constitution Louisiana was admitted into the Union by Act of Congress, April 8, 1812, and the Baton Rouge district, as far as Pearl river, having been added a few days later, the boundaries of Louisiana were fixed as they stand at the present day.

Claiborne Elected Governor of the State.—According to the new constitution, the governor was to be chosen by the people, instead of being appointed by the President. The two candidates who received the highest number of votes were Wm. C. C. Claiborne and James Villeré, the son of the patriot that lost his life during O'Reilly's administration. As Claiborne had a larger number of votes than Villeré, he became governor of the new State. This was certainly a high compliment to his services. He had been governor of the Territory for eight years, and now, by the choice of the people, he was once more raised to that high office. By his sterling integrity he had withstood all the attacks of his enemies and defeated all their plans.

The first secretary of state was L. B. Macarty, a member of a distinguished Louisiana family. There was no lieutenant-governor in Louisiana till a new constitution was framed in 1845.

The First Steamboat.—On the 10th of January, 1812, New Orleans was thrown into a great state of excitement by the announcement that a steamboat had arrived at the levee. It was the first ever seen on the Mississippi. Up to this time nothing had been known on Western waters except flat-boats, barges, and lighter craft. But Robert Fulton, who some years before had built a steamboat to run between New York and Albany, now drew the model of a second one to ply between Natchez and New Orleans. It was one hundred and sixteen feet long and twenty feet wide, and cost thirty-eight thousand dollars. When this new kind of vessel left Pittsburg and glided down the Ohio into the Mississippi, wondering crowds gathered along the banks and predicted that it would never be able to ascend the swift current. The only cabin passengers were N. J. Roosevelt, who was one of the owners, and his wife. At Cincinnati, Louisville, and Natchez the voyagers were received with great rejoicings.

The trip, however, was not without its dangers. Once the vessel caught on fire and came near being consumed. Moreover, during the latter part of the year 1811, the channel of the Mississippi was considerably changed by severe earthquake shocks, many of which occurred while the boat was making the trip; and several times the voyagers made narrow escapes from immense trees which were hurled into the stream by these sudden movements of the earth. No serious accident, however, occurred, and the "New Orleans," as the vessel was named, arrived safely at the Crescent City. The actual time from Pittsburg was only 259 hours, which was considered a very quick passage in those days.

The success of this steamboat made a great change in the development of the whole Western country. Cotton and other products began to come down the river in vast quantities, and New Orleans sent back all kinds of supplies. After the

war, which now broke out, was over, the Crescent City prospered as it had never prospered before.*

Why did the Northern Congressmen still object to having Louisiana
made a State?   When was Louisiana admitted as a State?   Who was
made governor, and how was he chosen?   Describe the first trip of
the first Mississippi steamboat.   Tell some of the changes made by
the use of steamboats.

WAR OF 1812-15.

CHAPTER XXV.

BEFORE THE LOUISIANA CAMPAIGN.

Causes of the War.—The Act of Congress making
Louisiana a State had not been approved more than a few
months when the United States declared war against Great
Britain (June 18, 1812). The principal cause of the war
was this: Great Britain had determined to crush Napoleon
Bonaparte, and as she needed sailors to man her ships, she
had boarded some nine hundred American vessels on the
high seas and impressed into her service several thousand
American sailors. It was claimed that these sailors had
been born in England, and that "once an Englishman"
meant "always an Englishman;" but a great many of them
were citizens of the United States and our Government determined to put a stop to these unjust seizures.

The First Years of the War.—For two years the war

---

* It is related that an old negro at Natchez, when he saw the " New Orleans"
temming the current, exclaimed: "Ole Mississippi got her massa dis time." See
laiborne's History of Mississippi.

went on without any decisive battle on either side. The British marched up to Washington and burned the Capitol; but on the sea the Americans met with brilliant success, and a large number of British vessels were sunk or captured. This was what Bonaparte had predicted, and he doubtless heard with great pleasure the news of our victories. In 1814 the English decided to attack the United States on the north through Canada and on the south through New Orleans. In September of the same year the northern army was defeated by the Americans, and forced to return to Canada. Another army and a fleet, however, had already been sent to Florida, with the intention of attacking New Orleans. Thus the seat of war was transferred to the Gulf of Mexico.

Fort Bowyer and Pensacola.—The commander of the American forces in the South was General Andrew Jackson,* who was destined to be the hero of the Battle of New Orleans. The first hostile movement of the British vessels was against Fort Bowyer on Mobile Point; but Major Lawrence, who was in command of the fort, repulsed the attack so successfully that they retired to Pensacola, at that time in the possession of Spain. Jackson marched against Pensacola, and forced the English to withdraw from the town. Then hastening to the defence of Louisiana, he arrived in New Orleans December 1, 1814.

John and Pierre Lafitte, the Smugglers.—The British had hoped that their designs against New Orleans were unknown to the Americans. But as early as September 5th of this year (1814), John Laffitte had warned Governor Claiborne of the approaching army and naval forces. As this Laffitte played an important part in the conflict, we must inquire who he was.

---

* Jackson was born in North Carolina, March 15, 1767. He was not well educated, but possessed great natural ability. Brave and skilful in war, he always won the confidence and affection of his soldiers. He was twice elected President of the United States, but he did not prove himself a wise statesman.

On the southern coast of Louisiana lies a beautiful little
island called Grande Terre.   Just behind this island is Lake
Barataria, which forms one of the safest harbors west of the
Mississippi.   On the inner coast of Grande Terre we find on
the old maps of Louisiana one spot marked as " Smuggler's
Anchorage."   For some years before the Battle of New Orleans this spot was the favorite haunt of a number of desperate men, who brought rich prizes into their little harbor and
defied the revenue laws of the United States.   Whether they
were sailors who fitted out privateers under the flag of Car-
thagena to seize the rich vessels of Spain, or whether they
acted on their own account as pirates, has been disputed.   It
is certain, however, that they were smugglers, and that they
established a kind of auction exchange at Grande Terre,
where they sold their rich goods to any one that dared to
come and buy them.   They even sent fine stuffs to New Orleans, and disposed of them through some of the merchants,
who were induced by the large profits to violate the laws.
The rules of the Spanish custom house had been so strict
that many people of New Orleans had fallen into the bad
habit of regarding smuggling as an innocent occupation.   The
most prominent of these Baratarian smugglers were Pierre
and John Lafitte.   The two brothers had come from France,
and had opened a blacksmith shop on St. Philip street in
New Orleans.   Soon growing weary, however, of following
this slow road to wealth, they betook themselves to Grande
Terre, where, amid the dark bayous overhung with Spanish
moss, they became chiefs of " a rebellious clan."   Their
swift vessels would dart out into the open sea, capture a
Spanish ship laden with rich goods, and bring it into the bay,
where the cargo, which cost them nothing, except perhaps a
little bloodshed, would be sold at a price far below its value.
It was as wild and fascinating a life as Robin Hood used to
lead in the forests of England, when every man was a law
unto himself.

The Governor of Louisiana, who strongly objected to these constant violations of the law, declared the inhabitants of Barataria to be pirates and outlaws; but for some years no serious attempt was made to break up this nest of evil-doers. On one occasion the Lafittes were tried for introducing contraband goods, but they boldly employed Livingston and Grymes, two of the most famous lawyers in New Orleans, to defend them, and nothing was proved against them.*

Finally Pierre Lafitte was arrested on another charge and thrown into the calaboose in New Orleans. After remaining there awhile he escaped in some mysterious way, and was soon back at Lake Barataria. During his absence important events had been taking place at Grande Terre.

The British Visit John Lafitte.—Colonel Nichols, who was commanding the British forces, sent one of his officers with a letter to "Mr. Lafitte, Barataria." It was dated August 31, 1814, and proved to be an offer from the British commander to take Lafitte and his company into the English service. "If you will join us with your men and vessels," said the letter, "you shall have a large sum of money, and " the rank of captain. After the war is over you and your " followers will receive large estates as a reward."

In order to gain time to warn Claiborne of the approaching danger, Lafitte asked for two weeks to consider the matter. This was granted, though the British officer begged him to decide immediately. "Your brother," said he, "has " been put in irons by the American Government; you your- " self have been declared an outlaw. Why not aid the " English to fight against a government that has treated you " so unjustly?"

Lafitte Writes to Claiborne.—But Lafitte secretly sent off to Claiborne a full account of the British plans, and asked

* The lawyers were to receive ten thousand dollars each for their services, and Grymes ventured down to Barataria to collect the fees. He was well received, and the money was promptly paid. See Gayarré, in Mag. Amer. Hist.

permission to serve his adopted country against the enemy.
As a sign of his repentance he described himself as a stray
sheep that wished to return to the fold. It was about this
time that Pierre Lafitte escaped from prison, and when he
reached Grande Terre he also wrote to a gentleman in New
Orleans, approving what his brother had done, and asking
to be taken into the service of Louisiana. No answer was
sent to these letters, and the Lafittes kept the English officer
waiting until he began to suspect some snare, and sailed
away.

Expedition Against the Lafittes.—In the meantime
Claiborne had called a council of officers (General Jackson
had not yet arrived) to decide whether the smugglers should
be pardoned and taken into the American service. The majority of the officers voted to have no friendly communication
with the Lafittes. Therefore, instead of returning a favorable answer, a body of troops under Commodore Patterson
was sent to break up the settlement at Barataria. The expedition was successful and a large amount of rich booty was
seized. The two brothers, however, escaped to the German
settlement on the Mississippi, whence they afterwards fled to
Last Island, which lies south of Terrebonne parish.

Lafitte Visits Jackson.—When General Jackson arrived
in New Orleans, John Lafitte paid him a visit, and again
offered his services and those of the other Baratarian outlaws.
The stern General had once declared that the Lafittes were a
set of bandits with whom he would have no dealings. But
now that he found himself face to face with the daring outlaw, he seems to have been won over by his manly bearing
and his attractive manners. Jackson liked a brave man, and
he knew that he needed every one he could find to defend the
city of New Orleans. So he accepted the services of the
Baratarians. Some of them were placed at the forts on the
Rigolets; others at Fort St. Philip; while Captain Dominique (who afterwards lived for many years in New Orleans),

commanded an important battery on the field of Chalmette. Everywhere that they were placed the Baratarians fought like tigers. Jackson himself admired their courage so much that, it is said, he never failed to stop and chat with them wherever he saw them.

QUESTIONS.

What was the cause of the war of 1812? What happened during the first years of the war? Who was Andrew Jackson? How did the English begin operations in the South? Who were the Lafittes? Why did Lafitte write to Claiborne? Tell of the expedition to Barataria. What was the result of Lafitte's visit to Jackson? Find Barataria Bay on large map of Louisiana.

CHAPTER XXVI.

THE BRITISH IN LOUISIANA.

Jackson in New Orleans.—We have seen that Jackson reached New Orleans December 1. Governor Claiborne had already been very active in organizing the militia to meet the British invasion. His proclamations had stirred the patriotism of the people, and every one was ready to do his duty.* As Louisiana had become a self-governing State, all classes felt that they had a common interest in protecting her. It was soon seen that Jackson was the right man to defend New Orleans. Though his constitution was weakened by constant sickness, his energy was untiring. He seemed to rise above bodily weakness by means of his indomitable spirit. Wherever he went he inspired the inhab-

---

*The following incident is given by Major Latour, who served under Jackson: "Madame Bienvenu, a rich widow of Attakapas, after sending her four sons to the defence of their State, wrote to Governor Claiborne that she regretted having no other sons to offer her country, but that if her services in taking care of the wounded should be thought useful, notwithstanding her advanced ege and the great distance of her residence, she would hasten to New Orleans.''

itants with confidence. "The streets," says Latour, "re-
sounded with Yankee Doodle, the Marseilles Hymn,* and
other martial airs, while those who had long been unaccus-
tomed to military duty were polishing up their arms and
preparing for battle. The women of New Orleans presented themselves at the windows and balconies to applaud
the troops in their evolutions and to encourage their husbands, sons, fathers, or brothers to protect them from the
insults of the enemy."

On the day of his arrival Jackson reviewed the militia
companies of Creoles and Frenchmen, and declared that he
was much pleased with their appearance and manœuvres.
Besides the white companies, two battalions were formed of
the " free-men-of-color," who were put under distinguished
white officers, and who were afterwards highly complimented
by Jackson for their bravery.

Defences.—With many hundred miles of sea coast, Louisiana was almost without defences; for the various forts
were in a bad condition. However, Jackson strengthened,
as best he could, Fort St. Philip, Spanish Fort, and a fort
on the Rigolets called Petites Coquilles (now Fort Pike).
There was not enough ammunition, and arms were so scarce
that he ordered private houses to be searched for fowling-
pieces. At his suggestion, moreover, an order was given
that all the bayous leading into the interior should be closed
with logs or other obstructions, so that the English vessels
could not pass. Unfortunately one important bayou was
neglected, and the consequences were very serious.

Battle of Lake Borgne, December 14, 1814.—To protect the entrance to Lake Pontchartrain, there were on Lake
Borgne five United States gunboats. These were under
Lieutenant Thos. Ap Catesby Jones, and were armed with
twenty-three guns and one hundred and eighty-two men. As
soon as Jones saw the English fleet approaching from Ship

---

*The national hymn of France,

Island, he decided to retire towards the Rigolets. But when he reached a point about fifteen miles off, he found the water so low that he had to cast anchor and await the enemy. The British sent against him a little fleet of forty-five barges and launches, armed with forty-three cannon and more than one thousand men. Though this force was far superior to his own, Jones made a fierce resistance, and many of the enemy's barges were sunk. But finally he himself was wounded in the shoulder, and the British, boarding the gunboats, captured them all. Their loss, however, was about three hundred, while the Americans had only ten killed and thirty-five wounded.

Martial Law.—The report of this disaster reached Jackson on the following day, and having heard that there were some British spies in New Orleans, he promptly declared the city to be under strict martial law. This meant that the city was to be controlled by the military orders of the General himself. Such a regulation was doubtless necessary at the time, but it will be seen that trouble grew out of it later on.

Landing of the British.—After the battle on Lake Borgne, the British decided to land some of their forces and march towards New Orleans. As they knew that their army was twice as large as that of the Americans, they expected to meet with very little resistance, and they actually imagined that the Creoles would come over to their side. We shall soon see what a mistake they made.

Bayou Bienvenu, leading from Lake Borgne to the plantations just below the city, had for some unknown reason been overlooked by the Americans, and there were no obstructions at its mouth. Some Spanish fishermen, who lived near by, doubtless acted as guides to the invading forces. About sixteen hundred men and two pieces of artillery were landed and placed in barges, which were silently rowed up the bayou. General Jackson had sent out some pickets to

watch the movements of the enemy, but these, being taken
unaware by the British, were all captured except one who
escaped through the marshes.

The British had never before seen a Louisiana marsh. As
they gazed around upon the tall reeds and the "trembling
prairies," with no human being and no dwelling in sight,
they declared that they had never beheld a more desolate
country. It was just the kind of country, however, that they
needed to conceal their movements. Their plan was to reach
solid ground and then send the boats back for reinforcements
from the ships. So during the morning hours of December
23rd they rowed up the bayou until they came to General
Villeré's plantation, about nine miles from New Orleans.
Sending out detachments, they surrounded Villeré's house and
captured two of his sons, who were stationed there with some
troops. The elder of these, Major Villeré, jumped through
a window, and though he was fired at several times, he escaped, and was one of the first to inform Jackson of the
enemy's approach.

The British now marched towards the river and camped
on Villeré's and LaRonde's plantations, within nine miles of
the city. They took their time, for they felt confident of
capturing New Orleans whenever they chose to advance.

They then drew up a proclamation, which was signed by
the British commander, and copies of which were posted on
all the fences. It was in these words: "Louisianians, re-
" main quiet in your houses. Your slaves shall be preserved
" to you and your property respected. We make war only
" against Americans." This proclamation excited nothing
but indignation among the Creoles; they were more determined than ever to show the British that they were not traitors, but patriots.

Jackson Marches to Meet the Enemy.—General Jackson was quietly sitting in his headquarters at New Orleans
when Major Villeré and two other gentlemen came rushing

in to inform him that the British were approaching. When the General heard this news, it is said that he started up, and striking the table with his fist, cried out: "By the Eternal, they shall not sleep on our soil." As we shall see, no British soldier closed his eyes that night.

All the available troops under Jackson's command were ordered to march out to meet the enemy. The General took a position in the lower part of the city, where the mint now stands, to see the battalions go by. - The right, composed of eight hundred and eighty-four men, was to be commanded by Jackson himself. Then came Major Plauché's battalion of Frenchmen and Creoles; next, the free-men-of-color under Major D'Aquin, and next, the left, under General Coffee, which was composed of Tennesseeans, Mississippians, and the Orleans Rifle Company.

Jackson's whole force was only two thousand, one hundred and thirty-one men.

Commodore Patterson, of the United States navy, was ordered by Jackson to let two gunboats, the *Carolina* and the *Louisiana* drop down the river and bombard the enemy. As there was little wind, the *Louisiana*, which was a heavy vessel, could not be steered; and so the *Carolina*, which was much lighter, sailed down alone and took up her position opposite the British camp.

In the meantime it had grown dark, and when the British saw the *Carolina* they thought she might be one of their own cruisers, and hailed her from the levee. All at once they heard some one on board cry: " Give them this for the honor of America!" Then the guns flashed out, and a deadly hail of shot swept over the British camp, and in ten minutes covered the ground with dead bodies. Those who were able, rushed to take refuge under the levee, where they lay for an hour shivering in the dark, but afraid to move.

Suddenly the rapid firing of the pickets informed the English that the Americans were attacking them on the land side.

Rushing to their arms, they defended themselves as best they could. At first the contest was in the dark, but the moon, then in her first quarter, afterwards gave a feeble light. The fighting lasted from 7 o'clock till 9:30.

During the battle the English landed and brought up additional troops till they had about five thousand on the field. Both sides fought with great bravery, but the advantage remained with the Americans. The English fell back to their camp, where they passed the night under arms. Jackson, fearing that he might come within range of the *Carolina's* guns, stopped his men. His loss in killed, wounded, and prisoners was two hundred and thirteen, while the English lost over four hundred. For the most part it was a hand-to-hand contest. An English officer, who afterwards went over the field, declares that in some places he found two soldiers lying dead together, each pierced with the other's bayonet.

Jackson was seen in the very front of the battle, exposing himself to every danger, and exhorting his men until their courage rose to the level of his own.

This bold attack on the British saved New Orleans. If the enemy had been allowed to march forward with their large army, Jackson would not have had time to build the fortifications necessary to resist them. But after the battle of the 23d of December, the British, seeing that the way was not open and that the Creoles would not join them, did not venture to advance till they had received large reinforcements.

QUESTIONS.

Tell about Jackson's arrival in New Orleans. How did he defend the city? Describe the battle of Lake Borgne. What is martial law? Describe the landing of the British. Describe the battle of December 23.

CHAPTER XXVII.

THE BATTLE OF NEW ORLEANS.

Preliminary Skirmishing.—Jackson now fell back two miles nearer the city and fortified the Rodrigues canal on the plain of Chalmette. The English spent the next few days in bringing up more troops, landing heavy artillery, and preparing for a vigorous campaign. This delay was fatal to them, for it gave Jackson time to build those terrible breastworks which the English long remembered.

Until the 25th instant, the British had been commanded by General Keane; but on Christmas morning the army was delighted by the arrival of the commander-in-chief, Sir Edward Pakenham, brother-in-law of that famous Duke of Wellington who, some months later, was to overthrow Napoleon at Waterloo.

The *Louisiana*, the other American war ship, had now dropped down the river and anchored above the *Carolina*. As these two vessels rendered any advance very dangerous, Pakenham's first step was to attack them. Bringing up his artillery, he threw red-hot shot at the *Carolina* until she took fire and blew up. The crew, however, escaped, and the *Louisiana*, finding herself in danger, succeeded in sailing up the river.

On the 27th of December the British troops advanced once more as if to attack the breastworks that Jackson was completing along the Rodrigues canal. But it was a useless attempt; for the American batteries poured a heavy fire into their ranks and forced them to retire.

On the 31st instant, Pakenham threw up embankments in front of the American lines, and having placed his heaviest artillery, he prepared to silence the American guns. The morning of January 1, 1815, dawned upon a thick Louisiana fog; but as soon as the mist cleared away both sides began a

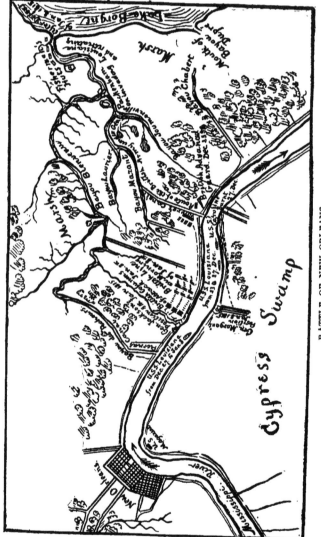

BATTLE OF NEW ORLEANS.

tremendous cannonading, which was continued till late in the afternoon. The Americans proved themselves so much more skilful in the use of artillery that the English despaired of overcoming them by this method of fighting. Nearly all the British batteries were silenced.

Arrival of the Kentuckians.—On January 5th the Kentucky militia arrived in New Orleans, and were put under the command of Major-General John Thomas. These troops, however, as well as many soldiers from other States, were in want of proper clothing to protect them from the intense cold and the rains of the month of January. " The Legisla-" ture of Louisiana," says Latour in his history, " voted six " thousand dollars, and this amount was increased to sixteen " thousand dollars by the private subscriptions of the New " Orleans Volunteers and the inhabitants of Attakapas and " the German Coast. With some of this money blankets " were bought, and the ladies of New Orleans quickly made " them into clothes. The rest was expended in the purchase " of shoes, mattresses, and other necessities, till all the needy " soldiers were well provided." In this noble way did Louisiana show her gratitude to those who had come to her defence.

Preparations for the Fight.—The 8th of January was the day chosen by the British to decide the fate of New Orleans and Louisiana. From the first of that month to the seventh they had busied themselves in digging out and extending Villeré's canal till it reached the Mississippi. It was Pakenham's intention to transport a body of troops on barges through this canal and land them on the opposite bank of the river. Colonel Thornton, who was put in command of these troops, was directed to cross the river before day on the morning of January 8, seize the American batteries on the right bank, and turn them against Jackson's lines as soon as Pakenham's army advanced. Unfortunately for Thornton, his barges stuck in the heavy mud of the canal, and when he reached the other bank with six hundred men, day had dawned and he was too late to render any assistance to Pakenham.

Jackson's Line.—Jackson's breastworks, which were one mile long, extended from the Mississippi back to a cypress swamp. They were thrown up behind an old mill race, or canal, which separated the plantation of Rodrigues from that of Chalmette.* At first some bales of cotton had been used to strengthen portions of the embankment, but this inflammable stuff had been set·on fire by the enemy's shot, and the heavy Louisiana mud was found to be far more useful.† In some places the works were twenty feet across the top and seven feet high, in others they covered the men only to the breast. The long line was defended by eight batteries and 3200 men. In the rear there were 800 more troops, consisting of the Mississippi cavalry and Attakapas dragoons, to act as a reserve and rear guard.

The line of 3200 was composed of various bodies of troops. Among them may be mentioned the uniformed militia of Creoles, under Major Plauché; Captain Beale's company of riflemen, stationed near the river, and the two battalions of free-men-of-color, under Lacoste and D'Aquin. Further on were the Kentuckians and Tennesseeans, under Major General Carroll and General Coffee; nor must we forget the Baratarian privateers under Captain Dominique, who commanded Battery No. 3.

The Fight.—Long before dawn on the morning of the 8th, the Americans, lying in their intrenchments, had heard sounds in the British camp which told them there was to be an attack on their lines. They waited calmly for the sun to rise and show them the enemy. It was a cold foggy morning. At dawn two rockets went up from the British camp. They were the signal of attack. The mist that covered the

---

* Alexander Walker's Life of Jackson.
† Hence the old story that Jackson fought behind cotton bales on January 8th is a mistake.

plains as with a veil slowly lifted, and revealed the English
columns approaching under General Gibbs. In front was
the famous 44th regiment, composed largely of Irish soldiers.
It was intended that these should bring up bundles of sugar
cane to fill up the canal, and short ladders to mount the
American fortifications. But by the negligence of their colonel they came unprovided, and had to be sent back to get
them. Before they could fall back, however, the American
batteries had opened upon them a murderous fire, which
cut great gaps in their ranks. Jackson was everywhere along
his lines, crying out: "Stand to your guns; don't waste
your ammunition; see that every shot tells!" The Tennesseeans and Kentuckians came forward in turn and
poured a shower of bullets into the advancing British columns, while the American batteries on the other side of the
river broke the enemy's lines with their shells. The effect
was terrible; the field in front of Jackson's works was strewed
with dead bodies. The 44th, headed by Pakenham himself, now advanced; but what could bravery do against
opponents that never showed themselves, while they swept
the field with volley after volley of grape-shot and shell and
bullet? All that was left of Gibbs' command had to give
way, and Keane brought to the front his splendid body of
troops, headed by the Scottish Highlanders. As these gallant soldiers swept forward, Pakenham raised himself in his
stirrups and cheered them.* But all was in vain. Out of the
body nine hundred strong that advanced, only one hundred
and thirty left that bloody field alive. Pakenham himself, as
he bravely led his men, was wounded in the arm; but still he
pressed forward. Suddenly a shell burst near by, killing
his horse and wounding him in the thigh. He fell into
the arms of his aid, and, as he was raised up, another shot
struck him. Borne to the shelter of an oak near by, the
young commander-in-chief expired before he witnessed the

* Walker's Life of Jackson.

total defeat of his army. Nor did the other principal officers escape. Gibbs received a mortal wound and welcomed death as a release from pain, while Keane was wounded too severely to take command.

Still the British pushed forward under Major Wilkinson, who succeeded in climbing to the top of the American fortifications. Here he too fell, pierced by twenty bullets. His

PAKENHAM'S OAK.

men were glad to fall upon their faces in the muddy canal and thus escape the hail of lead. Near the levee the British, under a brave officer named Rennie, rushed forward and captured the redoubt that guarded this point. But to take it was one thing, and to hold it another. The American riflemen soon forced them to retire with the loss of their commander.

General Lambert, who on Pakenham's death became commander-in-chief, brought up his reserve to shelter the columns as they fell back, but he did not venture to renew the attack on Jackson's lines. As the British retired, the American artillery continued to fire upon them, and the cannonading did not cease till 2 o'clock in the afternoon.

The Contest on the Right Bank.—Jackson had placed General Morgan on the right bank to oppose the advance of

the British. Morgan's position, though it was protected by
a canal, was not a strong one, and could easily be turned by
the enemy. His force was composed partly of Louisiana and
partly of Kentucky troops—in all about six hundred men.
These troops, however, seem to have been without discipline, and General Morgan did not manage them wisely. On
the morning of the 8th, as we have seen, General Thornton
crossed the river with about six hundred men. He immediately began to advance up the right bank towards Morgan's
lines. Almost no resistance was offered by the Americans.
The Kentuckians fled in disorder, and were followed by the
rest of Morgan's command.

The British, however, when they heard of Pakenham's
defeat on the other bank, retired across the river, and the
Americans occupied their former position. The flight of
Morgan's troops, though they seem to have had some excuse
for their conduct, brought a sharp rebuke from General
Jackson, who did not understand how an American could
retire before an Englishman.

British and American Losses.—An English writer who
was present at the battle of New Orleans, states that Pakenham
had seven thousand men on the field, and lost two thousand.
Jackson lost only eight killed and thirteen wounded!

Fort St. Philip. Retreat of British.—The British fleet
sailed up the Mississippi and attacked Fort St. Philip, but it
was so bravely defended by the Americans under Major
Overton that, though the English bombarded it from the 9th
to the 18th of January, they were unable to take it. Finally,
on the 18th, they retired down the river. On the same day
General Lambert commenced his retreat across the marshes
to Lake Borgne. He had given up all hope of taking New
Orleans.

QUESTIONS.

Who commanded the British? What was Pakenham's first step?
Tell about the arrival of the Kentuckians. Give the date of the Battle

of New Orleans. How did the British prepare for the battle? Did
Jackson fight behind cotton bales? What troops fought under Jack-
son? Describe the battle. Tell about the contest on the right bank.
What were the losses on both sides? Describe the retreat of the
British. Point out on the map the position of the British and the
Americans.

CHAPTER XXVIII.

AFTER THE BATTLE.

Rejoicings in New Orleans.—What had been happening
in the city during this time? The roar of the cannon on the

JACKSON'S STATUE.

morning of the 8th had been
distinctly heard by the inhabitants. Some veterans, who
were no longer fit for active
service in the field, had been
left to defend the city; but the
women and children were in a
state of great excitement. Few
persons believed that Jackson
would be able to resist such a
splendid army as Pakenham
was known to have. There
was a rumor, moreover, that
the British had sworn to give
over the city to a pillage of the
most dreadful kind. Every
one trembled at the thought of
such a fate. From the battle-
eld no message had come. Suddenly, however, the sound
f a horse's hoofs was heard, and a messenger, almost breath-

less, galloped through the streets, crying: "Victory! Victory! Pakenham is defeated! Hurrah for General Jackson!"

Then the people poured out into the public square, and there was shouting and rejoicing such as had never been heard before in New Orleans. Not only had Jackson won a ⁓great victory, but he had lost only a few of his brave soldiers; and had not these met a glorious death in dying for their country?

All hatred of the English was lost in pity. The wounded British soldiers were brought up to the city on the steamboat, and everything was done for their comfort. Many of them were nursed by the colored women of New Orleans, who volunteered their services.

The Treaty of Peace.—Two weeks before the battle of New Orleans a treaty of peace between Great Britain and America had been signed at Ghent in Belgium; but alas! this was not known in Louisiana till February 10th. For the war took place before there was any telegraph and before a steamer had ever crossed the Atlantic, so that news traveled very slowly.

Jackson's Praise of His Troops.—On Jannary 21st, Jackson issued general orders praising in the highest terms the conduct of the soldiers under his charge. The volunteers from the other States were thanked for their brave services, as were also the Creoles, many of whom he mentioned by name. The free-men-of-color, he declared, had acted with courage and perseverance; and the Baratarians, under the Lafittes and Dominique, had all deserved the thanks of the country. At his suggestion, the President of the United States pardoned the Baratarians for all their past misdeeds.

Jackson's Reception in New Orleans.—The 23d of Janury was appointed as a day of thanksgiving for the great victory. A triumphal arch was erected in the middle of the large square in which Jackson's equestrian statue now stands. The scene that followed is thus described by an eye-witness,

Major Latour: "The windows and balconies of the city
"hall (the old Cabildo) and all the adjacent buildings were
"filled with spectators. When General Jackson, accom-
"panied by the officers of his staff, arrived at the entrance
"of the square, he was requested to proceed to the cathe-
"dral by the way prepared for him. As he passed under the
"arch he received crowns of laurel from two children, and
"was congratulated in an address spoken by Miss Kerr, who
"represented the State of Louisiana. The General then pro-
"ceeded to the church amidst the salutations of young ladies
"representing the different States, who strewed his passage
"with flowers. At the entrance of the church he was re-
"ceived by the Abbé Dubourg, who conducted him to a seat
"prepared for him near the altar. Te Deum was chanted
"with solemnity, and soon after a guard of honor attended
"the General to his quarters; and in the evening the town,
"with its suburbs, was splendidly illuminated."

The Trial of Jackson.—It would be pleasant to record
that General Jackson left New Orleans with the praises of
the whole population ringing in his ears. But such was not
the case. By a mistake of the authorities at Washington the
General did not receive official notice that the Treaty of
Peace had been ratified by Congress till March 13th, 1815.
It is true that he had heard the news of the peace on the 10th
of February; but as he believed in strict discipline, he insisted on keeping New Orleans under martial law till the
official notice reached him; and he even went so far as to arrest Dominic Hall, judge of the District Court, who had dis-
pleased him.

After the official notice arrived the hero of Chalmette was
summoned before Judge Hall, and fined one thousand dollars
for having made an "unnecessary and arbitrary use of martial
law." This fine the General promptly paid. As he left the
Court House his friends hauled a carriage to the door, and,
forcing the General to enter, they dragged him in triumph to

a neighboring coffee-house. Here he made a speech, which concluded with these noble words: "Considering obedi-"ence to the laws, even when we think them unjustly ap-

COURT HOUSE IN WHICH JACKSON WAS TRIED.

"plied, as the first duty of every citizen, I do not hesitate to "comply with the sentence you have heard pronounced. Re-"member the example I have given you of respectful sub-"mission to the administration of justice."*

QUESTIONS.

How did New Orleans receive the news of Jackson's victory? If the telegraph had been in use at this time, would the Battle of New Orleans have been fought? How was Jackson received in New Orleans? Tell about Jackson's trial. What did Jackson say about obedience to law?

---

* Soon after this General Jackson left Louisiana. When he visited New Orleans again in 1828, he came as the guest of the State, and was received as a national hero. In the same year he was elected President of the United States. In 1845 Congress paid back to him the fine of one thousand dollars, with interest for thirty years; the Legislature of Louisiana offering at the same time to give the required amount out of the State Treasury. A few years later a splendid equestrian statue of the General was placed in the old *Place D'Armes*, which was re-christened "Jackson Square."

PERIOD OF DEVELOPMENT.

CHAPTER XXIX.

GROWTH OF THE STATE.

James Villere, Governor. 1816–1820.—After the British retired from Louisiana, no war came for many years to disturb the peace and happiness of the State, and Louisiana began to enjoy a period of wonderful prosperity. As soon as the soldiers who had served under Jackson laid down their arms, they returned to their various occupations and went to work with a new spirit. The fame of Louisiana's fertile lands had spread in all directions; and very soon settlers from Georgia, South Carolina and Virginia came crowding in to find homes in the new State. For many years, however, no great events took place; as we glance over the period, there seems to be nothing worth relating. But if we look more closely we find that what an English historian calls a "noiseless revolution" was going on. It was the revolution caused by the increase of population and the development of industries. In 1815 the population of the State, white and black, was only 90,000, but in 1820 it had grown to 153,407. Sugar and cotton were produced in greater quantities; and before many years had passed new methods of refining sugar had made this staple more profitable than ever before.

In 1816 Claiborne's term as governor came to an end. For twelve years he had held this office; and as a mark of their esteem for his high qualities, the legislature, in 1817, elected him as a representative of Louisiana in the United States Senate. A few months afterwards, however, he died. His successor as governor was General James Villeré, a Creole, who had distinguished himself alike in war and peace. It will be remembered that he was a rival candidate in the election of 1812.

GOVERNOR JAMES VILLERE.

Governor Villeré found that with the new population a great many persons of bad character had slipped into the State, and that the morals of New Orleans needed correction. Measures were quickly taken to put down all lawlessness in the city by establishing a Criminal Court and by passing severe regulations. By this means good order seems to have been very soon restored, for we hear no further complaint of the evil-doers.

Yellow Fever and Overflow.—The only things that interrupted the prosperity of the State at this time were the yellow fever and the overflows of the Mississippi, both of which came with terrible regularity. There was a great deal of discussion in regard to the necessity of building better levees, but very little work seems to have been done. In fact the native inhabitants appear to have regarded the overflows and fever as a matter of fate—something that could not be avoided. Moreover those who were acclimated soon ceased to fear the fever; its victims were to be found chiefly among the new settlers. According to Gayarré, many of the old Creoles even welcomed its coming, because they hoped it would keep out the bustling, pushing Americans, who threatened to take possession of the State. This jealous feeling toward the Americans continued for some years, and kept the Creoles a kind of separate race in Louisiana. Finally, however, the two mingled freely, and all ill-feeling was for-

gotten.   In our day it is hard to believe that any such trouble
ever existed; for the Creoles, though they like to preserve
the French language, take pride in being Americans, and
welcome settlers from all parts of the Union.

   Banks and Speculation.—The business of New Orleans
increased with the prosperity of the State.   Great warehouses
were built, fine residences were seen on every hand, and city
property rose rapidly in value.   As forty millions of dollars
had been invested in sugar plantations, many banks were
necessary for the large transactions that were taking place.
In 1818 the Bank of Louisiana, with a capital of two millions, had been incorporated.   Others soon followed, and
every one was eager to take stock in them.   Unfortunately,
however, this craze for new banks went too far.   As these
institutions lent money freely, the planters borrowed large
sums on their lands, and, as the money seemed easy to get,
they spent it lavishly.   On their estates they displayed a
splendid hospitality and lived like princes.   The State itself
took shares in the new banks, and for a time all went well.
But soon there was a period of wild speculation.   Property
in and around New Orleans was bought at prices far exceeding its value; even the swamp lands back of the city, which
were useless for any purpose, were eagerly purchased by
speculators.

   The banks had been allowed to issue notes, which were
accepted as money; for it was supposed that there was sufficient specie in their vaults to exchange for these notes whenever the holders wished to have them redeemed.   Finally,
however, there was what is now called a "panic."   It was
discovered that the banks had gone far beyond their means,
and were not able to redeem their notes.   In the year 1837,
the crisis came, and in one day fourteen banks suspended.
Of course the paper money became of no value, and many
persons were ruined.   Property that during these times of
rash speculation had risen very high, now fell very low.   But

this bitter experience taught every one to be more cautious in conducting business. and the general prosperity of the State was not long interrupted. As nothing could prevent the rich soil from producing fine crops of sugar and cotton, and as a ready market was found for these staples, the planters rapidly recovered from the " panic." *

Lafayette.—In the year 1825, the Marquis de la Fayette, the distinguished Frenchman who had fought for the independence of America in the Revolution of 1776, came over to the United States. He was received everywhere with great honor, and was invited by the people of Louisiana to visit their State. He consented, and on the 9th of April he arrived at Chalmette field. Here he was met by a committee of citizens and escorted to the city. The State legislature having voted fifteen thousand dollars for his entertainment, the old Cabildo on Jackson Square was fitted up as a residence. In this historic building Lafayette received the citizens, who came in great numbers to do him honor. Triumphal arches were erected; there were many splendid banquets; and the city gave itself up to enjoyment. Louisiana had not been one of the American colonies in 1776, but the Spanish governor of that day, it will be remembered, had aided the struggling colonies as much as he could; and now, in 1825, the people of Louisiana wished to show that they joined the rest of America in their love and respect for this noble "guest of the nation." After leaving New Orleans Lafayette ascended the Mississippi river. Everywhere that he stopped he was received with the highest honors. The United States Government presented him with the sum of two hundred thousand dollars and a large tract of land in Florida.

The Capital Removed.—In the same year (1825) an act of the legislature was passed to remove the Capital from

---

* Our present State National Banks, which issue paper money secured by bonds deposited in the U. S. Treasury, and which consequently can not refuse to redeem their notes, were not established until 1863.

New Orleans to Donaldsonville. This was done partly because the country parishes wished a more central location than New Orleans, and partly because it was thought that the legislators would do their work better in a quiet country town than in a gay city. The sum of five thousand dollars was expended on a building in Donaldsonville, and the transfer was made. But the legislators found the little town so dull after the pleasant life to which they had been accustomed, that they longed to return. Finally, in 1831, they adjourned the house one day, and taking the steamboat, were soon back in the Crescent City, which thus became the Capital once more.*

First Railroad.—Before it left Donaldsonville, the legislature passed an act incorporating the Pontchartrain Railroad Company. This railroad is the oldest in Louisiana, and the second that was completed in the United States. It is still in existence, and connects New Orleans with the pleasant little town of Milneburg. Some years passed before other railroads were built.

New Orleans Lighted by Gas.—Just four years later (1834), New Orleans was for the first time lighted by gas. Up to this time, as we learn from old newspapers, the privilege of furnishing oil and matches to light the city had been sold every year to the lowest bidder. When gas was introduced it was soon found that the increase of light diminished very much the number of crimes committed on the streets at night. But it is only since the introduction of electricity within the last ten years, that it has been clearly shown that plenty of light will do as much to free a city from criminals as will the best of laws.

---

* New Orleans remained the Capital till 1849, when the legislature met for the first time in Baton Rouge, which had been made the seat of government. After the Civil War the legislature assembled in New Orleans till 1882 when a transfer to Baton Rouge once more took place.

QUESTIONS.

Tell about the noiseless revolution in Louisiana. Who succeeded Claiborne as governor? What interrupted the prosperity of the State? What caused the bank failures in 1837? Who was Lafayette? How was he honored on his return to America? Why was the Capital removed from New Orleans? What was the first railroad in Louisiana?

---·◆·---

CHAPTER XXX.

GROWTH OF THE STATE — CONTINUED.

During the period which we have been reviewing Louisiana was blessed with a succession of excellent governors. As there was little political strife in these times, and as the State was generally very prosperous, some modern writers have named this period the " Golden Age of Louisiana."

Public Domain.—In 1820 Governor Villeré was succeeded by Thos. B. Robertson, a distinguished lawyer, who greatly endeared himself to the people by his wise and useful administration. After nearly four years' service he retired,* and the governor's chair was occupied from 1824–28 by Henry Johnson, who had previously held a seat in the United States Senate. The messages of these governors declare that the State was then in a prosperous condition ; but they contain constant complaints of the United States authorities for their management of the public lands in Louisiana. In making Louisiana a State the Government at Washington had reserved for itself large tracts of land that were not then occupied. As the population increased, the State Government wished to get possession of these lands, which were becoming more valuable every day ; but for some time the General Gov-

---

* Governor Robertson, having been appointed United States district judge, resigned the office of governor one month before his term expired.

ernment refused to surrender them. Finally, however, an arrangement was made by which Louisiana received a great part of this public domain, as it was called, and from the sale of certain portions money was obtained to build levees, to found institutions of learning, and to pay a part of the State debt. Large areas are still owned by the State.*

Pierre Derbigny.—In 1828, Johnson was succeeded as governor by Pierre Derbigny, who had previously been a

judge of the Supreme Court and secretary of state. In the following year, however, Governor Derbigny was thrown from his gig and killed.   As there was no

PIERRE DERBIGNY.

lieutenant-governor under the old constitution, the president of the senate, A. Beauvais, acted as governor until the legislature met, when he was followed by a second president of the senate, Jacques Dupré. Finally, in 1830, a regular

GOVERNOR A. B. ROMAN.

election was held, and the governor chosen was A. Bienvenu Roman.

---

*The University at Baton Rouge is partly supported by funds obtained from the sale of public domain. The United States Government still owns many thousands of acres in the upper parishes of Louisiana. This land is given away in certain quantities to settlers.

A. B. Roman, Governor. 1831-1835.—Governor Roman was a fine type of the Louisiana Creole, and his services to his native State were very important. He founded Jefferson College in St. James parish, and when the legislature made an appropriation for its support, he added a subscription from his own fortune. Professors were brought over from Europe, and many students were educated in the new college. In managing the affairs of the State, Governor Roman showed great ability. Being violently opposed to the wild speculations of his time, he did all that he could to keep the State from indulging in them. To him also, we owe the establishment of the first experimental farm to advance the study of agriculture. As we shall see he was the first gov-. ernor of the State to enjoy the honor of a second term.

Refining of Sugar.—During Roman's first term, and in the next few years, great progress was made by some prominent planters in the refining of sugar. Up to this time it

CARRYING CANE TO THE MILL.

had been often said that Louisiana sugar was not suitable for refining, and there were many complaints of its inferior quality. About the year 1830 some of the richest planters

determined to show that a fine grade of sugar could be produced in the State. The result of their experiments was
watched with the same interest that was shown when Etienne
de Boré made his successful attempt to produce granulation.
What is called the " vacuum process " had been introduced
by two planters, Messrs. Gordon and Forstall, and was very

PICKING COTTON.

successful. Two other rich planters, Valcour Aime and Thos.
Morgan, of St. James parish, now purchased expensive machinery and the best chemicals for the refining process.
Their first experiment succeeded beyond their expectations.
They produced a high grade of refined sugar, several tons
of which were sent to the North as a proof that Louisiana
could compete with other countries in supplying the markets
of the United States. It was even hoped that all the inhabitants of America could be supplied with Louisiana sugar.

Cholera.—In 1832, Louisiana was visited by a terrible disease called Asiatic Cholera. It proved to be a far worse
scourge than ever the yellow fever had been. Beginning in
Asia it had spread over Europe, and was then brought by a

ship to Canada. From Canada it finally reached Louisiana. Here as many as five thousand persons died of it. The negroes, who generally escaped the yellow fever, died in large numbers of this new disease.

Edward D. White, Governor. 1835–39.—In 1835, E. D. White,* who had for several years been an able representative in the Congress of the United States, was elected governor. During his administration there was a great increase in the amount of cotton produced. The price of sugar fell to six cents a pound, which in those days was considered too low for a profit. Every one, therefore, began to neglect sugar and cultivate cotton. In 1836 Louisiana produced 225,000 bales, which was nearly double the crop of 1834. After 1840, however, a new tariff brought up the price of sugar, which became once more the great staple of Louisiana. Nineteen of the southern parishes devoted themselves to its cultivation, while Rapides, Avoyelles, Concordia, Catahoula, and Calcasieu, which had, before this, raised only cotton, now prepared to try the cane. The result was that in 1844 the crop was 200,000 hogsheads.

Growth of New Orleans.—New Orleans, which always prospers with the State, had grown rapidly. The city was spreading beyond its old limits of Canal and Esplanade streets; for its population, which in ten years had more than doubled, now reached 102,000. In one year 2000 sailing vessels and 1600 steamboats arrived at its levees.

Overflow of 1840.—In the meantime Governor White had been succeeded by A. B. Roman, whose second term lasted until 1843. During his administration there was an unusual rise in the Mississippi river. There had not been such a flood, says an old historian, since that of 1782, when the prairies of the Attakapas and Opelousas country were partly overflowed. The Mississippi now spread over the parishes of Lafourche and Concordia, while the waters of Red river covered the

---

* The father of our present United States Senator.

extensive cotton lands along its banks.   When the flood disappeared, however, it was found that the overflowed district had received a rich deposit of mud, and the next year a fine crop was produced.

What was the trouble about public domain? Name the governors that preceded Roman. Tell the chief services of Governor Roman. Give an account of the refining of sugar. What was the change in agriculture while White was governor? Give an account of the overflow.

CHAPTER XXXI.

INCREASE OF DEMOCRACY—TROUBLE IN TEXAS.

A. Mouton, Governor.—In 1843 Alexander Mouton was elected governor.   He had previously been a United States Senator.   Open-hearted, frank, and endowed with good judgment, Mouton enjoyed great popularity among the people of Louisiana. He always showed himself ready to sacrifice his personal interests for the good of his State. During his administration Louisiana paid off a large portion of the debts she had contracted when she took stock in the new banks.

The New Constitution.—In 1845 a new constitution was framed for Louisiana, which differed in some important points from that of 1811.

ALEXANDER MOUTON.

It was far more democratic—that is, it gave more privileges to the people than they had possessed before.   Thus, under the old constitution no one was allowed to vote who had not a certain amount of property. Now all this was changed; the right of suffrage was granted to any male white twenty-one years of age who had resided two years in the State.

Formerly the governor was obliged to own a landed estate worth five thousand dollars; but now the poorest man in Louisiana could be elected to the highest office. Moreover, a change was made in the method of electing the governor— a change which is found in all the subsequent constitutions. By the constitution of 1812, the general assembly was permitted to choose the governor by ballot from the two candidates that had received the highest number of popular votes. Thus it was in the power of this assembly, if it wished, to choose the candidate that had received a smaller number of popular votes than his opponent; though such a disregard of the people's wishes never occurred. The new constitution, however, provided that the general assembly must declare the candidate receiving the highest number of popular votes to be the duly elected governor.

It was under this constitution, also, that the office of lieutenant-governor and that of superintendent of public education were created.

During this early period duelling had been very common in Louisiana, and the framers of the constitution determined to try to check it. Hence we find a provision that no State officer could enter upon his duties unless he swore that, since the adoption of the constitution, he had not engaged in a duel. A still severer article is found in the later constitution of 1852, which declared that no one who had been engaged in a duel should be allowed to vote. In our latest constitutions, those of 1868 and 1879, all provisions in regard to duelling have been dropped; and the practice itself seems to be disappearing.

Isaac Johnson, Governor. 1846-50. The Mexican War. —Under the new constitution, Isaac Johnson, who had held

the office of district judge, was elected governor. Scarcely
had he begun his duties when a serious war began between
the United States and Mexico. The cause of the war was

this: When Louisiana was purchased, Texas remained a part of
Mexico. As many American settlers, however, had moved into this
territory, the United States Government tried to purchase it, but Mexico would not sell. In 1835 Texas
boldly took the matter into her own
hands. Throwing off her allegiance
to Mexico, she declared herself a
free republic, and asked to be
admitted into the Union as a
State. At first Congress would

ISAAC JOHNSON.

not consent, for there was a party in the North who wished
to abolish slavery, and who opposed the admission of Texas
because she would be admitted as a slave State. In spite,
however, of this and other objections, Texas was finally
made a State in 1845. It was a fine thing for the United
States to acquire this splendid piece of territory; but Mexico
was very angry at the interference of the American Government, and before a year had passed war was declared between the two countries.

General Zachary Taylor, who owned an estate near Baton
Rouge, was sent with a small army to defend the border of
the new State. As the Mexicans threatened him with a
superior force, he called upon Governor Johnson for additional troops. When the governor brought the matter before
the legislature, the sum of one hundred thousand dollars
was immediately voted for the purpose of sending help. New
Orleans was wild with enthusiasm. The military companies
seemed as anxious to fight as they had been some thirty years
before at Chalmette. "In a few days," says General Owen,

in his account of the Mexican War, "the Washington Regi-
"ment, of New Orleans, 1000 strong, was on its way on
"transports down the Mississippi." Other troops followed
until Louisiana had sent a considerable force to aid her sister
State against the Mexicans. The details of the war that followed can not be given here. It is sufficient to say that the
Mexicans were defeated on every side, and that finally the
American army under General Scott fought its way to the
City of Mexico and captured it. The last defence of the
city was the fortress of Chapultepec, which was taken by
storm. In this portion of the campaign as well as in the
battles of Monterey and Buena Vista, the Louisiana troops
served with splendid courage. General G. T. Beauregard
(then major), distinguished himself, and was twice wounded.
As we look over the list of officers from Louisiana we see
such well known names as Dessommes, Musson, Blanchard,
Bourgeois, Soniat, and Hunt.

With the surrender of the Mexican capital the war ended,
and the Mexicans were glad to make peace. It was agreed
that Texas should take as her southern boundary the Rio
Grande river—a boundary which Mexico had not been willing to grant before the war.

General Joseph Walker, Governor. 1850–53.—The successor of Isaac Johnson was General Joseph Walker, who
had previously held high offices in the State. During his
administration, the people, having already become dissatisfied with the constitution of 1845, decided to have another
framed. The result was the constitution of 1852, which was
still more democratic than the previous one. Among other
things it declared that the judges of the State Supreme
Court instead of being appointed by the governor, as they
are at the present day, should be elected by the vote of the
people. The object of this measure was to limit the power
of the governor, but it was not a wise step. Moreover, the
privilege of creating new debts for the State, which had

been denied the legislature by the constitution of 1845, was now once more granted.

Paul Hebert, Governor. 1853-56.*—Under the new constitution Paul Hebert was elected governor.   He had previously occupied, says Gayarré, the position of State engineer, and had been president of the late constitutional convention.   During his administration there occurred one of the most terrible yellow fever epidemics that Louisiana had ever seen.   Formerly the disease had generally confined itself to New Orleans, but now it spread over every part of the State, and thousands of the inhabitants died.   Never since the coming of the cholera had such sorrow and dismay been felt throughout the State.   When the fever was over, however, trade was resumed and the State began once more to prosper.   Among the signs of this prosperity it may be mentioned that during this period the public school system, which up to this time had not been successful, was aided by State funds and put upon a better basis.   A few years before (1847) the University of Louisiana (now Tulane) had been established in New Orleans.   The State now made appropriations to complete the University buildings and to aid other institutions of learning.

R. C. Wickliffe.—In 1856 Governor Hebert was succeeded by Robert C. Wickliffe, a native of Kentucky, who had settled in West Feliciana.   Here Mr. Wickliffe had won prominence as a lawyer, and had afterwards been elected a State senator.   During his administration there was much political excitement in Louisiana, in which the leading lawyers took an active part.   Among these, three of the most prominent were Pierre Soulé, John Slidell, and Judah P. Benjamin.   Before the war all three served in the United States Senate, where they courageously defended the Southern Cause in the discussions that arose.

---

* Hebert was installed as governor in January, 1853, but by a special article of the new constitution the terms of all officers were regarded as beginning in January, 1852.

QUESTIONS.

What was the character of Governor Mouton? Tell about the changes made by the new constitution. What important event occurred during the administration of Governor Johnson? Give an account of the Mexican War. What changes were made by the constitution of 1852? Tell about the yellow fever in Hebert's administration. Who was the successor of Governor Hebert?

---•◆•---

THE CIVIL WAR—1861-65.

CHAPTER XXXII.

BEGINNING OF THE WAR.

The Approach of War.—The annual messages of Hebert and Wickliffe show that the great topics of discussion in Louisiana were slavery and secession. The war was not far off, and these messages, full of fiery sentiments, were like the low thunder that announces the coming of a storm.

The party opposed to slavery, known as the Republican party, had been rapidly growing at the North, and seemed likely at an early day to gain control of the National Government at Washington. Louisiana and the other Southern States thought that, if this happened, an attack would be made upon the institution of slavery; perhaps a law would be passed to do away with it altogether. At this period the North no longer had any slaves; while the South depended upon them for the cultivation of her plantations, which, it was believed, could not be worked by white labor.

The Causes of the War.—From the beginning of the nineteenth century there had been some jealousy between

the Northern and the Southern States; and this feeling, unfortunately, increased as the differences between the two sections became more marked.   Slavery never flourished in the
cold North as it did in the warm South.   Moreover, the
Northern people had no large plantations, and generally preferred manufactures to agriculture.   In the South the slaves
were suited both to the climate and to the occupation of the
people.   Now it was very difficult to make satisfactory tariff
laws for two portions of a large country, which depended for
their support upon different kinds of products.   A tariff, for
instance, that protected the manufacturer of the North often
threatened to ruin the planter of the South.   Whichever section of the country, therefore, had the majority in Congress
was able, if it wished, to pass laws very injurious to the
other.   Thus we have seen that, in 1811, Josiah Quincy, of
Massachusetts, declared in Congress that if Louisiana were
admitted as a State, the older States would be justified in
breaking up the Union; for, as he argued, Louisiana could
not have the same interests as the Northern and Eastern States.

   Twenty-four years later (1833), there was a great debate
in the United States Senate between Daniel Webster and
John C. Calhoun.   Webster, who was from Massachusetts,
declared that the Constitution of the United States did not
permit a State under any circumstances to withdraw from
the Union.   Thus Massachusetts had changed her opinion of
the Constitution since the days of Josiah Quincy.   Calhoun,
who was from South Carolina, maintained that the right to
withdraw from the Union belonged to every State; for, in
ratifying the Constitution, the States had reserved to themselves this power.   Such was the famous "State Rights
Doctrine."   In general the North took the side of Webster,
while the South took the side of Calhoun.*   The debate in

---

* It is interesting, however, to note that Webster's distinguished biographer,
Henry C. Lodge, though a Northern man and a violent opponent of secession, ad-
mits that, in this great debate, Calhoun proved his interpretation of the Constitution to be the true one.

this case had arisen over a tariff law passed by Congress. As this law was regarded as a violation of the Constitution, South Carolina "nullified" or refused to obey it, and prepared to secede, in case the President attempted to enforce obedience. The trouble, however, ended in a compromise. Each side gave up something, and a tariff diminishing yearly till it ceased, was finally adopted. Thus the great question of what rights belonged to the States and to the General Government respectively, was not settled, but only deferred.

When, therefore, some years later, the party in the North opposed to slavery grew very strong and seemed to be on the point of getting possession of the Government, the South naturally began to discuss once more the question of secession. Would the North dare to interfere with slavery, which had so long been an established institution in the South? If a Southern State submitted to such interference it would lose its self-respect; secession was the only means of preserving its rights. This was the general feeling in the South; while the North was determined to preserve the Union at all hazards. Each side thought itself in the right, and it looked as if the long contest over the question of secession, which slavery had thus brought to the front once more, could be decided only by a war between the two sections.

As soon, therefore, as the Republicans, in 1860, succeeded in electing as President Abraham Lincoln, the Southern States prepared to secede from the Union, and to defend their action, if necessary, by an appeal to arms.

Louisiana Secedes.—The first State to pass an ordinance of secession was South Carolina, which many years before had so boldly asserted her rights through the statesman, John C. Calhoun. Other Southern States followed. In Louisiana a convention was called at Baton Rouge to decide what course the State should pursue. The officer elected to preside on this important occasion was the venerable Ex-Governor Alexander Mouton, a man highly respected by all the people of the State. By a vote of 113 yeas to 17 nays, the convention decided that Louisiana would join her sister States in withdrawing from the Union (January 26, 1861).* This decision was destined to bring sorrow and disaster upon the State, but the Louisianians believed that under the Constitution of the United States they had the right of secession, and they were determined to fight, if necessary, to maintain it. The governor of Louisiana at this time was Thos. O. Moore, a rich planter and man of large influence. He strongly supported the course pursued by his State.

The New Government.—In February, 1861, the various States that had seceded sent representatives to a Southern

---

*The ordinance of secession was as follows:

"THE STATE OF LOUISIANA.

"*An ordinance to dissolve the Union between the State of Louisiana and other States united with her under the compact entitled*

"'THE CONSTITUTION OF THE UNITED STATES OF AMERICA.'

" We, the people of the State of Louisiana, in convention assembled, do declare and ordain, and it is hereby declared and ordained, that the ordinance passed by us in convention on the 22d day of November, in the year 1811, whereby the Constitution of the United States of America, and the amendments of the said Constitution, were adopted; and all laws and ordinances by which the State of Louisiana became a member of the Federal Union, be and the same are hereby repealed and abrogated; and that the Union now subsisting between Louisiana and other States, under the name of 'The United States of America,' is hereby dissolved.

" *We do further declare and ordain*, That the State of Louisiana hereby resumes all rights and powers heretofore delegated to the Government of the United States of America; that her citizens are absolved from all allegiance to said Government; and that she is in full possession and exercise of all those rights of sovereignty which appertain to a free and independent State.

" *We do further declare and ordain*, That all rights acquired and vested under the Constitution of the United States, or any Acts of Congress, or treaty, or under any law of this State, and not incompatible with this ordinance, shall remain in force and have the same effect as if this ordinance had not been passed."

On the 18th of February, 1861, the legislature passed the following joint resolution:

"1. *Be it resolved by the Senate and House of Representatives of the State of Louisiana, in general assembly convened*, That the right of a sovereign State to secede or withdraw from the Government of the Federal Union and resume her original sovereignty when in her judgment such act becomes necessary, is not prohibited by the Federal Constitution, but is reserved thereby to the several States, or people thereof, to be exercised, each for itself, without molestation.

"2. *Be it further resolved, etc.*, That any attempt to coerce or force a sovereign State to remain within the Federal Union, come from what quarter and under whatever pretence it may, will be viewed by the people of Louisiana, as well on her own account as of her sister Southern States, as a hostile invasion, and resisted to the utmost extent.

" C. H. MORRISON,
" *Speaker of the House of Representatives.*
" B. W. PEARCE,
" *President of the Senate.*
"THOS O. MOORE,
" *Governor of the State of Louisiana.*"

Congress, which met at Montgomery, Ala. A new government was formed under the title of the "Confederate States of America," a new constitution was adopted, and Jefferson Davis, of Mississippi, was elected President.*

The Fall of Fort Sumter.—For a short time it was thought that the North and the South could agree on some plan of compromise and that there would be no war. But on April 12, 1861, General G. T. Beauregard,† of Louisiana, who was in charge of the South Carolina defences, was instructed by the Confederate Government to fire on Fort Sumter in Charleston Harbor. This step was taken because a fleet, with a large supply of provisions, was on its way from New York to aid Sumter in withstanding any attack. The fort was at this time occupied by United States troops under Major Robert Anderson, and it refused to surrender until it

had been bombarded for thirty hours. This bombardment opened the war, for the "Fall of Sumter" aroused the North, and President Lincoln called for 75,000 volunteers to compel the South to come back into the Union. The terrible contest lasted four long years. Its course was marked by famous battles and great deeds of valor. Among the soldiers of the South

GEN. G. T. BEAUREGARD.

none gained greater fame than those from this State, but if

* The list of Confederate States was as follows: South Carolina, Mississippi, Alabama, Georgia, Louisiana, Florida, Texas, Virginia, Arkansas, Tennessee, and North Carolina. Missouri and Kentucky did not secede, but the Southern sympathizers in these States formed revolutionary governments, which were recognized by the Confederacy.

† General G. T. Beauregard became one of the most prominent generals on the Confederate side. As we have seen, he opened the war by the capture of Fort

we followed them in all their campaigns, we should have to give an account of the whole war. In this little volume, therefore, we shall relate only those events that occurred on Louisiana soil.

Preparations for War.—When the cry To Arms! was heard in Louisiana, the greatest enthusiasm filled the hearts of the people. Business was forgotten, and preparations were made to send as many troops as possible to Virginia, which, it was known, would be the chief battle ground of the war. Those who failed to enlist were regarded as traitors to the South. The famous Washington Artillery paraded the streets of New Orleans amid the cheers of the people, and after listening to a stirring address from an eloquent preacher, took its departure for Richmond. Other companies followed, until the old city had few troops to defend her in case she was attacked. The soldiers of Louisiana had gone to win laurels for themselves on battle fields far from their native State. At this time hardly any one thought that the war would ever reach Louisiana; for the South believed she could successfully defend her territory against the Northern armies.

QUESTIONS.

Describe the approach of war. Give the causes of the war. Who was elected President in 1860? When did Louisiana secede? Name the Confederate States. Describe the fall of Sumter, and the preparation for war in Louisiana.

Sumter. Subsequently he won great fame at Manassas and on other battle fields. After the war General Beauregard lived in New Orleans, where he died February 20, 1893 His body lay in state at the City Hall. In his honor the business of New Orleans was practically suspended and all public institutions were closed.

CHAPTER XXXIII.

THE WAR IN LOUISIANA.

Importance of New Orleans. Its Defences.—For nearly a year the State remained undisturbed; but in the

winter of 1862 a Federal fleet and an army arrived at Ship Island, with the intention of attacking New Orleans. The main object was to get possession of the great highway of

America, the Mississippi river, and thus cut off the troops
and supplies which the South could bring over from Louisiana and Texas to aid her army.   But the North knew that
unless New Orleans were captured, it would not be possible
to hold the lower Mississippi.   Extensive preparations, therefore, had been made to seize the Crescent City.

On the other hand, the Confederate Government does not
seem to have appreciated the importance of New Orleans,
for again, as in the days of the English invasion, the city
was by no means well protected.   At the Rigolets, Barataria Bay, and other inlets, there were some batteries, but they
were very weak, and the only strong defences were on the
Mississippi, about thirty miles from its mouth.   These were
Fort Jackson and Fort St. Philip, the latter of which had
resisted the English so successfully in the days of Andrew
Jackson.   Besides the guns of these forts, there were in the
Mississippi, just above them, eighteen war vessels to protect
the passage of the river and prevent an enemy from slipping
past.   Below the forts the river was obstructed by a line of
mastless vessels, placed across the channel and bound
together by a number of iron chains.   The entire river defence was under the command of General J. R. Duncan.

Farragut's Fleet.—The Federal fleet at Ship Island was
under Flag-Officer David G. Farragut, who was afterwards
made an admiral for his splendid services on the Mississippi.
He was a Southern man, and had once lived in New Orleans,
but when the war broke out he remained in the Northern
service.   He was one of the bravest and most skilful commanders that the American navy has ever had.   His fleet consisted of four powerful sloops of war, each one carrying over
twenty guns, together with a number of gunboats and mortar schooners—amounting in all to forty-three vessels.   Part
of these were under Commander D. D. Porter.

Farragut's plan was to come up the Mississippi, bombard
the forts, and try to reach New Orleans.   If this could be

accomplished, General B. F. Butler, at the head of 15,000 troops, was to follow him and occupy the city.

The Passing of the Forts. April 23, 1862.—When this formidable fleet came within about half a mile of the forts, a terrible bombardment began and continued several days. Fort Jackson received the greatest part of the attack, and returned the fire of the Federal vessels with great spirit and accuracy. On the second day, the 19th of April, a shot from this fort struck one of Farragut's schooners, passed through her bottom, and sunk her. As there seemed to be no chance of reducing the forts, the bold Flag-officer determined to break through the obstructions and run past. On the 20th, after dark, two vessels were sent forward to investigate. One of these, the *Itasca*, ran boldly against the chains which bound the old hulks together. These chains, not being sufficiently strong, snapped in two, and an opening large enough for the passage of the war vessels was made. For three more days, however, Farragut continued to bombard the forts, while he was busy making preparations to run the gauntlet. At 2 o'clock on the morning of the 23d, everything was ready, and the signal for the advance was made from the flag-ship. The excitement on both sides was intense. The forts knew that an attempt to run by them was about to be made; but in the darkness the gunners could not aim very accurately. Still they made ready, and as the fleet began to pass, they poured upon it a terrible discharge of shot and shell. Fire rafts were sent down to render the passage dangerous, and the flag-ship *Hartford* was soon in flames; but her crew extinguished the fire and she pressed on. The little Confederate fleet above the forts fought gallantly to defend the passage. The *Governor Moore*, a Confederate gunboat, commanded by a skilful officer named Beverly Kennon, rammed and fired into the Federal vessel *Varuna*, which was so disabled that she sunk. But the Northern fleet was too powerful to be stopped, and though many of his gunboats were riddled with shot, Farragut soon scattered or destroyed the Confederate vessels.

The Confederates had made an heroic defence, but the enemy had fought their way through, and New Orleans. was lost. On the 25th of April Farragut reached some batteries placed by the Confederates on both sides of the river near Chalmette. Having quickly silenced these, he anchored before New Orleans.

Burning of the Cotton.—As soon as the news reached New Orleans that Farragut had passed the forts, the dismay of the inhabitants was so great that at first nothing was done. Then as the people realized that the troops in the city were not sufficient for its defence, they decided to destroy everything that might aid the enemy. The South had refused to let any cotton be exported, imagining that the factories of the North would thereby be crippled, and that the want of this important staple would force foreign nations to aid the Confederacy. "Cotton is king," was the cry, "and by withholding it from the markets the South will win the day." Hence, there was at this time a large quantity of cotton in New Orleans, and the authorities were determined that it should not fall into the hands of the invaders. Twelve thousand bales were quickly piled upon the levee and set on fire; warehouses were broken open, and barrels of sugar and molasses were added to the burning mass. The very gutters ran with molasses, and the banquettes were covered with sugar. Many of the steamers at the levee were set on fire; and a powerful gunboat called the *Mississippi*, which had not been finished in time to be of any use, was sent down the river a mass of flames to meet Farragut's fleet. A cloud of black smoke rested over the city like a symbol of ruin and destruction.

New Orleans Occupied by the Federals.—When Farragut had anchored in front of New Orleans, he sent an officer to Mayor Monroe to demand that the city should be surrendered and that the Louisiana flags should be removed from all public buildings. The mayor, probably hoping that something might still be done to save the city, refused to surrender, and for some days negotiations were carried on between him and Farragut. In the meantime, however, the Confederate forces in New Orleans under Gen. M. S. Lovell, being too weak to make a successful resistance, retired from the city. If any resistance had been made Farragut would have bombarded New Orleans and killed thousands of the inhabitants. The retreat of Lovell, therefore, was a wise measure. Moreover, the forts on the river had surrendered to Porter, who had been left in charge of the mortar schooners. Finally, on the 30th of April, Farragut sent two of his officers, with a strong guard, to the present City Hall, with orders to pull down the flag that waved there, and run up the "Stars and Stripes" in its stead. An immense crowd of citizens looked on; but resistance was now useless, and none was made. New Orleans was in the hands of the enemy.*

On May 1, the city was handed over by Farragut to the control of General B. F. Butler, who had followed with a large army. Butler was a coarse, rough man, who treated the people with great indignity. His tyrannical behavior will long be remembered in New Orleans. The only thing that has been said to his credit is that he cleansed the city and kept it in the best sanitary condition that it has ever known. This task, however, was rendered easy by the fact that the city had been deserted by a large number of the inhabitants. Moreover, the absence of foreign trade during the war helped to keep all Southern cities free from disease.

* Before Farragut had taken possession of New Orleans, a United States flag was placed over the Mint by the crew from one of his vessels. As the city had not surrendered, this act caused a great deal of indignation, and some bold citizens determined at the risk of their lives to pull it down. Accordingly four men, among whom was W. B. Mumford, mounted to the roof of the building. Mumford, taking the lead, let the flag drop from the staff and dragged it through the streets. It was a rash deed; for when General Butler took command of the city he had Mumford arrested, tried, and put to death. As the flag had been placed on the Mint without the orders of Farragut, the execution of Mumford was unjust and cruel.

The fall of New Orleans was a great blow to the Southern Cause. It was held till the close of the war by Union soldiers, who thus controlled the mouth of the Mississippi, and at the same time had a convenient point from which to attack the Confederates.

QUESTIONS.

How was New Orleans defended? Why was New Orleans an important city to capture? Describe the passing of the forts. What was the effect of the news in the city? Describe the occupation of New Orleans.

————— · ◆ · —————

CHAPTER XXXIV.

THE WAR IN LOUISIANA—CONTINUED.

The Opening of the Mississippi.—As a Federal fleet had already descended the Mississippi to a point some distance above Vicksburg, Farragut determined to join it and thus complete the "clearing" of the river. Accordingly, after the capture of New Orleans, he sent up the river seven of his war vessels. When these reached Baton Rouge, that town, which was not fortified, quickly surrendered. Such, also, was the fate of Natchez; but Vicksburg refused to surrender. Farragut now arrived from New Orleans, and taking a number of his vessels, he ran past the batteries at Vicksburg to join the Union fleet above. As he went by, the guns on the heights of Vicksburg rained down shells upon his fleet, but though they killed fifteen of his men and wounded thirty, they did not succeed in stopping him. His guns answered those on the heights, but did no damage to the Confederates.

Thus Farragut had shown that he could pass the fortifica-
s, though he had clearly seen that Vicksburg was too
g to be captured without the help of a land army. After

joining the upper fleet and remaining with it awhile, he returned to New Orleans. The river was falling rapidly and the malaria had attacked so many of his sailors that he was glad to escape from the unhealthy district around Vicksburg. Some powerful vessels, however, were left above Baton Rouge to watch a dangerous Confederate ram named the *Arkansas.* This ram was armed with ten guns and covered with railroad iron three inches thick; and when Farragut was above Vicksburg she had come down the Yazoo river, run the gauntlet of the whole Union fleet, and taken refuge under the batteries of the city.

The Confederates Attack Baton Rouge.—When Farragut retired, a strong Federal force under General Thomas Williams took possession of Baton Rouge. This was the Capital of Louisiana, and the Confederates determined to make a desperate attempt to drive away the Federals and recover the town. If Baton Rouge could be retaken, the Mississippi from that point to Vicksburg would be practically under the control of the South, and the Red river, from the banks of which all sorts of supplies could be brought for the support of the Southern army, would be open to Confederate steamboats. Accordingly a large force under General John C. Breckinridge, a brave Kentuckian, was sent down from Vicksburg to attack General Williams. As the Federal gunboats were still in the river, General Breckinridge ordered the ram *Arkansas* to drop down the Mississippi, clear the river, and join him at Baton Rouge. With the assistance of the ram on the water side, he hoped to make a successful attack upon the town. As soon as the *Arkansas* left Vicksburg, the telegraph announced the fact to Breckinridge, and he waited to hear her guns upon the river. But alas! the famous boat never reached Baton Rouge. Her engines, which had been badly constructed, were now out of order. As she descended the river every effort was made to repair them; the loud blows of hammers were distinctly heard from

the banks.   Nothing, however, could be done, and when she
reached a point a few miles above the town, there was a
crash in the machinery, and the *Arkansas* lay almost helpless
upon the Mississippi.   Without the power to move quickly
she was useless.   And now the enemy began to draw near.
What was to be done?   The decision was prompt.   Head-
ing the vessel for the bank, the men jumped ashore, and her
commander, Lieutenant Stevens, set her on fire and turned
her adrift.   It was a memorable scene.   The Confederate
flag still waved above her, and every gun was loaded.   As
the flames began to spread, her great guns pealed out, one
after another, threatening destruction to the approaching
enemy.   Then when the fire reached her magazine there was
a mighty report, and the fragments of the powerful Confederate
iron-clad were hurled in every direction.   Though no *Arkansas*
came to his aid, Breckinridge bravely attacked the Federal
troops in the town, and in his first assault carried everything
before him.   General Williams on the Union side was killed at
the head of his men, and if Breckinridge had been supported
from the river, the capture of Baton Rouge would have been
complete.   But in the face of the Federal gunboats, which
were now rapidly firing, the Confederates could not hold
their position, and Breckinridge was compelled to order a
retreat.   The attack was one of the boldest feats of the war,
for the Federals were superior in numbers and were
splendidly equipped, while Breckinridge's soldiers were,
many of them, without coats, shoes, or socks.   Already the
greater wealth of the North was shown by the bountiful supplies that came for her soldiers ; the poor Confederates often
lacked the necessities of life.   The very table covers in New
Orleans had been cut into coats for Southern soldiers shivering with cold upon the bleak hills of Virginia.

   After the failure to take the Capital, the Confederates
·tified Port Hudson, and the Union soldiers soon after gave
Baton Rouge and retired to New Orleans.

General Taylor in Southern Louisiana.—Some weeks after the attack on Baton Rouge there arrived at Opelousas one of the most gallant of the Confederate generals. This was General "Dick" Taylor, who had already distinguished himself in Virginia under Stonewall Jackson, and who was now

GENERAL RICHARD TAYLOR.

sent to take command of all the forces in Louisiana. He was a native of the State, and was a son of General Zachary Taylor, who, after his famous campaign in the Mexican war, had been elected President of the United States. Having inherited his father's skill in battle, General "Dick" proved himself a splendid officer.

As soon as he arrived, General Taylor, with great energy, undertook the raising of an army to defend the State against the advance of the Federals, and to keep open a road for the passage of supplies to the Confederate troops east of the Mississippi. The Governor of Louisiana, Thos. O. Moore, met him at Opelousas and turned over to him a few State troops. To these were soon added some companies from Texas. Great assistance was given by Ex-Governor Mouton, of Lafayette, who was very popular in that portion of the country, and who brought many of the Acadians under the Confederate flag.* Five companies of soldiers from St. Mary parish, under Colonel Fournet, took service, and thus Taylor's little army gradually increased. When he arrived there seemed to be no money and no troops; but he tells us that the brave Creoles of that portion of the State were devoted to the Confederacy, and gave him invaluable help. Very

---

* See Taylor's "Destruction and Reconstruction," a work to which we wish to acknowledge our great obligations for the account of the Louisiana campaign.

soon, also, Taylor was joined by General Alfred Mouton, a son of Governor Mouton. This general served with great gallantry till he met his death at Mansfield.

The Salt Mines.—About this time an important discovery was made on Avery's Island, near New Iberia, a discovery which may best be described in General Taylor's own words. "Salt wells had long been known to exist on Avery's Island, "and some salt had been boiled there. The want of salt "was severely felt in the Confederacy, our only considerable "source of supply being in Southwestern Virginia, whence "it was not easily obtained. Judge Avery, the owner of "the island, began to boil salt for h s neighbors, and desir- "ing to increase the flow of brine by deepening the wells, "came unexpectedly upon a bed of pure rock salt, which "proved to be of immense extent. Intelligence of this "reached me at New Iberia, and induced me to visit the "island. Devoted to our cause, Judge Avery placed the "mine at my disposal for the use of the Government. Many "negroes were assembled to get out salt, and a packing "establishment was organized at New Iberia to cure beef. "During succeeding months large quantities of salt, salt "beef, sugar, and molasses were transported by steamers "to Vicksburg, Port Hudson, and other points east of "the Mississippi. Two companies of infantry and a "section of artillery were posted on the island to preserve "order among the workmen, and to secure it against a "sudden raid of the enemy, who later sent a gunboat "up the Petite Anse to shell the mine, but the gunboat "became entangled in the marsh, and accomplished "nothing."

Since the war this salt mine has been found to be practi-
~ally inexhaustible, and it will long continue to be a source
wealth to its owners. At the present day the mine is one
the most remarkable sights in Louisiana. Vast halls
orned with pillars have been cut out of the solid salt, and

when the whole is illuminated by artificial light, it resembles some enchanted subterranean palace.

QUESTIONS.

Tell about the "clearing" of the Mississippi. Tell about the ram *Arkansas*. Why did the Confederates attack Baton Rouge? Describe the attack. Tell about the hardships of the Southern soldiers. What general now took command of the forces in Louisiana? What troops did he muster? Tell about the discovery of the Avery salt mines.

———•♦•———

CHAPTER XXXV.

THE WAR IN LOUISIANA — CONTINUED.

Fighting on Bayou Lafourche and the Teche.—General Taylor had not long to wait for the enemy. On the 27th of October, 1862, General Weitzel, with a large body of Federal troops, advanced from Donaldsonville towards Labadieville in Assumption parish. The Confederates, under General Mouton, were on both sides of Bayou Lafourche, and as there was no bridge, they could not combine against the enemy. At Labadieville, however, Colonel Armand, with about five hundred men and a battery, opposed the advance of Weitzel's army, which numbered four thousand. The contest was brief but sharp. Many were killed on both sides; but Armand, having used all his ammunition, was forced to retire. General Mouton then fell back with all his troops to Berwick Bay below Morgan City.

Finding here that Federal gunboats were preparing to come up from Atchafalaya Bay, he retreated along the Teche. Weitzel followed slowly, and there were a number of skirmishes. In one of these the Federal gunboats attacked the *Cotton*, a river steamer which the Confederates had armed, and forced her commander, Captain Fuller, to burn her in the Teche.   Weitzel seems now to have been content with his success, for he remained quiet during several months at Berwick Bay.

In the month of April, 1863, he was reinforced by large bodies of troops until the Federal army numbered 16,000 men. The officer in command was General N. P. Banks, who had succeeded General Butler in New Orleans.   Though Taylor's entire force was only 3000 men, he felt that some effort must be made to resist the enemy, and he determined to throw up breastworks at Bisland, between Franklin and Morgan City.   Here the Confederates made a magnificent stand for two days, but finding that a portion of the Federal army was trying to cut them off in the rear, they were forced to retreat.   As the Confederates fell back, the Union army advanced northwards through Louisiana until it reached Alexandria on Red river, while General Taylor stationed himself at Natchitoches.*

Trans-Mississippi Department.—In March of this year (1863) Lieutenant-General E. Kirby Smith† had been sent by President Davis to take charge of the whole Trans-Mississippi department, which consisted of Missouri, Arkansas, Texas, Louisiana, and some of the Territories.   Great powers were given to the new commander; he was to conduct the campaign as he thought best, and all the other generals west of the Mississippi, including General Taylor, were to obey his orders. His headquarters were at Shreveport on Red river.

Port Hudson and Vicksburg.—After remaining some weeks at Alexandria, General Banks retired from Louisiana, and crossing the Mississippi laid siege to Port Hudson,

---

* On the 20th of April Fort Butte à la Rose had fallen into the hands of the enemy. This little fort had been established on the Atchafalaya, not very far distant from St. Martinsville. With four guns and a garrison of only sixty men, it had bravely defended the Atchafalaya and driven off some of the enemy's gunboats; but it was finally captured by a superior force of Federals.

† After the war General Smith became a professor at Sewanee, Tenn., where he died in 1893.

which, as we have seen, was held by the Confederates.   At
this time Vicksburg, also, was undergoing the horrors of a
siege.   General Grant had shut up there the Confederate

army under General Pemberton,
and with the assistance of a fleet,
he was bombarding the city.   If
Vicksburg and Port Hudson fell,
the Mississippi would be in the
power of the Federals, and the
prospects of Louisiana would be
indeed gloomy.

Taylor at Berwick Bay.—
When the enemy retired across
the Mississippi, General Taylor
determined to return to Southern
Louisiana and attack a body of
Federals that had been left at

LIEUT. GEN. E. KIRBY SMITH.
(Taken in 1893.)

Berwick Bay.   His expedition was planned with great skill
and was entirely successful.   The forces under General
Thos. Green and General Mouton, who were then about one
hundred miles apart, were ordered to meet at the Bay on
the 23d of June.   They arrived on time, and General
Green planted a battery on the west side of the Bay.   His
object was to drive off a Federal gunboat, which had been
left there to protect the camp of the enemy on the east
bank.   General Taylor then ordered Major Hunter with a
body of Texas troops to await the opening of Green's
guns, and then dash in upon the enemy from the rear.
All this was well executed.   Before the astonished Federals could arouse themselves, Green had charged with his
Texans and captured the whole camp, with the exception
of a few men who escaped on a railroad train.   General
Taylor describes the scene as one of great excitement and
confusion.   Seventeen hundred prisoners were taken, but
three-fourths of them were wounded and convalescents left by

General Banks. These were cared for, and as many as possible were sent to New Orleans with their surgeons. The spoils found in the camp were immense. They consisted of twelve cannon, many small arms, and a great quantity of ammunition, provisions, and medicines. So much rich booty the poor Confederates had not seen for a long time, and during several months they lacked nothing that was necessary for their comfort.

Fall of Vicksburg and Port Hudson—Taylor's Retreat.—After this successful expedition, General Taylor marched over to the Mississippi, and placed a battery of twelve guns on the river, with the hope of cutting off the Federal communication between Port Hudson and New Orleans. In about a week, however, sad news reached him. On the 4th of July, 1863, Vicksburg had surrendered to General Grant. Five days later Port Hudson, finding further resistance useless, had capitulated to General Banks.* Thus at last the Mississippi was wholly in the power of the North; the Confederacy was split into two parts, which could no longer communicate with each other. As we shall see, however, General Taylor did not despair of holding Western Louisiana.

Having accomplished their object on the east bank of the river, the Federals under General Weitzel—six thousand strong—crossed over to Donaldsonville. Taylor, who had a force of only three thousand men, and who feared that the enemy might come down the Atchafalaya and cut him off, retired with his little army to Berwick Bay. This he crossed, carrying with him the rich plunder which he had captured. During the next few months there was lively skirmishing in the country between Opelousas and New Iberia. The only considerable engagement was at Bayou Bourbeau near Ope-

---

* The defence of Port Hudson by Louisiana troops under General Gardner, who was ably seconded by his chief of artillery, Col. Marshall J. Smith, was one of he most gallant that occurred during the war.

lousas, where the Federals were defeated by General Green and six hundred prisoners taken.

Southern Losses in 1863.—During the rest of the year 1863, and the first months of 1864, there was no fighting of importance in Louisiana.   But the year 1863 had been marked by great misfortunes for the Confederates.   On the 1st of January President Lincoln had issued his famous Emancipation Proclamation, by which he declared all the slaves to be free.   Many of them still remained faithful to their old masters; but some ran away from the South and enlisted in the Northern armies.   Moreover, not only had Vicksburg fallen and the Mississippi passed into the hands of the Federals; but on the 3d of July, General Lee had been defeated at Gettysburg, Pennsylvania, with a loss of 21,000 men.   This was a series of disasters from which the South could never entirely recover.   Her means of carrying on the war were diminishing every day, while the North seemed to be as rich as ever.   Still many brilliant victories were yet to be won by Southern leaders, especially by Lee in Virginia; and the war was to last nearly one and a half years longer.

QUESTIONS.

Tell something about the fighting around Bayou Lafourche. Where are Bayou Lafourche, the Teche, Berwick Bay? What power was given to General Kirby Smith? Who was in charge of the Union army? Tell about the seige of Vicksburg. Taylor at Berwick Bay. Fall of Vicksburg and Port Hudson. Tell about the Southern losses in 1863.

CHAPTER XXXVI.

THE CLOSE OF THE WAR.

Banks' Raid ; the Federals Attempt to Occupy Western Louisiana.—In the spring of the year 1864, the Federals seemed determined to crush all opposition in Louisiana. On the 12th of March seventeen gunboats under the command of Admiral Porter entered the mouth of Red river. This fleet protected 10,000 men under General A. J. Smith. The troops landed at Simmsport on the Atchafalaya, and marching forward the next day, reached De Russey, a little fort on the Red. As the fortifications here had not been completed, there could be no successful resistance, and the enemy seized the garrison and ten guns. Another Federal army of 18,000 men, under General Franklin, now marched up the Teche to join Smith at Alexandria. Thus the force that was intended to overwhelm Louisiana consisted of 28,000 men and a strong fleet of gunboats. The commander-in-chief of the expedition was General N. P. Banks, who had occupied Alexandria the year before. Besides his present army, Banks was informed that General Steele, with 7000 men, would march down from Arkansas and join him at Shreveport.

Taylor's Retreat to Pleasant Hill and Mansfield.— General Taylor had been warned of the arrival of this great force, and he had fallen back towards Pleasant Hill and Mansfield. General Kirby Smith, who had fortified himself at Shreveport, thought it unwise for Taylor to try to make a stand against so large an army. But Taylor determined to risk a battle as soon as he saw a good opportunity. His army had been reinforced, and he had under him some excellent soldiers, and several distinguished officers. The chief of these were General Mouton, General Thos. Green, and General Charles Polignac. The last was a French Prince, who

had come over to America to fight for the South. He had
charge of a Texas Brigade, who did not at first like to be
commanded by a Frenchman, but Polignac soon proved himself so brave and so skilful that his men regarded him with
admiration and affection.

　　The Battle of Mansfield, April 8, 1864.—When Taylor
had collected his troops at Pleasant Hill and Mansfield, he
discovered that Banks was following him. Banks' army,
however, was divided into large bodies, which were separated from one another by considerable distances. Taylor
immediately decided to attack each body in turn, and thus
try to rout the whole army. On the 8th of April he drew
up his forces at Sabine Cross Roads, three miles in front of
Mansfield. He had 8800 men—3000 horse, 500 artillerymen,
and 3300 infantry. Of Banks' large army only 5000 were
in sight, but more troops were rapidly coming up. When
the advance columns of the enemy appeared, it was impossible to restrain the Louisiana troops, for they felt
that they were defending their native soil. Rushing forward under General Mouton they carried everything before them. The other brigades were equally successful;
but as the Louisianians approached the Federal lines, they
had to meet a deadly fire from the enemy's artillery. One
of the first to fall was the brave Mouton. It is said that
he stopped to protect some Federal soldiers who had
thrown down their arms and surrendered. While he sat
upon his horse, waving to his men not to fire, some of the
Federals picked up the guns they had thrown down and shot
their protector through the breast. Not one of them, however, survived this act of treachery. Polignac quickly took
Mouton's place, and the Confederates pressed on, routing
each new body of Federal troops as it was met. The pursuit was stopped only by the darkness. " The fruits of the
victory of Mansfield," says Taylor, " were twenty-five hun-
" dred prisoners, twenty pieces of artillery, several stands of

"colors, many thousands of small arms, and two hundred "and fifty wagons." It is estimated that Banks' force engaged in this battle amounted to about 13,000 men.

Pleasant Hill, April 9.—To complete his victory by attacking Banks on the following morning was Taylor's immediate decision. By that time, however, the enemy had taken a strong position at Pleasant Hill, and being reinforced by fresh troops, had in line about 18,000 men. Taylor, therefore, waited till he could be joined by General Churchill, who was coming up with several brigades composed of Arkansas and Missouri troops. With the addition of these, his army amounted to 12,500, but the new men were so wearied from a long march that the attack on the Federal lines could not be made before 3 o'clock in the afternoon. Churchill's troops were ordered by Taylor to march around through some woods and "turn the enemy's left." Having passed through the woods, the Missouri troops charged with great bravery, but unfortunately they made a mistake in choosing the point of attack, and were finally forced to retreat. Polignac's division, however, and General Green's dismounted horsemen drove back the enemy on their front, and at nightfall the Confederates were in possession of the field. Under cover of the darkness the Federals retreated as fast as possible to Grand Ecore on Red river. Banks afterwards claimed a victory at Pleasant Hill, and declared that he retired because his army lacked water and provisions; but Admiral Porter, in his report, describes the whole expedition up the Red river as a complete failure. The Confederates, on their side, considered that they had won the day, and General Smith issued the following general orders:

"Shreveport, La., April 19, 1864: God has blessed our "arms with signal victories at Mansfield and Pleasant Hill. "The General commanding finds it an appropriate occasion "to pay a well merited tribute to the endurance and valor

" of the troops engaged in these battles. Collected from re-
" mote points—from Missouri, Arkansas, Louisiana, and
" Texas—after long and tedious marches, their combined
" courage has gained on the soil of Louisiana the patriot sol-
" dier's highest reward, victory. * * * In the name of
" a grateful people I thank them for this splendid result.
" While we mourn for the glorious dead and sympathize
" with the heroic wounded, let us take courage for the
" future. * * * The names of Mansfield and Pleasant
" Hill will be inscribed on the colors of the regiments en-
" gaged in these battles. By command of General E.
" Kirby Smith."

The Pursuit of Banks.—General Kirby Smith and General Taylor did not agree as to the best manner of conducting
the campaign after the battle of Pleasant Hill. Taylor
thought that Banks should be pursued with all the available
forces, and every effort made to destroy his army. General
Smith feared that General Steele with 7000 Federals
would advance to attack Shreveport, and taking a portion of Taylor's infantry, he set out to meet Steele. The
latter retired into Arkansas, and as Smith pursued him, Taylor was left without sufficient force to do more than worry
Banks on his retreat. Taylor thought that he had been badly
treated by his commanding officer; but it was simply an honest difference of opinion as to what was the best course to
pursue.

From Grand Ecore, Banks retired to Alexandria, destroying property as he went; while the Federal fleet, a part of
which had ascended as high as Springfield Landing, about
thirty miles below Shreveport, now dropped down the Red
to cover Banks' retreat. A small battery of four guns (the
Federals maintain that there were eighteen) under Captain
Cornay, a brave officer, had been placed by the Confederates near the junction of Cane river and Red river. It
was supported by two hundred riflemen. As Porter's fleet

reached this point the little battery opened fire upon his gunboats.   One of them was cut to pieces, while the others suffered terribly.   Captain Cornay, however, was killed, and
Porter succeeded in passing.   The battery's fire, Porter afterwards declared, was the heaviest he ever witnessed.

  When the Federal fleet reached the Red River Falls, near
Alexandria, it was discovered that the water was too low to
allow the gunboats to pass.   There was a depth of only
three feet four inches, while the largest boats required about
seven feet.   At first it looked as if the fleet must fall into the
hands of the Confederates.   But finally an engineer, Colonel
Joseph Bailey, proposed a plan by which a dam might be
built across the river.   The task was a very difficult one, for
at this point the river is seven hundred and fifty-eight feet
wide and the current is swift.   For eight days, however, several thousand men worked day and night, and finally the dam
was completed.   But as a portion of it was carried away by
the current, it became necessary to build an additional one
above.   By means of the two the depth of the water was increased sufficiently to allow all the vessels to pass over.   This
was a splendid piece of engineering work, the remains of
which were still visible a few years ago.   Colonel Bailey,
who planned it, was raised to the rank of brigadier general,
and received the thanks of the United States Congress.   With
the protection of the fleet, Banks now retreated to Simmsport.
The Confederates, hanging upon his flanks, succeeded in
cutting off many of his men; but on May 20th he crossed
the Atchafalaya.   Here, as the Mississippi was in the possession of the Federals, the Confederates had to give up
the pursuit.

  End of the War.—From this time on there was no more
fighting in Louisiana.   Nearly a year later General Robert
E. Lee, the great Southern commander-in-chief, surrendered to General Grant in Virginia, and thus put an end to
the war.   The South had fought a noble fight, but it was

impossible for her to struggle any longer against the over-whelming numbers of the North.

By this terrible contest between the two sections, the question of secession was settled forever. Perhaps it could not have been settled in any other manner. At the present day the Southern people, while they still maintain that their interpretation of the Constitution was the true one, have accepted "the judgment of war," and are now firm in their loyalty to the Union.*

General H. W. Allen, Governor.—In 1864, while the war was going on, an election for governor was held in

Louisiana. In the New Orleans district, Michael Hahn, a Union man, was chosen; but his authority was recognized only in that portion of the State which was controlled by the Northern soldiers. The rest of the State chose as governor General Henry W. Allen, who, though born in Virginia, was an adopted son of Louisiana. General Allen had been a gallant soldier, and had served under Breckinridge in the famous attack on Baton Rouge. Here he was wounded so desperately that it was thought he must die. Thanks to a good doctor, however, he recovered. As governor he won the love and respect of all Louisianians. Shreveport became the capital of the State, and it was here that Allen resided. The State had been de-

---

* The Fourteenth Amendment to the Constitution of the United States, passed after the war (1868), declares: "All persons born or naturalized in the United States, and subject to the jurisdiction thereof, are citizens of the United States and of the State wherein they reside." This amendment abolishes forever the constitutional right of secession. No "citizen of the United States" can take up arms against the General Government.

vastated by the armies that had occupied it so long; and at the close of the war the misery and want were such that, in many cases, the inhabitants of the parishes were on the point of starvation. Governor Allen nobly came to their relief. To raise money for the purchase of provisions was almost an impossibility; but, by his heroic exertions, it was accomplished. Not only was food sent wherever it was needed, but a great number of the poor were aided in their efforts to begin life anew. Other good deeds of the "War Governor" are held in grateful remembrance. When, however, peace was finally made, Governor Allen, whose health had been shattered by his wounds, retired to Mexico, where he died in 1866. His remains are buried in Baton Rouge.

QUESTIONS.

What was Banks' whole force? What was the difference of opinion between Taylor and Smith? Tell about the battle of Mansfield. How many soldiers fought on each side? Tell about the battle of Pleasant Hill? What was the result of Banks' Red river campaign? Describe the pursuit of Banks. How did Porter pass Red River Falls? How did the war end? Give an account of Governor Allen.

RESTORATION TO THE UNION.

CHAPTER XXXVII.

AFTER THE WAR.

Reconstruction.—Louisiana had suffered terribly during the war. Her rich fields had been laid waste, her sugar houses had been burned, and, saddest of all, thousands of her brave sons had perished on the battle field. When the survivors returned to their homes, they took up once more the duties of life with the hope of restoring their fortunes by courage and industry.* The war had served one good purpose; it had taught those who fought in it to bear misfortunes bravely. But alas! for the next twelve years Louisiana was destined to suffer almost as much as during the war itself.

In December, 1865, there was added to the Constitution of the United States the Thirteenth Amendment, which declared that slavery was forever abolished. But Congress, which was now largely composed of Republicans, was afraid that the freedmen might not obtain the right of suffrage in the South. It decided, therefore, that the Southern States should not send representatives to Congress and should not control their own governments until they had been "reconstructed." This meant that in these States strong military governments were to be established by the President, and that these were to frame new constitutions, guaranteeing to the freedmen the right to vote, and excluding from office all prominent Confederates.† As soon as the rights of the freedmen had been

---

* General Richard Taylor tells us that at the close of the war his plantation had been confiscated, and that his whole fortune consisted of two horses, one of which was lame and unfit for service.

†After "reconstruction" these Confederates were not admitted to Congress until they had been pardoned.

thus secured, the States. were to be readmitted to the Union.

Political Adventurers.—In 1868, Louisiana having been duly "reconstructed," was readmitted to the Union.* But this was not to be the end of her troubles. Crowds of Republican adventurers, who had hurried down from the North, got possession of the State Government. This was easy to do ; for according to the new constitution, framed in 1868, the Southern Democrats who had taken a prominent part in the war were not allowed to vote, and the freedmen naturally thought that they must support the Republicans, who had abolished slavery. Hence, a bitter contest arose between the Democrats, who owned all the property in the State, and the political adventurers, who held all the offices. These latter were called in the South "carpet-bag" politicians, because it was said that they brought with them from the North nothing but their carpet-bags.

The new-comers soon began to seize the public money, large sums of which they put into their own pockets or spent in keeping themselves in office. All their actions were supported by a band of soldiers called the Metropolitan Police, and by United States troops, which had been sent by the President " to keep order in Louisiana." Hence there followed a period of shameless corruption. In a few years the public debt of Louisiana was increased by the sum of $40,-000,000. Taxes became extremely high, and the people of the State, who had been much impoverished by the war, were now overwhelmed with debt. After a while, however, the Republicans began to quarrel among themselves. H. C. Warmoth, who had been elected governor in 1868, was impeached and suspended from office in 1872 by a hostile wing of his own party. For one month P. B. S. Pinchback acted

* Michael Hahn, who was elected governor in 1864, resigned in 1865, and was succeeded by another Union man, J. M. Wells. The "reconstruction" governors were B. F. Flanders and Joshua Baker. The former served from June, 1867, to January, 1868, and the latter from January, 1868, till July of the same year.

as governor.   In 1873 he was succeeded by another Republican, Wm. P. Kellogg.   *

The White League.—The Louisianians soon saw that if
they wished to enjoy their right of free government, they must
take up arms against the oppressors. A great number of the
most prominent men in various parts of the State, therefore,
formed themselves into what was called the White League.
The object of this organization was to rescue the State from
the "carpet-bag" government and restore it to the white
Democrats. "Resistance to tyranny!" was the cry in all the
parishes. At St. Martinsville the people rose and drove
back an armed vessel called the "Ozark," which the Republican governor, Wm. Pitt Kellogg, had sent to arrest the
principal citizens of town because they refused to pay taxes
for the support of his government. Finally, on the 14th of
September, 1874—a day ever memorable in the annals of
New Orleans—there was a battle between a detachment of
the League and Kellogg's Metropolitan Police. Some fire-
arms for the League had been brought to the city by steamer,
and Kellogg declared that they should not be delivered to
their owners. The forces of the White League, under General Fred N. Ogden, marched to the foot of Canal street
with the intention of taking possession of the arms. Here
they were met by the Metropolitan Police under General
Longstreet, and there was a sharp contest, in which forty
men were killed and one hundred were wounded. The
White League was victorious. The Metropolitans were
scattered, and the pieces of artillery which they had placed
upon the levee were turned against themselves.

When the battle was over it was found that sixteen members of the League lay dead upon the street.* With their

---

* On the 14th of September, 1891, a monument to the memory of these heroes
was dedicated with appropriate ceremonies. It stands at the foot of Canal street,
and bears the names of those who fell in defence of free government, These names
should never be forgotten: Bozonier, Betz, Brulard, Crossin, Considine, Feuil-
lan, Gautier, Gourdain, Graval, Lindsey, Mohrmann, Newman, Robbins, Tole-
dano, Wells, and West.

deaths, however, began a new era in Louisiana; for the people of the State felt that their cause had been sanctified by the blood of these brave citizens, and that they must never give up the struggle until they had won back the right to govern themselves.

Kellogg's troops had been defeated; but he himself had taken refuge in the Custom House. While here he appealed to the President for help. His request was granted, and with the aid of United States troops he was once more installed as governor.*

F. T. Nicholls, Governor.—In 1876, however, a new election was held. The Democrats, by a majority of 8,000,

FRANCIS T. NICHOLLS.

carried the State for Francis T. Nicholls. Many of the colored people, preferring to live in peace with the white landowners, left the Republican party of their own free will, and voted with the Democrats. Kellogg's party, however, maintained that a majority of the votes had been cast for their candidate, a United States marshal named Packard, whom they hoped to keep in office by means of United States soldiers. Nicholls, who had been a brave soldier, now showed that he was a devoted patriot. With calm courage he declared that at all hazards he would guard the rights of his State. "I "have been elected governor," he said, "and I intend to "be governor." The Louisianians rallied around him, ready to defend him at the point of the bayonet.

---

* The Democrats had elected John McEnery governor, and D. B. Penn lieutenant-governor, but both were now forced to retire.

In January, 1877, therefore, two governors were inaugurated in Louisiana; Nicholls openly on the balcony of the court building that overlooks Lafayette Square, and Packard behind closed doors in the State House (now Hotel Royal). Here, guarded by Federal troops, Packard and his followers remained for several months, while the White League held all the courts for Nicholls.* Finally, in April, 1877, a committee sent down from Washington to to investigate the strange condition of affairs in Louisiana, advised the President to withdraw the Federal troops. Without troops, Packard could do nothing, and his government immediately fell to pieces. The "carpet-baggers" soon after departed from Louisiana, and the State once more enjoyed a free government.

Such is a brief summary of the important events from the close of the war to the year 1877. It is a far more agreeable task to take up the subsequent history of Louisiana, and tell how the State drew herself out of the " slough of despond " and began again that career of wonderful prosperity which had been interrupted by the war.

QUESTIONS.

What was the Thirteenth Amendment? What was "reconstruction?" Tell about the "carpet-bag politicians," and the increase of the State debt. What was the White League? Tell about the "Ozark." Tell about the Fourteenth of September. Whom did the Democrats elect governor in 1876? Tell about the two governors. How did the contest end?

---

*The seizure of the Supreme Court on Jackson Square by Governor Nicholls' troops was one of the most exciting and important events that occurred during this period. It was on the 9th of January, a bitter cold day. At six o'clock in the morning the White League, well armed, gathered around the court, in which Packard had stationed a guard of Metropolitans. Cannon were placed at the head of neighboring streets; for it was expected that the Republicans would make a fierce resistance and that the United States troops would lend them aid. At the last moment, however, the courage of the Metropolitans failed them, and they decided to surrender. There being no actual conflict the United States troops refused to interfere. As Packard's judges had already left the building and sought places of safety, Nicholls' appointees took their seats. They were Judges Manning, Marr, Egan, Spencer, and De Blanc, with Alfred Roman as clerk. The other courts having been surrendered soon after, the judicial business of the State was conducted wholly by the Nicholls government.

CHAPTER XXXVIII.

PROGRESS.

Nicholls and the New Constitution.—We have seen that, in 1868, under the Republican administration, a new constitution was framed for Louisiana; but it was clear that this constitution contained many unwise provisions, which must be corrected or removed. Accordingly the leading men of the State assembled in convention at New Orleans and drew up the constitution of 1879, under which we are now living. It is given in full, at the end of this volume.

This constitution contained some important changes. In all previous constitutions (except in one framed in 1864, during the military rule of General Banks), there was a provision that the governor should not be elected for a second term until four years after the expiration of his first term. This provision was now abolished. Moreover, the courts of the State were remodeled on a novel plan, the chief feature of which was the establishment of courts of appeal, subject to the supervision of the Supreme Court. In general, we may say that this constitution made provision for the immense debt that had been contracted by the State; it established a better system of public schools than had ever before existed in Louisiana; and it confined within very narrow limits the powers of the legislature, so that the State might not be injured by unwise laws.

Louis A. Wiltz, Governor, 1880-81—S. D McEnery, Governor, 1881-88.—Louis A. Wiltz, who had been elected governor under the new constitution, was inaugurated in January, 1880. One of the provisions of the constitution was that the seat of government should be removed from New Orleans to Baton Rouge. The old Capitol building in the latter city had been burned during the war, but immediate steps were now taken to rebuild it. Wiltz, who had been lieutenant-governor under Nicholls, and had won an enviable reputation for himself as mayor of New Orleans in 1872-74, did not live through his term. At his death, in 1881, the lieutenant-governor, S. D. McEnery, succeeded him, and after serving the unexpired term, he was elected governor in 1884. Governor McEnery thus held the highest position in the gift of the people for seven years.

GOVERNOR LOUIS A. WILTZ.

The Jetties.—Up to the year 1879 New Orleans lacked a good channel through the mouths of the Mississippi. Dredging machines had been used to remove the sand bars that constantly formed in the passes, and at various times iron harrows had been dragged over the obstructions; but nothing permanent had been accomplished. Vessels containing a million dollars' worth of goods were often aground on the bar for days, and the commerce of New Orleans was seriously injured. In 1874, however, Captain Jas. B. Eads, a distinguished engineer, proposed to try a plan that had been suggested by a French engineer soon after the founding of New Orleans. This was to build jetties, which, by confining the immense volume of water between them, would force the river to dredge itself. The United States Government thought favorably of this proposition, and made large appropriations for the work. Thus encouraged, Eads began his jetties in 1875 and finished them

GOVERNOR S. D. M'ENERY.

in four years.   They are built in what is called the South
Pass, and consist of two long lines of willow " mattresses,"
ballasted with stone and held in place by piles.   The
east jetty is a little over two miles long, while the west
one is about a mile and a half.   The work was a perfect
success; for a channel from twenty-six to thirty feet in depth
was obtained where there had not been fifteen feet before;
and large vessels can now come up to New Orleans without
any detention.   Up to the year 1881, nearly six millions of
dollars had been spent on the jetties; and the success of the
plan gained for Captain Eads the gratitude of Louisiana and
a world-wide reputation.

THE JETTIES.

The Levees.—About the time the jetties were completed
(1879), important progress was made in protecting Louisiana against the overflows and crevasses which every year
seemed to become more destructive. In 1882, however, there
came a great flood, which produced 284 crevasses. The extent
of levee embankment swept away amounted in all to more
than fifty-six miles.   At first it seemed impossible to raise
enough money to rebuild these levees, though it was clear that

the prosperity of the State depended upon the protection of the rich plantations that lie along the banks of the rivers. In 1883, however, a levee convention was called in Baton Rouge; great interest was aroused; money was raised; and levee building on a large scale was undertaken. Timely assistance, moreover, came from the United States Government, which had already begun to appreciate the fact that the care of the levees on the Mississippi is a matter of national importance. In meeting the terrible difficulties of this period, Governor McEnery showed such zeal and ability that he gained for himself the gratitude of the whole State.

This good work was continued on a larger scale than ever before during the second term of Governor Nicholls. From the time of the convention down to the year 1893, the sums spent upon the levees by the General Government and the State Boards amounted to many millions of dollars. The results of this wise policy were seen in the flood of 1890. In this year the water rose higher than in 1882; but the whole breakage in eleven hundred miles of levees was only four and one-quarter miles in extent.* Since then the United States Government has made an appropriation of ten million dollars for the Mississippi. With this sum and the amounts raised by the States most interested, it is promised by the engineers that the South shall have "a system of levees capable of controlling all floods in the Mississippi."

Maritime Sanitation.—In 1878 over four thousand persons died of yellow fever in Louisiana. Some years later, however, Dr. Joseph Holt, of New Orleans, established at the mouth of the Mississippi a system of disinfecting vessels which won for him a national reputation. Improvements were made by his successor, Dr. C. P. Wilkinson, and by Dr. S. R. Oliphant, until the quarantine station is now the best equipped in the world. Since the establishment of this new system there has been no yellow fever in Louisiana; at last

---

* "Memoirs of Louisiana."

the State seems to have been freed from the terrible scourge
which formerly did so much to injure commerce and to prevent immigration.   Many physicians once believed that the
disease originated in New Orleans and could not be kept out
by quarantine; but the present admirable system has proved
the contrary.   It may be added that Louisiana is now one of
the healthiest States in the Union; for the mildness of the climate, and the out-door life which such a climate renders possible, preserve the inhabitants from many of the terrible dis-
eases so common in the North.

THE CAPITOL AT BATON ROUGE.

The Cotton Centennial Exposition.—In the year 1784
the earliest shipment of cotton was made from Charleston,
S. C.   It consisted of six bags (about one bale).   To celebrate the one hundredth anniversary of this event, a great
Centennial Exposition was opened in New Orleans during
the year 1884.   The largest exposition building the world

had ever seen was built, and thousands of visitors flocked to Louisiana from the North, the East, and the West. They saw the beauty of our Southern land and enjoyed the hospitality of our Southern people. The Exposition, if it accomplished nothing else, enabled the Northern and Southern people to know each other better, and removed much of the bitterness that had been handed down as a relic of the war.

The annual Carnival of New Orleans, probably the most splendid pageant ever seen in the world, has also played its part in drawing the two sections of the country more closely together.

THE LEVEE AT NEW ORLEANS.

Nicholls' Second Term as Governor. 1888-1892.— In 1888, Francis T. Nicholls was called once more to the governor's chair. His great services in asserting the rights of his State and standing firm during the troublous times of 1876-77, had greatly endeared him to the people of Louisiana, and they showed their appreciation of his sterling qualities by giving him a second term. During his administration a fierce contest arose over the renewal of the Louisiana Lottery charter. As the Lottery Company offered a large annual sum to the State for this renewal, many people were in favor of granting it. But the Governor and some other prominent men declared themselves opposed to the continuance of lotteries, and a strong anti-lottery party sprung up. As both sides canvassed the State, there was a great deal of excitement. Finally, however the United States Government refused the Lottery Company the use of the mails; whereupon the managers of that corporation withdrew their offer.

Murphy J. Foster, Governor. 1892. —.—Murphy J. Foster, "the man from St.

GOVERNOR MURPHY J. FOSTER.

Mary," who had been the anti-lottery candidate for governor, was soon after elected over three opponents. The lieutenant-governor chosen at the same time was Charles Parlange, of Pointe Coupée. Coming into office after this bitter contest, in which the passions of two parties were greatly excited, Governor Foster, by his personal magnetism and his wise administration, has won the praise even of his political enemies.

Prosperity.—During the last sixteen years the prosperity of the State has been very remarkable. Now that there is deep water at the mouth of the Mississippi, thousands of vessels visit every year the docks of New Orleans, and bear away to all parts of the world not only sugar and cotton, the products of the South, but also great cargoes of grain sent down by the Western States.

Sugar and Cotton.—Improved methods have made great changes in the sugar industry. "A quarter of a century ago " the yield of sugar was one pound from forty-five pounds of

" cane; at the present day in large factories the yield is one
" pound from nine pounds of cane." Moreover, large central sugarhouses have been built, which buy the cane from
the small planter and save him a great deal of expense. This
economy in the manufacture, together with the bounty now
paid to the planters by the United States Government, has
given a new impulse to sugar planting.

The cotton crop of 1891-92 was the most extraordinary in
the history of the South. It amounted to nearly nine millions
of bales. Of this crop Louisiana produced about 740,000
bales—more than her usual share.

Immigration from the West—Cultivation of Rice.—
Within the last few years a thousand families of settlers from
Iowa, Kansas, and other Western States have crowded into
the parishes of Southwestern Louisiana. The changes that
these worthy people have produced in this portion of the
State are so remarkable that they seem to be the result of a
magical transformation.

The chief settlements of the new-comers are in Calcasieu,
and in parts of Vermillion and Cameron. At first they devoted themselves more particularly to grass-growing, fruit-
raising, and the breeding of fine stock. In all these they were
very successful on account of the new and improved methods
which they introduced. Their greatest success, however,
has been won in the cultivation of upland rice. This was
first tried on a small scale, but the crop was made with so
little expense, and was so profitable, that more lands were
soon drained and more rice was planted, until an immense
area is now under cultivation. In St. Charles, Plaquemines,
and other river parishes, rice has been cultivated for a number of years. In 1880, however, the crop of the State was
only 80,000 barrels; while in 1893, with the addition of the
new plantations in Southwestern Louisiana, it is estimated
that the crop will be about 850,000 barrels. Hence r¹
must now be placed among the great staple products of

State.   Formerly it was grown chiefly in the Atlantic States ;
but Louisiana now yields far more than all these States together.   As the quality of the Louisiana rice is very fine,
and as the crop can be produced here at less expense than in
any other State, the planters have a new source of wealth.

The settlers from the West, therefore, have introduced a
wonderful spirit of activity and enterprise into Louisiana.
The Acadians themselves, who have generally been slow in
accepting improvements, are now imitating their Western
brethren, and are trying new methods of agriculture.   As a
result the assessed value of property in this portion of Louisiana has been trebled during the last ten years.   No wonder,
then, that the Louisianians appreciate the importance of
bringing good immigrants into their State.

Education and Literature.—Louisiana may well boast
of her progress in education and literature.   Every year her
public school system is improving.*   It is now clearly seen
that the State can not depend upon private schools, however
useful they may be ; a public system is the true method of
preparing the youth of the land to become good citizens.   In
the higher education, also, there has been much progress.
The Universities for white and colored in New Orleans, the
University at Baton Rouge, the Normal School at Natchitoches, together with the numerous colleges scattered over
the State, are offering better advantages than ever before.
The young men of Louisiana no longer need to seek an education in Northern colleges or in foreign countries.

Finally, with peace and prosperity, there has sprung up in
the South a new literature, and in the production of it Louisiana has played an important part.   Brilliant writers in
French and English are to be found within the State. Creole
and American authors are successfully describing to the outside world the manners, the customs, and the scenery of our

* New Orleans owes a debt of gratitude to John McDonogh, who gave a large
im of money for the erection of handsome school buildings in the city.

Southern land. This new literature has excited great enthusiasm in the North, and we may predict that Louisiana will gain a high place for herself in the literary world. Her writers have an interesting field to explore, for no history is richer in romantic incidents than that of Louisiana.

With a glorious past to be proud of, and splendid opportunities before her, the Pelican State can not fail to win still greater fame for herself and greater happiness for her people.

QUESTIONS.

Tell about the constitution of 1879. What two governors served after Nicholls ? To what city was the capital removed ? Tell about the jetties. Tell about the levees. The quarantine system. What did the Exposition of 1884 celebrate ? Influence of the New Orleans Carnival. Nicholls' second term and the lottery contest. Who succeeded Nicholls in 1892 ? Give some evidences of the prosperity of Louisiana. Tell about sugar. Cotton. Tell about the Western immigrants and the cultivation of rice. Education and literature in Louisiana.

PHYSICAL FEATURES, POPULATION, AND RESOURCES.

The area of Louisiana is 45,420 square miles. The population in 1810 was 75,556; it was in 1890 1,118,587. The State is divided into fifty-nine parishes, the names of which are as follows:

Acadia, Ascension, Assumption, Avoyelles, Bienville, Bossier, Caddo, Calcasieu, Caldwell, Cameron, Catahoula, Claiborne, Concordia, De Soto, East Baton Rouge, East Carroll, East Feliciana, Franklin, Grant, Iberia, Iberville, Jackson, Jefferson, Lafayette, Lafourche, Lincoln, Livingston, Madison, Morehouse, Natchitoches, Orleans, Ouachita, Plaquemines, Pointe Coupée, Rapides, Red River, Richland, Sabine, St. Bernard, St. Charles, St. Helena, St. James, St. John the Baptist, St. Landry, St. Martin, St. Mary, St. Tammany, Tangipahoa, Tensas, Terrebonne, Union, Vermillion, Vernon, Washington, Webster, West Baton Rouge, West Carroll, West Feliciana, Winn.

The chief cities, with their population in 1890, are:

New Orleans, 242,039; Shreveport, 11,979; Baton Rouge, 10,478.

Rivers and Streams.—Besides the three great rivers, the Mississippi, the Red and the Ouachita, there are innumerable little lakes and over two hundred bayous; so that Louisiana doubtless has more water courses than any other State in the Union.

Soil and Products.—The geological features of Louisiana are very simple. The three formations found in the State are the *cretaceous or chalky*, the *tertiary*, and the *post-tertiary*.* It is said that the *chalky* formation underlies the whole State; it may be seen cropping out in the limestone hills of St. Landry and Winn. All the salt deposits are found in this formation. Above this comes the *tertiary*, which underlies the bluff lands; and on top of this is the *post-tertiary*, of which the rich alluvial lands of the State are composed.

The following is the description which Prof. Lockett, formerly of the Louisiana State University, has given of the formation of these bluff and alluvial lands:

"It is likely," says he, "that a broad estuary or arm of the sea once

---

*This term in geology is applied to all the most recent formations.

extended as far inland as the junction of the Ohio and the Mississippi. Fine mud and silt, however, were washed into this estuary from the higher lands, and floating gently towards the sea, were deposited in a deep stratum, whose upper surface was a broad submerged plain. This stratum of silt completely filled up what we now call the Mississippi bottom, and the broad plain extended out to the hill-side slopes on the east and west to a distance of twenty miles from the limits of the present alluvial lands. But a great continental upheaval took place, and this plain was raised several hundred feet above its old-time level. The old Mississippi had then to wash out for itself a new channel to the sea, and having the easily dissolved silt to work upon, the mighty river swept much of its former bed into the gulf. In so doing it left those high bluffs on which Baton Rouge, Natchez, and Vicksburg now stand."

Products.—South of 31 deg. north latitude the State is well adapted to the production of sugar, cotton, and rice; but north of that line the great staple is cotton. Indian corn, also, is grown in considerable quantities. In the parishes of St. James and Natchitoches the light, sandy soil produces the famous strong tobacco called "perique." This tobacco derives its name from Senor Perique, a Spaniard, who first planted it many years ago. It is much sought after in Europe and America. In the southern part of the State, tropical fruits reach great perfection, especially oranges, bananas, and figs. The Louisiana oranges are superior in sweetness to those of Florida.

Animals.—Deer, wild-cats, panthers, and bears are found in Louis-

iana. The birds of the State, which are very numerous, have been made known to the world by the illustrious John James Audubon. Audubon was born on a Louisiana plantation in 1780. When he was young he showed his fondness for birds by keeping a number of them as pets. When he grew up he published the "Birds of America," a work that contained life-sized drawings made by himself. It was sold by subscription at one thousand dollars a copy, and made Audubon famous. He died in New York, and on

JOHN JAMES AUDUBON.

the 26th of April, 1893, a beautiful monument to his memory was unveiled in that city.

Minerals.—One of the most important minerals in Louisiana is salt, which is found in various parts of the State, but chiefly, as we have seen, on Avery's Island. From this island the exports in one day frequently amount to 400 tons. Near Lake Charles there is a large deposit of sulphur and gypsum. The other mineral products of Louisiana are not important.

The Lands of Louisiana.—According to Prof. Lockett, there are eight kinds of land in the State: good uplands, pine hills, bluff lands, pine flats, prairies, alluvial lands, wooded swamps, and coast marsh.

Thus we see that Louisiana has a very diversified surface. Besides the rich plantations and the broad prairies for cattle raising, there are immense forests containing oak, cypress, pine, and many other valuable kinds of trees. According to the report of the Hon. T. W. Poole, Commissioner of Immigration, from which we draw many of the following details, the good uplands embrace chiefly the parishes of Sabine, De Soto, Caddo, Bossier, Red River, Bienville, Webster, Lincoln, Jackson, Union, and portions of Morehouse and Ouachita.

These, which are the northwestern parishes of the State, were settled principally by worthy people from Georgia, Alabama, and other Atlantic States. They have adopted various professions; but most of them are industrious and successful farmers, who have raised this portion of the State to a high degree of prosperity. Instead of large plantations, such as exist in Southern Louisiana, we find here a num, ber of small farms, with numerous towns and villages.

The pine hills embrace chiefly the following parishes: Vernon-Grant, Winn, Catahoula, Rapides, St. Helena, Tangipahoa, Washington, and St. Tammany. The timber in these parishes is extremely valuable.

In the bluff lands are included parts of the following parishes: West Carroll, Richland, Franklin, Livingston, East and West Feliciana, and East Baton Rouge. The pine flats are found in the western portion of Calcasieu parish. They form an area of poor lands, generally covered with water.

The prairie lands are found in St. Landry, Lafayette, Acadia, St. Martin, Iberia, Vermillion, and St. Mary. "These seven parishes," says Col. Hillyard, "contain more than 3,000,000 acres of tillable land, most of it of inexhaustible fertility. Even most of the sea-marsh, and all of the swamp lands, may be reclaimed by local levees and draining machines, and may become the most productive rice an ' sugar lands of the State. On thousands of acres the grass grows a smooth surface under the waving branches of noble trees. The fat herds grazing upon these green prairies help in giving the finishing touch to this magnificent landscape scenery." Five of these parishes, St. Mary, Iberia, Vermillion, St. Martin, and Lafayette, once formed the Attakapas region, and they are still called the "Attakapas parishes."[1]

Through this beautiful region runs the lovely Teche, which has been described in the "Evangeline" of Longfellow. For it was the Teche that the heroine of this poem ascended, seeking in vain for her husband Gabriel, from whom she had been separated in her native country. The following is Longfellow's description of the Attakapas region:

> " Beautiful is the land with its prairies and forest and fruit trees;
> Under the feet a garden of flowers, and the bluest of heavens
> Bending above, and resting its dome on the walls of the forest.
> They who dwell there have named it the ' Eden of Louisiana.' "

In this "Eden of Louisiana" still reside the descendants of the Acadian exiles. Until they began the cultivation of rice their manner of life had changed very little since they settled the country about the middle of the eighteenth century. They are industrious, prosperous, and many of them rich. When the day's work is done they delight to assemble and spend the evening in dancing and merry-making. They still weave the wonderful Attakapas cloth, so well known in Louisiana. Some of the most distinguished men in the State are descended from Acadian ancestors.

In St. Mary parish it is said that there is not an acre of poor land. The chief product is sugar, and the quantity produced is so great that St. Mary has won for herself the title of the " banner parish " of the State.

Alluvial Lands.—These lands are so-called from *alluvium*, which means "earth, sand, and gravel, transported by rivers, floods, and other causes, and deposited upon land not permanently submerged beneath the waters of lakes or seas." The alluvial lands constitute the plantations along the banks of all the streams in Louisiana. They are exceedingly rich, and form an area of about 12,300 square miles.

Wooded Swamps and Coast Marsh.—The last divisions of which we have to speak are the wooded swamps and coast marsh. These swamps, which were formerly very extensive, are now being redeemed by drainage. Many of them, when they are properly drained, and the trees are felled, will be classed as alluvial lands. The coast marsh is valuable for game and for pasturage. A large quantity of it is owned by the State, and may be purchased for less than one dollar an acre.

The South-Eastern Parishes.—It has been impossible within our limits to give an account of all the parishes in the State; though the history of many of them is extremely interesting. A few words, however, may be added in regard to St. Bernard, Plaquemines, and Orleans. The first two produce large quantities of sugar, rice, and vegetables. They contain also the most important orange groves in the State. There is no more beautiful sight in Louisiana than the acres of orange trees along the banks of the Mississippi, from New Orleans to Ft. Jackson. These lands are extremely valuable. A one hundred acre grove, says Commissioner Poole, produced in 1890, a crop of oranges that sold for $12,000. Of late years Cameron, in Southwestern Louisiana, has also become a great orange-raising parish.

The whole of the parish of Orleans is included within the limits of the city of New Orleans, so the city may be said to have an area of about 187 square miles, a larger area than that of any other city in the Union * New Orleans is now a magnificent city, and is increasing every year in manufactures, in population, and in wealth. It has taken its position as one of the great commercial centres of the world.

QUESTIONS.

What is the area of Louisiana? Increase of population from 1810 to 1890? How many parishes are there? Chief cities and their population. Three great rivers. How many bayous? Give the main geological features of Louisiana. Tell about the formation of the "Mississippi bottom" and the origin of bluff lands. What are the chief products of Louisiana? Its minerals? What animals are found? Who was Audubon? Tell about Louisiana uplands. Pine hills. Bluff lands. Pine flats. Prairie lands. Tell about the Teche and the Attakapas region. What are the alluvial lands? Wooded swamps? Coast marsh? Where are the orange groves of Louisiana? What is the area of New Orleans?

---

* The actual area of the city is estimated at 37 square miles.

LIST OF STATE OFFICERS, 1893.

Governor, MURPHY J. FOSTER, of St. Mary.

Lieutenant-Governor, CHARLES PARLANGE, of Pointe Coupée.

Secretary of State, T. S. ADAMS. *Treasurer*, W. W. HEARD.

Auditor, JOHN PICKETT, *Att'y-General*, M. J. CUNNINGHAM.

Superintendent of Education, A. D. LAFARGUE.

JUDICIARY.

Supreme Court—Chief Justice, F. T. NICHOLLS; Associate Justices, S. D. McENERY, CHAS. E. FENNER, L. B. WATKINS, and JOS. A. BREAUX.

LEGISLATURE.

The number of Senators is 37. The number of Representatives is 98. The list of names can not be given here.

STATE BOARD OF EDUCATION.

This Board consists of the Governor, the Attorney-General, and the Superintendent of Education, who are all *ex-officio* members, and of the following citizens, appointed by the Governor, one from each Congressional district: ALCEE FORTIER, of New Orleans; MAX HELLER, of New Orleans; THOMAS OVERTON, of Marksville; WILLIAM CLEGG, of Lafayette; F. SEIP, of Alexandria, and FRANKLIN GARRETT, of Monroe.

CONSTITUTION OF LOUISIANA.

ADOPTED JULY 23, 1879.

With the Amendments down to 1893 inserted in their proper places.

PREAMBLE.

We, the people of the State of Louisiana, in order to establish justice, insure domestic tranquillity, promote the general welfare and secure the blessings of liberty to ourselves and our posterity, acknowledging and invoking the guidance of Almighty God, the author of all good government, do ordain and establish this constitution.

BILL OF RIGHTS.

ARTICLE 1. All government of right originates with the people, is founded on their will alone, and is instituted solely for the good of the whole, deriving its just powers from the consent of the governed. Its only legitimate end is to protect the citizen in the enjoyment of life, liberty and property. When it assumes other functions it is usurpation and oppression.

ART. 2. The right of the people to be secure in their persons, houses, papers and effects against unreasonable searches and seizures shall not be violated; and no warrant shall issue except uponprobable cause, supported by oath or affirmation, and particularly describing the place to be searched and the persons or things to be seized.

ART. 3. A well regulated militia being necessary to the security of a free State, the right of the people to keep and bear arms shall not be abridged. This shall not prevent the passage of laws to punish those who carry weapons concealed. D. sec. 915, 2309.

ART. 4. No law shall be passed respecting an establishment of religion or prohibiting the free exercise thereof, or abridging the freedom of speech or of the press, or the right of the people peaceably to assemble and petition the government for a redress of grievances.

ART. 5. There shall be neither slavery nor involuntary servitude in this State otherwise than for the punishment of crime, whereof the party shall have been duly convicted. Prosecutions shall be by indictment or information; *provided*, that no person shall be held to answer for a capital crime unless on a presentment or indictment by a grand jury, except in cases arising in the militia when in active service in time of war or public danger; nor shall any person be twice put in jeopardy of life or liberty for the same offence, except on his own application for a new trial, or where there is a mistrial, or a motion in arrest of judgment is sustained. D. 977.

ART. 6. No person shall be compelled to give evidence against himself in a criminal case or in any proceeding that may subject him to criminal prosecution, except where otherwise provided in this constitution; nor be deprived of life, liberty or property without due process of law.

ART. 7. In all criminal prosecutions the accused shall enjoy the right to a speedy public trial by an impartial jury, except that, in cases where the penalty is not necessarily imprisonment at hard labor or death the general assembly may provide for the trial thereof by a jury less than twelve in number; *provided*, that the accused in every instance shall be tried in the parish wherein the offence shall have been committed, except in cases of change of venue. Acts 1880, p. 35, No. 35, sec. 4; D. sec. 1021, 1031.

ART. 8. In all criminal prosecutions the accused shall enjoy the right to be informed of the nature and cause of the accusation, to be confronted with the witnesses against him, to have compulsory process for obtaining witnesses in his favor, and to defend himself and to have the assistance of counsel, and to have the right to challenge jurors peremptorily, the number of challenges to be fixed by statute. D. sec. 992.

ART. 9. Excessive bail shall not be required, nor excessive fines be imposed, nor cruel and unusual punishments inflicted. All persons shall be bailable by sufficient sureties, unless for capital offences, where the proof is evident or the presumption great, or unless after conviction for any crime or offence punishable with death or imprisonment at hard labor. D. sec. 1010, 1011.

ART. 10. The privilege of the writ of *habeas corpus* shall not be suspended, unless when, in case of rebellion or invasion, the public safety may require it. C. P., art. 791.

ART. 11. All courts shall be open, and every person for injury done him in his rights, lands, goods, person or reputation, shall have adequate remedy by due process of law and justice, administered without denial or unreasonable delay.

ART. 12. The military shall be in subordination to the civil power.

ART. 13. This enumeration of rights shall not be construed to deny or impair other rights of the people not herein expressed.

DISTRIBUTION OF POWERS.

ART. 14. The powers of the government of the State of Louisiana shall be divided into three distinct departments, and each of them be confided to a separate body of magistracy, to-wit: Those which are legislative to one, those which are executive to another, and those which are judicial to another.

ART. 15. No one of these departments, nor any person or collection of persons holding office in one of them, shall exercise power properly belonging to either of the others, except in the instances hereinafter expressly directed or permitted.

LEGISLATIVE DEPARTMENT.

Apportionment.

ART. 16. Representation in the house of representatives shall be [q]ual and uniform, and shall be regulated and ascertained by the total population. Each parish shall have at least one representative. The first enumeration to be made by the State authorities under this constitution shall be made in the year eighteen hundred and ninety; and subsequent enumerations shall be made every tenth year thereafter, in such manner as shall be prescribed by law, for the purpose of ascertaining the total population and the number of qualified electors in each parish and election district. At its first regular session after each enumeration the general assembly shall apportion the representation among the several parishes and election districts on the basis of the total population as aforesaid. A representative number shall be fixed; and each parish and election district shall have as many representatives as the aggregate number of its population will entitle it to, and an additional representative for any fraction exceed-. ing one-half the representative number. The number of representatives shall not be more than ninety-eight nor less than seventy.

ART. 17. The general assembly, in every year in which they shall apportion representation in the house of representatives, shall divide the State into senatorial districts. No parish shall be divided in the formation of a senatorial district—the parish of Orleans excepted. Whenever a new parish shall be created it shall be attached to the senatorial district from which most of its territory was taken, or to another contiguous district, at the discretion of the general assembly, but shall not be attached to more than one district. The number of senators shall not be more than thirty-six nor less than twenty-four, and they shall be apportioned among the senatorial districts according to the total population contained in the several districts.

ART. 18. Until an enumeration shall be made in accordance with articles sixteen and seventeen the State shall be divided into the following senatorial districts, with the number of senators hereinafter designated to each district:

The first senatorial district shall be composed of the eighth and ninth wards of Orleans, and of the parishes of St. Bernard and Plaquemines, and shall elect two senators.

The second district shall be composed of the fourth, fifth, sixth and seventh wards of Orleans and shall elect two senators.

The third district shall be composed of the third ward of Orleans, and shall elect one senator.

The fourth district shall be composed of the second and fifteenth wards (Orleans right bank) of Orleans, and shall elect one senator.

The fifth district shall be composed of the first and tenth wards of Orleans, and shall elect one senator.

The sixth district shall be composed of the eleventh, twelfth, thirteenth, fourteenth, sixteenth and seventeenth wards of Orleans, and shall elect two senators.

The seventh district shall be composed of the parishes of Jefferson, St. Charles and St. John the Baptist, and shall elect one senator.

The eighth district shall be composed of the parishes of St. James and Ascension, and shall elect one senator.

The ninth district shall be composed of the parishes of Terrebonne, Lafourche and Assumption, and shall elect two senators.

The tenth district shall be composed of the parishes of St. Mary, Vermillion, Cameron and Calcasieu, and shall elect two senators.

The eleventh district shall be composed of the parishes of St. Martin, Iberia and Lafayette, and shall elect one senator.

The twelfth district shall be composed of the parish of St. Landry, and shall elect two senators.

The thirteenth district shall be composed of the parishes of Avoyelles and Pointe Coupée, and shall elect one senator.

The fourteenth district shall be composed of the parishes of Iberville and West Baton Rouge, and shall elect one senator.

The fifteenth district shall be composed of the parishes of East and West Feliciana, and shall elect one senator.

The sixteenth district shall be composed of the parish of East Baton Rouge, and shall elect one senator.

The seventeenth district shall be composed of the parishes of St. Helena, Livingston, Tangipahoa, Washington and St. Tammany, and shall elect one senator.

The eighteenth district shall be composed of the parishes of Rapides and Vernon, and shall elect one senator.

The nineteenth district shall be composed of the parishes of Natchitoches, Sabine, DeSoto and Red River, and shall elect two senators

The twentieth district shall be composed of the parish of Caddo, and shall elect one senator.

The twenty-first district shall be composed of the parishes of Bossier, Webster, Bienville and Claiborne, and shall elect two senators.

The twenty-second district shall be composed of the parishes of Union, Morehouse, Lincoln and West Carroll, and shall elect two senators.

The twenty-third district shall be composed of the parishes of Ouachita, Richland, Caldwell, Franklin and Jackson, and shall elect two senators.

The twenty-fourth district shall be composed of the parishes of Catahoula, Winn and Grant, and shall elect one senator.

The twenty-fifth district shall be composed of the parishes of East Carroll and Madison, and shall elect one senator.

The twenty-sixth district shall be composed of the parishes of Tensas and Concordia, and shall elect one senator.

Thirty-six senators in all.

And the representatives shall be apportioned among the parishes and representative districts as follows: For the parish of Orleans:

First representative district, first ward, one representative.

Second representative district, second ward, two representatives.

Third representative district, third ward, three representatives.

Fourth representative district, fourth ward, one representative.

Fifth representative district, fifth ward, two representatives.

Sixth representative district, sixth ward, one representative.

Seventh representative district, seventh ward, two representatives.

Eighth representative district, eighth ward, one representative.

Ninth representative district, ninth ward, two representatives.

Tenth representative district, tenth ward, two representatives.

Eleventh representative district, eleventh ward, two representatives.

Twelfth representative district, twelfth ward, one representative.

Thirteenth representative district, thirteenth and fourteenth wards, one representative.

Fourteenth representative district, sixteenth and seventeenth wards, one representative.

Fifteenth representative district, fifteenth ward, one representative.

The parishes of Ascension, West Baton Bouge, Bienville, Bossier, Calcasieu, Caldwell, Cameron, East Carroll, West Carroll, Catahoula, Concordia, West Feliciana, Franklin, Grant, Iberia, Jackson, Jefferson, Lafayette, Lincoln, Livingston, Morehouse, Ouachita, Plaquemines, Pointe Coupée, Red River, Richland, Sabine, St. Bernard, St. Charles, St. Helena, St. James, St. John the Baptist, St. Martin, St. Tammany, Tangipahoa, Union, Vermillion, Vernon, Washington, Webster and Winn, each one representative.

The parishes of Assumption, Avoyelles, East Baton Rouge, Caddo, Claiborne, DeSoto, East Feliciana, Iberville, Lafourche, Madison, Natchitoches, Rapides, St. Mary, Tensas and Terrebonne, each two representatives.

The parish of St. Landry four representatives.

This apportionment of senators and representatives shall not be changed or altered in any manner until after the enumeration shall have been taken by the State in eighteen hundred and ninety, in accordance with the provisions of articles sixteen and seventeen.

GENERAL ASSEMBLY.

ART. 19. The legislative power of the State shall be vested in a general assembly, which shall consist of a senate and house of representatives.

ART. 20. The style of the laws of this State shall be, Be it enacted by the general assembly of the State of Louisiana.

ART. 21. The general assembly shall meet at the seat of government on the second Monday of May, eighteen hundred and eighty-two, at twelve o'clock noon, and biennially thereafter. Its first session under this constitution may extend to a period of ninety days, but any subsequent session shall be limited to a period of sixty days. Should a vacancy occur in either house the governor shall order an election to fill such vacancy for the remainder of the term.

ART. 22. Every elector under this constitution shall be eligible to a seat in the house of representatives, and every elector who has reached the age of twenty-five years shall be eligible to the senate; *provided*, that no person shall be eligible to the general assembly unless at the time of his election he has been a citizen of the State for five years, and an actual resident of the district or parish from which he may be elected for two years immediately preceding his election. The seat of any member who may change his residence from the district or parish which he represents shall thereby be vacated, any declaration of a retention of domicile to the contrary notwithstanding; and members of the general assembly shall be elected for a term of four years.

ART. 23. Each house shall judge of the qualifications, election and returns of its own members, choose its own officers, except president of the senate, determine the rules of its proceedings, and may punish its members for disorderly conduct and contempt, and, with the concurrence of two-thirds of all its members elected, expel a member.

ART. 24. Either house, during the session, may punish by imprisonment any person not a member who shall have been guilty of disrespect by disorderly or contemptuous behavior, but such imprisonment shall not exceed ten days for each offence.

ART. 25. No senator or representative shall, during the term for which he was elected, nor for one year thereafter, be appointed or elected to any civil office of profit under this State which may have been created or the emoluments of which may have been increased by the general assembly during the time such senator or representative was a member thereof.

ART. 26. The members of the general assembly shall in all cases, except treason, felony and breach of the peace, be privileged from arrest during their attendance at the sessions of their respective houses, and in going to and returning from the same; and for any speech or debate in either house they shall not be questioned in any other place. D. sec. 1538.

ART. 27. The members of the general assembly shall receive a compensation not to exceed four dollars per day during their attendance, and their actual traveling expenses going to and returning from the seat of government; but in no instance shall more than thirty dollars each way be allowed for traveling expenses. D. sec. 1532, 1535.

ART. 28. Each house shall keep a journal of its proceedings and cause the same to be published immediately after the close of the session. When practicable the minutes of each day's session shall be printed and placed in the hands of members on the day following. The original journal shall be preserved after publication in the office of the secretary of State, but there shall be required no other record thereof.

ART. 29. Every law enacted by the general assembly shall embrace but one object, and that shall be expressed in the title.

ART. 30. No law shall be revived or amended by reference to its title, but in such cases the act revived or section as amended shall be re-enacted and published at length.

ART. 31. The general assembly shall never adopt any system or code of laws by general reference to such system or code of laws, but in all cases shall recite at length the several provisions of the laws it may enact.

ART. 32. Not less than a majority of the members of each house of the general assembly shall form a quorum to transact business; but a smaller number may adjourn from day to day, and shall have power to compel the attendance of absent members.

ART. 33. Neither house during the session of the general assembly shall, without the consent of the other, adjourn for more than three days nor to any other place than that in which it may be sitting.

ART. 34. The yeas and nays on any question in either house shall, at the desire of one-fifth of the members elected, be entered on the journal.

ART. 35. All bills for raising revenue or appropriating money shall riginate in the house of representatives, but the senate may propose r concur in amendments as in other bills.

Art. 36. No bill, ordinance or resolution, intended to have the effect of a law, which shall have been rejected by either house, shall be again proposed in the same house during the same session, under the same or any other title, without the consent of a majority of the house by which the same was rejected.

Art. 37. Every bill shall be read on three different days in each house, and no bill shall be considered for final passage unless it has been read once in full, and the same has been reported on by a committee; nor shall any bill become a law unless, on its final passage, the vote be taken by yeas and nays, the names of the members voting for or against the same be entered on the journal, and a majority of the members elected to each house be recorded thereon as voting in its favor.

Art. 38. No amendment to bills by one house shall be concurred in by the other, except by a vote of a majority of the members elected thereto, taken by yeas and nays, and the names of those voting for or against recorded upon the journal thereof. And reports of committees of conference shall be adopted in either house only by a majority of the members elected thereto, the vote to be taken by yeas and nays, and the names of those voting for or against recorded upon the journal.

Art. 39. Whenever a bill that has been passed by both houses is enrolled and placed in possession of the house in which it originated the title shall be read, and, at the request of any five members, the bill shall be read in full, when the speaker of the house of representatives or the president of the senate, as the case may be, shall act at once, sign it in open house, and the fact of signing shall be noted on the journal; thereupon the clerk or secretary shall immediately convey the bill to the other house, whose presiding officer shall cause a suspension of all other business to read and sign the bill in open session and without delay. As soon as bills are signed by the speaker of the house and president of the senate they shall be taken at once and on the same day to the governor by the clerk of the house or secretary of the senate.

Art. 40. No law passed by the general assembly, except the general appropriation act, or act appropriating money for the expenses of the general assembly, shall take effect until promulgated. A law shall be considered promulgated at the place where the State journal is published the day after the publication of such law in the State journal, and in all other parts of the State twenty days after such publication.

Art. 41. The clerical officers of the two houses shall be a secretary of the senate and clerk of the house of representatives, with such assistants as may be necessary; but the expenses for clerks and employés shall not exceed sixty dollars daily for the senate nor seventy dollars daily for the house.

Art. 42. All stationery, printing, paper and fuel used in the legislative and other departments of government shall be furnished, and the printing, binding and distributing of the laws, journal and department reports, and all other printing and binding, and the repairing and furnishing the halls and rooms used for the meetings of the general assembly and its committees, shall be done under contract, to be given to the lowest responsible bidder, below such maximum pric and under such regulations as shall be prescribed by law; *provided*, that such contracts shall be awarded only to citizens of the State. No member or officer of any of the departments of the government shall be in any way interested in such contracts; and all such contracts shall be subject to the approval of the governor, the president of the senate and speaker of the house of representatives, or of any two of them. D. sec. 2986, 3005.

LIMITATION OF LEGISLATIVE POWERS.

ART. 43. No money shall be drawn from the treasury except in pursuance of specific appropriation made by law; nor shall any appropriation of money be made for a longer term than two years. A regular statement and account of receipts and expenditures of all public moneys shall be published every three months, in such manner as shall be prescribed by law.

ART. 44. The general assembly shall have no power to contract or to authorize the contracting of any debt or liability, on behalf of the State, or to issue bonds or other evidence of indebtedness thereof, except for the purpose of repelling invasion or for the suppression of insurrection.

ART. 45. The general assembly shall have no power to grant or to authorize any parish or municipal authority to grant any extra compensation, fee or allowance to a public officer, agent, servant or contractor, nor pay nor authorize the payment of any claim against the State, or any parish or municipality of the State, under any agreement or contract made without express authority of law; and all such unauthorized agreements or contracts shall be null and void. D. sec. 2448. 2743.

ART. 46. The general assembly shall not pass any local or special law on the following specified objects:

For the opening and conducting of elections, or fixing or changing the place of voting.

Changing the names of persons.

Changing the venue in civil or criminal cases.

Authorizing the laying out, opening, closing, altering or maintaining roads, highways, streets or alleys, or relating to ferries and bridges, or incorporating bridge or ferry companies, except for the erection of bridges crossing streams which form boundaries between this and any other State.

Authorizing the adoption or legitimation of children or the emancipation of minors.

Granting divorces.

Changing the law of descent or succession.

Affecting the estates of minors or persons under disabilities.

Remitting fines, penalties and forfeitures, or refunding moneys legally paid into the treasury.

Authorizing the constructing of street passenger railroads in any ⁻rporated town or city.

gulating labor, trade, manufacturing or agriculture.

eating corporations, or amending, renewing, extending or lining the charter thereof; *provided*, that this shall not apply to the corporation of the city of New Orleans, or to the organization of levee districts and parishes.

Granting to any corporation, association or individual, any special or exclusive right, privilege or immunity.

Extending the time for the assessment or collection of taxes, or for the relief of any assessor or collector of taxes, from the due performance of his official duties, or of his securities from liability; nor shall any such be passed by any political corporation of this State.

Regulating the practice or jurisdiction of any court, or changing the rules of evidence in any judicial proceeding or inquiry before courts, or providing or changing methods for the collection of debts, or the enforcement of judgments, or prescribing the effects of judicial sales.

Exemption of property from taxation.

Fixing the rate of interest.

Concerning any civil or criminal actions.

Giving effect to informal or invalid wills or deeds, or to any illegal disposition of property.

Regulating the management of public schools, the building or repairing of schoolhouses, and the raising of money for such purposes.

Legalizing the unauthorized or invalid acts of any officer, servant or agent of the State, or of any parish or municipality thereof.

ART. 47. The general assembly shall not indirectly enact special or local laws by the partial repeal of a general law; but laws repealing local or special laws may be passed.

ART. 48. No local or special law shall be passed on any subject not enumerated in article forty-six of this constitution, unless notice of the intention to apply therefor shall have been published, without cost to the State, in the locality where the matter or thing to be affected may be situated, which notice shall state the substance of the contemplated law, and shall be published at least thirty days prior to the introduction into the general assembly of such bill, and in the same manner provided by law for the advertisement of judicial sales. The evidence of such notice having been published shall be exhibited in the general assembly before such act shall be passed, and every such act shall contain a recital that such notice has been given.

ART. 49. No law shall be passed fixing the price of manual labor.

ART. 50. Any member of the general assembly who has a personal or private interest in any measure or bill proposed or pending before the general assembly shall disclose the fact to the house of which he is a member, and shall not vote thereon.

ART. 51. No money shall ever be taken from the public treasury, directly or indirectly, in aid of any church, sect or denomination of religion, or in aid of any priest, preacher, minister or teacher thereof, as such; and no preference shall ever be given to, nor any discrimination made against any church, sect or creed of religion, or any form of religious faith or worship; nor shall any appropriations be made for private, charitable or benevolent purposes to any person or community; *provided*, this shall not apply to the State asylums for the insane and deaf, dumb and blind, and the charity hospitals and publi charitable institutions conducted under State authority.

ART. 52. The general assembly shall have no power to increase the expenses of any office by appointing assistant officials.

ART. 53. The general appropriation bill shall embrace nothing but appropriations for the ordinary expenses of the government, interest on the public debt, public schools and public charities, and such bill shall be so itemized as to show for what account each and every appropriation shall be made. All other appropriations shall be made by separate bills, each embracing but one object.

ART. 54. Each appropriation shall be for a specific purpose, and no appropriation shall be made under the head or title of contingent; nor shall any officer or department of government receive any amount from the treasury for contingencies or for a contingent fund.

ART. 55. No appropriation of money shall be made by the general assembly in the last five days of the session thereof. All appropriations, to be valid, shall be passed and receive the signatures of the president of the senate and speaker of the house of representatives five full days before the adjournment *sine die* of the general assembly.

ART. 56. The funds, credit, property or things of value of the State, or of any political corporation thereof, shall not be loaned, pledged or granted to or for any person or persons, association or corporation, public or private; nor shall the State or any political corporation purchase or subscribe to the capital or stock of any corporation or association whatever, or for any private enterprise; nor shall the State nor any political corporation thereof assume the liabilities of any political, municipal, parochial, private or other corporation or association whatsoever; nor shall the State undertake to carry on the business of any such corporation or association, or become a part owner therein; *provided*, the State, through the general assembly, shall have power to grant the right of way through its public lands to any railroad or canal. D. sec. 711, 724.

ART. 57. The general assembly shall have no power to release or extinguish, or to authorize the releasing or extinguishing, in whole or in part, the indebtedness, liability or obligation of any corporation or individual to this State, or to any parish or municipal corporation therein; *provided*, the heirs to confiscated property may be released of all taxes due thereon at the date of its reversion to them.

EXECUTIVE DEPARTMENT.

ART. 58. The executive department shall consist of a governor, lieutenant-governor, auditor, treasurer and secretary of State.

ART. 59. The supreme executive power of the State shall be vested in a chief magistrate, who shall be styled the governor of Louisiana. He shall hold his office during four years and, together with the lieutenant-governor, chosen for the same term, shall be elected as follows: The qualified electors for representatives shall vote for a governor and lieutenant-governor at the time and place of voting for representatives. The returns of every election for governor and lieutenant-nor shall be sealed up separately from the returns of election of officers, and be transmitted by the proper officer of every parish e secretary of State, who shall deliver them, unopened, to the al assembly then next to be holden. The members of the general assembly shall meet on the first Thursday after the day on which they assemble, in the house of representatives, to examine and count the votes. The person having the greatest number of votes for governor shall be declared duly elected; but in case two or more persons shall be equal and highest in the number of votes polled for governor, one of them shall be immediately chosen governor by the joint vote of the members of the general assembly. The person having the greatest number of votes for lieutenant-governor shall be lieutenant-governor; but if two or more persons shall be equal and highest in number of votes polled for lieutenant-governor, one of them shall be immediately chosen lieutenant-governor by joint vote of the members of the general assembly.

ART. 60. No person shall be eligible to the office of governor or lieutenant-governor who shall not have attained the age of thirty years, been ten years a citizen of the United States, and a resident of the State for the same space of time next preceding his election, or who shall be a member of congress, or shall hold office under the United States at the time of or within six months immediately preceding the election for such office.

ART. 61. The governor shall enter on the discharge of his duties the first Monday next ensuing the announcement by the general assembly of the result of the election for governor; and shall continue in office until the Monday next succeeding the day that his successor shall have been declared duly elected and shall have taken the oath or affirmation required by this constitution.

ART. 62. In case of the impeachment of the governor, his removal from office, death, refusal or inability to qualify, disability, resignation or absence from the State, the powers and duties of the office shall devolve upon the lieutenant-governor for the residue of the term, or until the governor, absent or impeached, shall return or be acquitted or the disability be removed. In the event of the death, or from whatever cause the office of lieutenant-governor shall become vacant, then, and in that event, the president *pro tem.* of the senate shall fill the office of lieutenant-governor, performing all the duties incident to the office and receiving its emoluments.

ART. 63. The lieutenant-governor or officer discharging the duties of governor shall, during his administration, receive the same compensation to which the governor would have been entitled had he continued in office.

ART. 64. The lieutenant-governor shall by virtue of his office, be president of the senate, but shall have only a casting vote therein. The senate shall elect one of its members as president *pro tempore* of the senate.

ART. 65. The lieutenant-governor shall receive for his services a salary which shall be double that of a member of the general assembly, and no more.

ART. 66. The governor shall have power to grant reprieves for all offences against the State; and, except in cases of impeachment or treason, shall, upon the recommendation in writing of the lieutenant-governor, attorney-general and presiding judge of the court before which conviction was had, or of any two of them, have power to grant pardons, commute sentences and remit fines and forfeitures after conviction. In cases of treason he may grant reprieves until the end of the next session of the general assembly, in which body the power of pardoning is vested.

ART. 67. The governor shall receive a salary of four thousand dollars per annum, payable monthly on his own warrant.

ART. 68. He shall nominate and, by and with the advice and consent of the senate, appoint all officers whose offices are established by this constitution, and whose appointments or elections are not herein otherwise provided for; *provided*, however, that the general assembly shall have the right to prescribe the mode of appointment or election to all offices created by it.

ART. 69. The governor shall have the power to fill vacancies that may happen during the recess of the senate, in cases not otherwise provided for in this constitution, by granting commissions, which shall expire at the end of the next session; but no person who has been nominated for office and rejected shall be appointed to the same office during the recess of the senate. The failure of the governor to send into the senate the name of any person appointed for office, as herein provided, shall be equivalent to a rejection. D. sec. 2606.

ART. 70. He may require information in writing from the officers in the executive department upon any subject relating to the duties of their respective offices. He shall be commander-in-chief of the militia of the State, except when they shall be called into the actual service of the United States.

ART. 71. He shall from time to time give to the general assembly information respecting the situation of the State, and recommend to its consideration such measures as he may deem expedient.

ART. 72. He shall take care that the laws be faithfully executed, and he may, on extraordinary occasions, convene the general assembly at the seat of government, or, if that should have become dangerous from an enemy or from an epidemic, at a different place. The power to legislate shall be limited to the objects enumerated specifically in the proclamation convening such extraordinary session. Therein the governor shall also limit the time such session may continue; *provided*, it shall not exceed twenty days. Any legislative action had after the time so limited, or as to other objects than those enumerated in said proclamation, shall be null and void.

ART. 73. Every bill which shall have passed both houses shall be presented to the governor. If he approve, he shall sign it; if not, he shall return it, with his objections, to the house in which it originated. which house shall enter the objections at large upon the journal and proceed to reconsider it. If, after such reconsideration, two-thirds of all the members elected to that house shall agree to pass the bill, it shall be sent, with the objections, to the other house, by which likewise it shall be reconsidered, and if passed by two-thirds of the members elected to that house it shall be a law; but in such cases the votes of both houses shall be taken by yeas and nays, and the names ʾhe members voting for and against the bill shall be entered on ɔurnal of each house respectively. If any bill shall not be re- d by the governor within five days after it shall have been pre- d to him, the same shall be a law in like manner as if he had signed it, unless the general assembly, by adjournment, shall prevent its return, in which case it shall not be a law.

ART. 74. The governor shall have power to disapprove of any item or items of any bill making appropriations of money, embracing distinct items; and the part or parts of the bill approved shall be law, and the item or items of appropriation disapproved shall be void, unless repassed according to the rules and limitations prescribed for the passage of other bills over the executive veto.

ART. 75. Every order, resolution or vote to which the concurrence of both houses may be necessary, except on a question of adjournment or on matters of parliamentary proceedings, or an address for the removal from office, shall be presented to the governor, and before it shall take effect be approved by him, or, being disapproved, shall be repassed by two-thirds of the members elected to each house.

ART. 76. The treasurer, auditor, attorney-general and secretary of State shall be elected by the qualified electors of the State for the term of four years; and in case of vacancy caused by death, resignation or permanent absence of either of said officers, the governor shall fill such vacancy by appointment, with the advice and consent of the senate; *provided*, however, that notwithstanding such appointment, such vacancy shall be filled by election at the next election after the occurrence of the vacancy.

ART. 77. The auditor of public accounts shall receive a salary of two thousand five hundred dollars per annum; the treasurer shall receive a salary of two thousand dollars per annum, and the secretary of State shall receive a salary of one thousand eight hundred dollars per annum. Each of the before named officers shall be paid monthly, and no fees or perquisites or other compensation shall be allowed to said officers; *provided*, that the secretary of State may be allowed fees as may be provided by law for copies and certificates furnished to private persons.

ART. 78. Appropriations for the clerical expenses of the officers named in the preceding article shall specify each item of such appropriations; and shall not exceed in any one year, for the treasurer, the sum of two thousand dollars; for the secretary of State, the sum of one thousand five hundred dollars, and for the auditor of public accounts, the sum of four thousand dollars.

ART. 79. All commissions shall be in the name and by the authority of the State of Louisiana, and shall be sealed with the State seal, signed by the governor and countersigned by the secretary of State.

JUDICIARY DEPARTMENT.

ART. 80 The judicial power shall be vested in a supreme court, in courts of appeal, in district courts and in justices of the peace.

ART. 81. The supreme court, except in cases hereinafter provided, shall have appellate jurisdiction only, which jurisdiction shall extend to all cases when the matter in dispute or the fund to be distributed, whatever may be the amount therein claimed, shall exceed two thousand dollars, exclusive of interest; to suits for divorce and separation from bed and board; to suits for nullity of marriage; to suits involving the rights to homesteads; to suits for interdiction,* and to all cases in which the constitutionality or legality of any tax, toll or impost whatever, or of any fine, forfeiture or penalty imposed by municipal corporation, shall be in contestation, whatever may be the amount thereof; and in such cases the appeal on the law and facts shall be directly from the court in which the case originated to the supreme court; and to criminal cases on questions of law alone, whenever the punishment of death or imprisonment at hard labor may be inflicted, or a fine exceeding three hundred dollars is actually imposed. D. sec. 1913.

ART. 82. The supreme court shall be composed of one chief-justice and four associate justices, a majority of whom shall constitute a quorum. The chief-justice and associate justices shall each receive a salary of five thousand dollars per annum, payable monthly on their own warrants. They shall be appointed by the governor, by and with the advice and consent of the senate. The first supreme court to be organized under this constitution shall be appointed as follows: The chief-justice for the term of twelve years; one associate justice for the term of ten years; one for the term of eight years; one for the term of six years; one for the term of four years; and the governor shall designate in the commission of each the term for which such judge is appointed. In case of death, resignation or removal from office of any of said judges the vacancy shall be filled by appointment for the unexpired term of said judge; and upon expiration of the term of any of said judges the office shall be filled by appointment for a term of twelve years. They shall be citizens of the United States and of the State, over thirty-five years of age, learned in the law, and shall have practised law in this State ten years preceding their appointment.

ART. 83. The State shall be divided into four supreme court districts, and the supreme court shall always be composed of judges appointed from said districts. The parishes of Orleans, St. John the Baptist, St. Charles, St. Bernard, Plaquemines and Jefferson shall compose the first district, from which two judges shall be appointed. The parishes of Caddo, Bossier, Webster, Bienville, Claiborne, Union, Lincoln, Jackson, Caldwell, Ouachita, Morehouse, Richland, Franklin, West Carroll, East Carroll, Madison, Tensas and Catahoula shall compose the second district, from which one judge shall be appointed. The parishes of De Soto, Red River, Winn, Grant, Natchitoches, Sabine, Vernon, Calcasieu, Cameron, Rapides, Avoyelles, Concordia, Pointe Coupée, West Baton Rouge, Iberville, St. Landry, Lafayette and Vermillion shall compose the third district, from which one judge shall be appointed. And the parishes of St. Martin, Iberia, St. Mary, Terrebonne, Lafourche, Assumption, St. James, Ascension, East Baton Rouge, East Feliciana, West Feliciana, St. Helena, Livingston, Tangipahoa, St. Tammany and Washington shall compose the fourth district, from which one judge shall be appointed.

ART. 84. The supreme court shall hold its sessions in the city of ew Orleans from the first Monday in the month of November to the

---

*As Amended in 1882.

end of the month of May in each and every year. The general assembly shall have power to fix the sessions elsewhere during the rest of the year. Until otherwise provided the sessions shall be held as heretofore. They shall appoint their own clerks and remove them at pleasure. D. 1894.

ART. 85. No judgment shall be rendered by the supreme court without the concurrence of three judges. Whenever three members can not concur, in consequence of the recusation of any member or members of the court, the judges not recused shall have authority to call upon any judge or judges of the district courts, whose duty it shall be, when so called upon, to sit in the place of the judge or judges recused, and to aid in the determination of the case.

ART. 86. All judges, by virtue of their office, shall be conservators of the peace throughout the State. The style of all process shall be "the State of Louisiana." All prosecutions shall be carried on in the name and by the authority of the State of Louisiana, and conclude, "against the peace and dignity of the same."

ART. 87. The judges of all courts, whenever practicable, shall refer to the law by virtue of which every definitive judgment is rendered; but in all cases they shall adduce the reasons on which their judgment is founded.

ART. 88. There shall be a reporter of the decisions of the supreme court, who shall report in full all cases which he may be required to report by law or by the court. He shall publish in the reports the title, numbers and head notes of all cases decided, whether reported in full or not. In all cases reported in full he shall make a brief statement of the principal points presented and authorities cited by counsel. He shall be appointed by a majority of the court, and hold his office and be removable at their pleasure. His salary shall be fixed by the court, and shall not exceed fifteen hundred dollars per annum, payable monthly on his own warrant. D. sec. 3221, 3229.

ART. 89. The supreme court and each of the judges thereof shall have power to issue writs of *habeas corpus* at the instance of all persons in actual custody, in cases where it may have appellate jurisdiction. C. P., art. 792.

ART. 90. The supreme court shall have control and general supervision over all inferior courts. They shall have power to issue writs of *certiorari*, prohibition, mandamus, *quo warranto* and other remedial writs.

ART. 91. The general assembly shall provide for appeals from the district courts to the supreme court upon questions of law alone, when the party or parties aggrieved desire only a review of the law.

ART. 92. Except as herein provided no duties or functions shall ever be attached by law to the supreme court, courts of appeal or district courts, or the several judges thereof, but such as are judicial; and the said judges are prohibited from receiving any fees of office or other compensation than their salaries for any official duties performed by them. No judicial powers, except as committing magistrates in criminal cases, shall be conferred on any officers other than those mentioned in this title, except such as may be necessary in towns and cities; and the judicial powers of such officers shall not extend further than the cognizance of cases arising under the police regulations of towns and cities in the State.

ART. 93. The judges of all courts shall be liable to impeachment for crimes and misdemeanors. For any reasonable cause the governor shall remove any of them on the address of two-thirds of the members elected to each house of the general assembly. In every case the cause or causes for which such removal may be required shall be stated at length in the address, and inserted in the journal of each house.

ATTORNEY-GENERAL.

ART. 94. There shall be an attorney-general for the State, who shall be elected by the qualified electors of the State at large every four years. He shall be learned in the law, and shall have actually resided and practised law as a licensed attorney in the State five years next preceding his election. He shall receive a salary of three thousand dollars per annum, payable monthly on his own warrant.

COURTS OF APPEAL.

ART. 95.* The courts of appeal, except in cases hereinafter provided, shall have appellate jurisdiction only, which jurisdiction shall extend to all cases, civil or probate. when the matter in dispute or the funds to be distributed shall exceed one hundred dollars, exclusive of interest, and shall not exceed two thousand dollars, exclusive of interest.

ART. 96. The courts of appeal shall be composed of two circuit judges, who shall be elected by the two houses of the general assembly in joint session. The first judges of the courts of appeal under this constitution shall be elected for the following terms: One judge for each court for the term of four years and one judge for the term of eight years. They shall be learned in the law, and shall have resided and practised law in this State for six years, and shall have been actual residents of the circuit from which they shall be elected for at least two years next preceding their election.

ART. 97. The State, with the exception of the parish of Orleans, shall be divided into five circuits, from each of which two judges shall be elected. Until otherwise provided by law the parishes of Caddo, Bossier, Webster, Bienville, DeSoto, Red River, Claiborne, Union, Lincoln, Natchitoches, Sabine, Jackson, Winn and Caldwell shall compose the first circuit.

The parishes of Ouachita, Richland, Morehouse, West Carroll, Catahoula, Franklin, Madison, East Carroll, Concordia and Tensas shall compose the second circuit.

The parishes of Rapides, Grant, Avoyelles, St. Landry, Vernon, Calcasieu, Cameron, Lafayette, Vermillion, St. Martin and Iberia shall compose the third circuit.

The parishes of East Baton Rouge, West Baton Rouge, Iberville, ⁻ast Feliciana, St. Helena, Tangipahoa, Livingston, St. Tammany,

---

* As amended in 1882.

Washington, Pointe Coupée and West Feliciana shall compose the fourth circuit.

And the parishes of St. Mary, Terrebonne, Ascension, Lafourche, Assumption, Plaquemines, St. Bernard, Jefferson, St. Charles, St. John the Baptist and St. James shall compose the fifth circuit.

ART. 98. The judges of the courts of appeal, until otherwise provided by law, shall hold two terms annually in each parish composing their respective circuits.

ART. 99. Until otherwise provided by law the terms of the circuit courts of appeal shall be as follows:

First Circuit.

Caddo—First Mondays in January and June.
Bossier—Third Mondays in January and June.
Webster—First Mondays in February and July.
Bienville—Second Mondays in February and July.
Claiborne—Third Mondays in February and July.
Union—First Mondays in March and October.
Lincoln—Second Mondays in March and October.
Jackson—Third Mondays in March and October.
Caldwell—Fourth Mondays in March and October.
Winn—First Mondays in April and November.
Natchitoches—Second Mondays in April and November.
Sabine—Fourth Mondays in April and November.
De Soto—First Mondays in May and December.
Red River—Third Mondays in May and December.

Second Circuit.

Ouachita—First Mondays in January and June.
Richland—Fourth Mondays in January and June.
Franklin—First Mondays in February and July.
Catahoula–Second Mondays in February and July.
Concordia—Fourth Mondays in February and July.
Tensas—Second Mondays in March and October.
Madison—Fourth Mondays in March and October.
East Carroll—Second Mondays in April and November.
West Carroll—Fourth Mondays in April and November.
Morehouse—First Mondays in May and December.

Third Circuit.

St. Landry—First Mondays in January and June.
Avoyelles—Fourth Mondays in January and June.
Rapides—Second Mondays in February and July.
Grant—Fourth Mondays in February and July.
Vernon—First Mondays in March and October.
Calcasieu—Second Mondays in March and October.
Cameron—Fourth Mondays in March and October.
Vermillion—First Mondays in April and November.
Lafayette—Second Mondays in April and November.

Iberia—Fourth Mondays in April and November.
St. Martin—Second Mondays in May and December.

Fourth Circuit.

East Baton Rouge—First Mondays in January and June.
West Baton Rouge—Fourth Mondays in January and June.
Livingston—First Mondays in February and July.
Tangipahoa—Second Mondays in February and July.
St. Tammany—Fourth Mondays in February and July.
Washington—First Mondays in March and October.
St. Helena—Second Mondays in March and October.
East Feliciana—Fourth Mondays in March and October.
West Feliciana—Second Mondays in April and November.
Pointe Coupée—Fourth Mondays in April and November.
Iberville—Second Mondays in May and December.

Fifth Circuit.

St. Mary—First Mondays in January and June.
Terrebonne—Third Mondays in January and June.
Assumption—First Mondays in February and July.
Lafourche—Third Mondays in February and July.
St. Charles—First Mondays in March and October.
Jefferson—Second Mondays in March and October.
St. Bernard—Fourth Mondays in March and October.
Plaquemines—First Mondays in April and November.
St. John the Baptist—Second Mondays in April and November.
St. James—Third Mondays in April and November.
Ascension—Second Mondays in May and December.

ART. 100. Whenever the first day of the term shall fall on a legal holiday the court shall begin its sessions on the first legal day thereafter.

ART. 101.* Whenever the judges composing the courts of appeal shall concur their judgment shall be final. Whenever there shall be a disagreement the two judges shall appoint a lawyer having the qualifications for a judge of the court of appeals of their circuit, who shall aid in the determination of the case; a judgment concurred in by any two of them shall be final.

ART. 102. All causes on appeal to the courts of appeal shall be tried on the original record, pleadings and evidence in the district court.

ART. 103. The rules of practice regulating appeals to and proceedings in the supreme court shall apply to appeals and proceedings in the courts of appeal, so far as they may be applicable, until otherwise provided by law.

ART. 104. The judges of the courts of appeal shall have power to issue writs of *habeas corpus* at the instance of all persons in actual custody, within their respective circuits. They shall also have
 hority to issue writs of mandamus, prohibition and *certiorari*, in
 f their appellate jurisdiction.

_____

s amended in 1882.

ART. 105. The judges of the courts of appeal shall each receive a salary of four thousand dollars per annum, payably monthly on their respective warrants. The general assembly shall provide by law for the trial of recused cases in the courts of appeal. D. sec. 3190-3195.

ART. 106. The sheriff of the parish in which the sessions of the court are held shall attend in person or by deputy to execute the orders of the court.

District Court.

ART. 107. The State shall be divided into not less than twenty nor more than thirty judicial districts, the parish of Orleans excepted. D. sec. 1927.

ART. 108. Until otherwise provided by law there shall be twenty-six districts.

The parish of Caddo shall compose the first district.

The parishes of Bossier, Webster and Bienville shall compose the second district.

The parishes of Claiborne, Union and Lincoln shall compose the third district.

The parishes of Jackson, Winn and Caldwell shall compose the fourth district.

The parishes of Ouachita and Richland shall compose the fifth district.

The parishes of Morehouse and West Carroll shall compose the sixth district.

The parishes of Catahoula and Franklin shall compose the seventh district.

The parishes of Madison and East Carroll shall compose the eighth district.

The parishes of Concordia and Tensas shall compose the ninth district.

The parishes of DeSoto and Red River shall compose the tenth district.

The parishes of Natchitoches and Sabine shall compose the eleventh district.

The parishes of Rapides, Grant and Avoyelles shall compose the twelfth district.

The parish of St. Landry shall compose the thirteenth district.

The parishes of Vernon, Calcasieu and Cameron shall compose the fourteenth district.

The parishes of Pointe Coupée and West Feliciana shall compose the fifteenth district.

The parishes of East Feliciana and St. Helena shall compose the sixteenth district.

The parish of East Baton Rouge shall compose the seventeenth district.

The parishes of Tangipahoa, Livingston, St. Tammany and Washington shall compose the eighteenth district.

The parishes of St. Mary and Terrebonne shall compose the nineteenth district.

The parishes of Lafourche and Assumption shall compose the twentieth district.

The parishes of St. Martin and Iberia shall compose the twenty-first district.

The parishes of Ascension and St. James shall compose the twenty-second district.

The parishes of West Baton Rouge and Iberville shall compose the twenty-third district.

The parishes of Plaquemines and St. Bernard shall compose the twenty-fourth district.

The parishes of Lafayette and Vermillion shall compose the twenty-fifth district.

And the parishes of Jefferson, St. Charles and St. John the Baptist shall compose the twenty-sixth district.

ART. 109. District courts shall have original jurisdiction in all civil matters where the amount in dispute shall exceed fifty dollars, exclusive of interest. They shall have unlimited original jurisdiction in all criminal, probate and succession matters, and when a succession is a party defendant. The district judges shall be elected by a plurality of the qualified voters of their respective districts in which they shall have been actual residents for two years next preceding their election. They shall be learned in the law, and shall have practised law in the State for five years previous to their election. They shall be elected for the term of four years. All elections to fill vacancies occasioned by death, resignation or removal shall be for the unexpired term, and the governor shall fill the vacancy until an election can be held. The judges of the district courts shall each receive a salary of three thousand dollars per annum, payable monthly on their respective warrants. D. sec. 1930.

ART. 110. The general assembly shall have power to increase the number of district judges in any district whenever the public business may require.

ART. 111. The district courts shall have jurisdiction of appeals from justices of the peace in all matters where the amount in controversy shall exceed ten dollars, exclusive of interest. D. sec. 2047.

ART. 112. The general assembly shall provide by law for the trial of recused cases in the district courts by the selection of licensed attorney-at-laws, by an interchange of judges or otherwise. D. 3190-3195.

ART. 113. Wherever in this constitution the qualification of any justice or judge shall be the previous practice of the law for a term of years, there shall be included in such term the time such justice or judge shall have occupied the bench of any court of record in this State; *provided*, he shall have been a licensed attorney for five years before his election or appointment.

ART. 114. No judge of any court of the State shall be affected in his term of office, salary or jurisdiction as to territory or amount during the term or period for which he was elected or appointed. Any legislation so affecting any judge or court shall take effect only t the end of the term of office of the judges, incumbents of the court r courts to which such legislation may apply at the time of its enactment. This article shall not affect the provisions of this constitution relative to impeachment or removal from office.

ART. 115. The district judges shall have power to issue writs of *habeas corpus* at the instance of all persons in actual custody in their respective districts. C. P., art. 791.

ART. 116. The general assembly at its first session under this constitution shall provide by general law for the selection of competent and intelligent jurors, who shall have capacity to serve as grand jurors and try and determine both civil and criminal cases, and may provide in civil cases that a verdict be rendered by the concurrence of a less number than the whole. C. P., art. 493; D. sec. 2125, 2154; Act 1880, No. 54.

ART. 117.* In those districts composed of one parish there shall not be less than six terms of the district court each year. In all other districts there shall be in each parish not less than four terms of the district court each year, except in the parishes of Cameron, Franklin and Vernon, in which there shall not be less than two terms of the district court each year. Until provided by law the terms of the district court in each parish shall be fixed by a rule of said court, which shall not be changed without notice by publication at least thirty days prior to such change. There shall be in each parish not less than two jury terms each year, at which a grand jury shall be empaneled, except in the parishes of Cameron, Franklin and Vernon, in which there shall not be less than one jury term each year, at which a grand jury shall be empaneled. At other than jury terms the general assembly shall provide for special juries when necessary for the trial of criminal cases. D. sec. 1928.

SHERIFFS AND CORONERS.

ART. 118. There shall be a sheriff and coroner elected by the qualified voters of each parish in the State, except the parish of Orleans, who shall be elected at the general election and hold office for four years. (D 652, 676, 3538, 3539, 3238.) The coroner shall act for and in place of the sheriff whenever the sheriff shall be party interested, and whenever there shall be a vacancy in the office of sheriff until such vacancy shall be filled; but he shall not, during such vacancy, discharge the duties of tax collector. (C. P., art. 760; D. 676.) The sheriff, except in the parish of Orleans, shall be *ex officio* collector of State and parish taxes. He shall give separate bonds for the faithful performance of his duty in each capacity. Until otherwise provided the bonds shall be given according to existing laws. The general assembly, after the adoption of this constitution, shall pass a general law regulating the amount, form, condition and mode of approval of such bonds, so as to fully secure the State and parish; and all parties in interest. Sheriffs elected at the first election under this constitution shall comply with the provisions of such law within thirty days after its promulgation, in default of which the office shall be declared vacant and the governor shall appoint for the remainder of the term.

*ART. 117. As amended in 1886.

ART. 119. Sheriffs shall receive compensation from the parish for their services in criminal matters (the keeping of prisoners, conveying convicts to the penitentiary, insane persons to the insane asylum and service of process from another parish, and service of process or the performance of any duty beyond the limits of his own parish, excepted) not to exceed five hundred dollars per annum for each representative the parish may have in the house of representatives. (D. 3563, 3567.) The compensation of sheriffs as tax-collectors shall not exceed five per cent. on the amount collected and paid over; *provided*, that he shall not be discharged as tax-collector until he makes proof that he has exhausted the legal remedies to collect the taxes.

ART 120. The coroner in each parish shall be a doctor of medicine, regularly licensed to practise, and *ex officio* parish physician; *provided*, this article shall not apply to any pari-h in which there is no regularly licensed physician who will accept the office. D. 650.

CLERKS.

ART. 121. There shall be a clerk of the district court in each parish, the parish of Orleans excepted, who shall be *ex officio* clerk of the court of appeals. (D. 462, 484.) He shall be elected by the qualified electors of the parish every four years, and shall be *ex officio* parish recorder of conveyances, mortgages and other acts, and notary public. He shall receive no compensation for his services from the State or the parish in criminal matters. He shall give bond and security for the faithful performance of his duties, in such amount as shall be fixed by the general assembly.

ART. 122. The general assembly shall have power to vest in clerks of courts authority to grant such orders, and to do such acts as may be deemed necessary for the furtherance of the administration of justice; and in all cases powers thus vested shall be specified and determined.

ART. 123. Clerks of district courts may appoint, with the approval of the district judge, deputies, with such powers as shall be prescribed by law; and the general assembly shall have the power to provide for continuing one or more of them in office, in the event of the death of the clerk, until his successor shall have been appointed and duly qualified.

DISTRICT ATTORNEYS.

ART. 124. There shall be a district attorney for each judicial district in the State, who shall be elected by the qualified electors of the judicial district. He shall receive a salary of one thousand dollars per annum, payable monthly on his own warrant, and shall hold his office for four years. He shall be an actual resident of the district and a licensed attorney-at-law in this State (D. 1140). He shall also receive es; but no fees shall be allowed in criminal cases except on convic-
1. Any vacancy in the office of district attorney shall be filled by ointment by the governor for the unexpired term. There shall be parish attorney or district attorney *pro tempore*. (This article ll not apply to the parish of Orleans.) D. 1142, 1178, 1189.

JUSTICES OF THE PEACE.

ART. 125. In each parish, the parish of Orleans excepted, there shall be as many justices of the peace as may be provided by law (D. 2044, 2045). The present number of justices of the peace shall remain as now fixed until otherwise provided. They shall be elected for the term of four years by the qualified voters within the territorial limits of their jurisdiction. They shall have exclusive original jurisdiction in all civil matters when the amount in dispute shall not exceed fifty dollars, exclusive of interest, and original jurisdiction, concurrent with the district court, when the amount in dispute shall exceed fifty dollars, exclusive of interest, and shall not exceed one hundred dollars, exclusive of interest (D. 2047). They shall have no jurisdiction in succession or probate matters, or when a succession is a defendant. They shall receive such fees or salary as may be fixed by law.

ART. 126. They shall have criminal jurisdiction as committing magistrates, and shall have power to bail or discharge in cases not capital or necessarily punishable at hard labor. D. 2058, 2059.

CONSTABLES.

ART. 127. There shall be a constable for the court of each justice of the peace in the several parishes of the State, the parish of Orleans excepted, who shall be elected for the term of four years by the qualified voters within the territorial limits of the jurisdiction of the several justices of the peace (D. 631). The compensation, salaries or fees of constables and the amount of their bonds shall be fixed by the general assembly.

COURTS OF THE PARISH AND CITY OF NEW ORLEANS.

ART. 128.* There shall be in the parish of Orleans a court of appeals for said parish, with exclusive appellate jurisdiction in all matters, civil or probate, arising in said parish, when the amount in dispute or fund to be distributed exceeds one hundred dollars, interest excluded, and is less than two thousand dollars, exclusive of interest. Said court shall be presided over by two judges, who shall be elected by the general assembly in joint session. They shall be residents and voters of the city of New Orleans, possessing all the qualifications necessary for judges of circuit courts of appeal throughout the State. They shall each receive an annual salary of four thousand dollars, payable monthly upon their respective warrants. Said appeals shall be upon questions of law alone in all cases involving less than five hundred dollars, exclusive of interest, and upon the law and the facts in other cases. It shall sit in the city of New Orleans from the first Monday of November to the last Monday of June of each year. It shall have authority to issue writs of mandamus, prohibition, *certiorari* and *habeas corpus* in aid of its appellate jurisdiction.

ART. 129. The provisions of this constitution relating to the term of office, qualifications and salary of the judges of the circuit courts

---

* As amended in 1882.

of appeal throughout the State, and the manner of proceeding and determining causes, as applicable to such circuit courts of appeal, shall apply to this court and its judges, in so far as such provisions are not in conflict with the provisions specially relating to said court and its judges. Said court of appeals shall have jurisdiction of all causes now pending on appeal from the parish of Orleans before the supreme court of the State where the amount in dispute or fund to be distributed is less. than one thousand dollars, exclusive of interest; and the supreme court shall at once transfer said causes to the court of appeals.

ART. 130.* For the parish of Orleans there shall be two district courts and no more. One of said courts shall be known as the civil district court of the parish of Orleans, and the other as the criminal district court for the parish of Orleans. The former shall consist of not less than five judges and the latter of not less than two judges, having the qualifications prescribed for district judges throughout the State. The said judges shall be appointed by the governor, by and with the advice and consent of the senate, for the term of eight years. The first appointments shall be made as follows: Three judges of the civil district court for four years and two for eight years; one judge of the criminal district court for four years and one for eight years—the terms to be designated in their commissions. The said judges shall receive each four thousand dollars per annum. Said civil district court shall have exclusive and general probate and exclusive civil jurisdiction in all causes where the amount in dispute or to be distributed exceeds one hundred dollars, exclusive of interest, and exclusive appellate jurisdiction from the city courts of the parish of Orleans when the amount in dispute exceeds twenty-five dollars, exclusive of interest. All causes filed in said court shall be equally allotted and assigned among said judges in accordance with rules of court to be adopted for that purpose. In case of recusation of any judge in any cause such cause shall be reassigned; or in case of absence from the parish, sickness or other disability of the judge to whom any cause may have been assigned, any judge of said court may issue or grant conservatory writs or orders. In other respects each judge shall have exclusive control over every cause assigned to him from its inception to its final determination in said court. The criminal district court shall have criminal jurisdiction only. All prosecutions instituted in said court shall be equally apportioned between said judges by lot. Each judge or his successor shall have exclusive control over every cause falling to him from its inception to final determination in said court. In case of vacancy or recusation, causes assigned shall be reassigned under order of court.

ART. 131. The general assembly may increase the number of judges of the civil district court, not, however, to exceed nine judges, and the number of the criminal judges not to exceed three.

ART. 132. The court of appeals and the civil and criminal district courts for the parish of Orleans shall respectively regulate the order ʿpreference and trial of causes pending, and adopt other rules to

_____

As amended in 1882.

govern the proceedings therein, not in conflict with the provisions of law.

ART. 133. The civil district court for the parish of Orleans shall select a solvent incorporated bank of the city of New Orleans as a judicial depository. Therein shall be deposited all moneys, notes, bonds and securities (except such notes or documents as may be filed with suits or in evidence, which shall be kept by the clerk of the court), so soon as the same shall come into the hands of any sheriff or clerk of court; such deposits shall be removable in whole or in part only upon order of court. The officer making such deposits shall make immediate and written return to the court of the date and particulars thereof, to be filed in the cause in which the matter is pending, under penalties to be prescribed by law. Act 1880, No. 33.

ART. 134. There shall be a district attorney for the parish of Orleans, who shall possess the same qualifications and be elected in the same manner and for the same period of time as the district attorneys for other parishes, as provided by this constitution. (D. 1140). He shall receive a salary of one thousand dollars per annum and such fees as may be allowed by law; but no fee shall be allowed in criminal cases except on conviction. (D. 1145, 1146.) He may appoint an assistant at a salary not to exceed fifteen hundred dollars per annum.

ART. 135.* There shall be in the city of New Orleans four city courts, one of which shall be located in that portion of the city on the right bank of the Mississippi river, presided over by judges having all the qualifications required for a district judge, and shall be elected by the qualified voters for the term of four years. They shall have exclusive jurisdiction over all sums not exceeding one hundred dollars, exclusive of interest, subject to an appeal to the civil district court when the amount claimed exceeds twenty-five dollars, exclusive of interest. The general assembly shall regulate the salaries, territorial division of jurisdiction, the manner of executing their process, the fee bill and proceedings which shall govern them. They shall have authority to execute commissions, take testimony and receive therefor such fees as may be allowed by law. (D. 2070-2101; Act 1880, No. 45, 67.) The general assembly may increase the number of city courts for said parish not to exceed eight in all. Until otherwise provided by law each of the said courts shall have one clerk, to be elected for the term of four years by the qualified voters of the parish, who shall receive a salary of twelve hundred dollars per annum and no more, and whose qualifications, bond and duties shall be regulated by law.

ART. 136. The general assembly may provide for police or magistrates' courts; but such courts shall not be vested with jurisdiction beyond the enforcement of municipal ordinances or as committing magistrates.

ART. 137. There shall be one clerk for the civil district court and one for the criminal district court of the parish of Orleans. The former shall be *ex officio* clerk of the court of appeals of said parish. Said clerk shall be removable in the manner provided for the removal of the sheriffs of said parish. The clerk of said civil district court

*As amended in 1882.

shall receive an annual salary of three thousand six hundred dollars
and no more; and the clerk of the criminal court an annual salary of
three thousand dollars and no more; both payable quarterly on their
warrants.   They shall be elected by the qualified voters of the parish
for a term of four years. (D. 507.) The amount and character of the
bonds, and qualification of the sureties to be furnished by said clerks
shall be prescribed by law. D. 462.

ART. 138. The court of appeals and each judge of the civil and
criminal district courts of the parish of Orleans shall appoint a min-
ute clerk, at an annual salary of not more than eighteen hundred
dollars, whose duties shall be regulated by law. Each clerk of court
shall appoint, by and with the consent of the district court of which
he is clerk, such deputies as may be necessary to perform efficiently
the duties of said office, at salaries to be fixed by law. He shall be
responsible for said deputies, and may require from each such security
as he may deem sufficient to secure himself; and said deputies shall
be removable at his pleasure.

ART. 139. There shall be a civil and a criminal sheriff for the parish
of Orleans. The civil sheriff shall be the executive officer of all the civil
courts, except city courts, and the criminal sheriff shall be the executive officer of the criminal district court. (D. 3537 *et seq.*) They
shall attend the sittings, and execute the writs and mandates of their
respective courts. They shall be elected by the voters of the parish
of Orleans every four years. They shall be citizens of the State,
residents and voters of the city of New Orleans, at least twenty-five
years of age, and shall be removable, each by the district court of
which he is the executive officer, upon proof after trial, without jury,
of gross or continued neglect, incompetency, or unlawful conduct,
operating injury to the court or any individual. The two district
courts for the parish of Orleans shall immediately, upon organization
under this constitution, in joint session, adopt rules governing the
lodging of complaints against and trial of such officers; and such
rules, once adopted, shall not be changed, except by the unanimous
consent of all the judges composing the said courts. D. 3537.

ART. 140. The civil sheriff of the parish of Orleans shall receive
such fees as the general assembly may fix. He shall render monthly
accounts, giving amounts and dates, number and title of causes,
wherein received or paid out, of all sums collected and disbursed by
him, which shall be filed in the civil district court of said parish and
form a part of its public records. He shall be responsible to the State
for all profits of said office over ten thousand dollars per annum, and
shall settle with the State at least once a year in such manner as the
general assembly may provide. The criminal sheriff shall receive an
annual salary of thirty six hundred dollars and no more. He shall
receive no other compensation. He shall charge and collect for the
State, from parties convicted, such fees and charges as may be fixed
by law and shall render monthly accounts of the same.

ART. 141. Said sheriffs shall appoint, each with the consent and
approval of the district court which he serves, such a number of
deputies as the said court may find necessary for the proper expedition of the public business, at such salaries as may be fixed by law.
Each sheriff shall be responsible for his deputies, may remove them

at pleasure and fill vacancies with the approval of the court, and may exact from all deputies security in such manner and amount as such sheriff may deem necessary. D. 3542.

ART. 142. The civil sheriff for the said parish shall execute a bond, with sureties, residents of said parish, conditioned for the lawful and faithful performance of the duties of his office, in the sum of fifty thousand dollars. The sureties shall be examined in open court by the judges of the civil district court for the parish of Orleans, and the questions and answers shall be reduced to writing, and form a portion of the records of said court. (D. 3538.) A similar bond shall be executed by the criminal sheriff of said parish in the sum of ten thousand dollars, with sureties to be examined and approved as to solvency by the criminal district court of said parish, as herein directed for the civil district court of said parish in the case of the civil sheriff.

ART. 143. There shall be one constable for each city court of the parish of Orleans, who shall be the executive officer of such court. He shall be elected by the qualified voters of the parish of Orleans for the term of four years. The general assembly shall define his qualifications and fix his compensation and duties, and shall assimilate the same so far as practicable to the provisions of this constitution relating to the civil sheriff of said parish. The judges of the city courts shall sit in *bunc* to examine such bonds, try and remove constables, and adopt rules regulating such trial and removal. They shall in such proceedings be governed so far as practicable by the provisions of this constitution regulating the proceedings of the district courts of the parish of Orleans in the case of the sheriffs of said parish. D. 642.

ART. 144. There shall be a register of conveyances and a recorder of mortgages for the parish of Orleans, who shall be elected by the qualified voters of said parish every four years. The register of conveyances shall receive an annual salary of twenty-five hundred dollars and no more, and said recorder of mortgages an annual salary of four thousand dollars and no more. The general assembly shall regulate the qualifications and duties of said officers, and the number of employés they shall appoint and fix the salaries of such employés, not to exceed eighteen hundred dollars for each. D. 3152, 3171.

ART. 145. The general assembly, at its first session after the adoption of this constitution shall enact a fee bill for the clerks of the various courts, including the city courts sitting in New Orleans, and for the civil and criminal sheriffs, constables, register of conveyances and recorder of mortgages of said parish. In the same act provision shall be made for a system of stamps or stamped paper for the collection by the State, not by said officers, of such fees and charges, so far as clerks of courts, register of conveyances and recorder of mortgages are concerned. D. 778, 3163, 3172.

ART. 146.* All fees and charges fixed by law for the various courts of the parish of Orleans, and for the register of conveyances and recorder of mortgages of said parish shall enure to the State; and all sums realized therefrom shall be set aside and held

---

* As amended in 1882.

as a special fund, out of which shall be paid by preference the expenses of the clerk of the civil district court, the clerk of the city courts, the registrar of conveyances, and the recorder of mortgages of the parish of Orleans; *provided*, that the State shall never make any payment to any sheriff, clerk, register of conveyances or recorder of mortgages of the parish of Orleans, or any of their deputies, for salary or other expenses of their respective offices, except from the special fund provided for by this article; and any appropriation made contrary to this provision shall be null and void.

ART. 147. There shall be one coroner for the parish of Orleans, who shall be elected every four years by the qualified electors of said parish, and whose duties shall be regulated by law. He shall be *ex officio* city physician of the city of New Orleans, and receive an annual salary of five thousand dollars, and no more. He shall be a practising physician of said city, and a graduate of the medical department of some university of respectable standing. He may appoint an assistant, having the same qualifications as himself, at an annual salary not exceeding three thousand dollars. The salaries of both coroner and assistant to be paid by the parish of Orleans. (D. 649, 674). The maintenance and support of prisoners confined in the parish of Orleans, upon charges or conviction for criminal offences, shall be under the control of the city of New Orleans.

GENERAL PROVISIONS.

ART. 148. No person shall hold any office, State, parochial or municipal, or shall be permitted to vote at any election or act as a juror, who, in due course of law, shall have been convicted of treason, perjury, forgery, bribery or other crime punishable by imprisonment in the penitentiary, or who shall be under interdiction.

ART. 149. Members of the general assembly and all officers, before they enter upon the duties of their offices, shall take the following oath or affirmation: " I, A B, do solemnly swear (or affirm) that I will support the constitution and laws of the United States, and the constitution and laws of this State; and that I will faithfully and impartially discharge and perform all the duties incumbent on me as ———, according to the best of my ability and understanding. So help me God." D. sec. 2550, 2558.

ART. 150. The seat of government shall be and remain at the city of Baton Rouge. The general assembly, at its first session after the adoption of this constitution, shall make the necessary appropriations for the repair of the statehouse and for the transfer of the archives of the State to Baton Rouge; and the city council of Baton Rouge is hereby authorized to issue certificates of indebtedness in such manner and form as to cover the subscription of thirty-five thousand dollars tendered by the citizens and the city council of said city to aid in repairing the capitol in said city; *provided*, the city of Baton Rouge shall pay into the State treasury said amount of thirty-five thousand dollars before the contract for the repairs of the statehouse be finally closed.

ART. 151. Treason against the State shall consist only in levying war against it, or adhering to its enemies, giving them aid and comfort. No person shall be convicted of treason except on the testimony of two witnesses to the same overt act, or on his confession in open court. D. 855.

ART. 152. All civil officers shall be removable by an address of two-thirds of the members elected to each house of the general assembly, except those whose removal is otherwise provided for by this constitution.

ART. 153. No member of congress nor person holding or exercising any office of trust or profit under the United States, or either of them, or under any foreign power, shall be eligible as a member of the general assembly, or hold or exercise any office of trust or profit under the State.

ART. 154. The laws, public records and the judicial and legislative written proceedings of the State shall be promulgated, preserved and conducted in the English language; but the general assembly may provide for the publication of the laws in the French language, and prescribe that judicial advertisements in certain designated cities and parishes shall also be made in that language. D. 1522, 2166; Act 1880, No. 38, p. 37.

ART. 155. No *ex post facto* law, nor any law impairing the obligation of contracts, shall be passed, nor vested rights be divested, unless for purposes of public utility and for adequate compensation previously made.

ART. 156. Private property shall not be taken nor damaged for public purposes without just and adequate compensation being first paid. D. 1479, 1493.

ART. 157. No power of suspending the laws of this State shall be exercised unless by the general assembly or its authority.

ART. 158. The general assembly shall provide by law for change of venue in civil and criminal cases. D. 3891, 3910.

ART. 159. No person shall hold or exercise at the same time more than one office of trust or profit, except that of justice of the peace or notary public.

ART. 160. The general assembly may determine the mode of filling vacancies in all offices for which provision is not made in this constitution. D. 2606.

ART. 161. All officers shall continue to discharge the duties of their offices until their successors shall have been inducted into office, except in case of impeachment or suspension. D. 2608.

ART. 162. The military shall be in subordination to the civil power, and no soldier shall, in time of peace, be quartered in any house without the consent of the owner.

ART. 163. The general assembly shall make it obligatory upon each parish to support all infirm, sick and disabled paupers residing within its limits; *provided,* that in every municipal corporation in a parish where the power of the police jury do not extend the said corporation shall support its own infirm, sick and disabled paupers. D. 2743 *et seq.*

ART. 164. No soldier, sailor or marine in the military or naval service of the United States shall hereafter acquire a domicile in this State by reason of being stationed or doing duty in the same.

ART. 165. It shall be the duty of the general assembly to pass such

laws as may be proper and necessary to decide differences by arbitra
tion.

ART. 166. The power of courts to punish for contempt shall be limited by law. D. 124.

ART. 167. The general assembly shall have authority to grant lottery charters or privileges; *provided*, each charter or privilege shall
pay not less than forty thousand dollars per annum in money into the
treasury of the State; *provided further*, that all charters shall cease
and expire on the first of January, eighteen hundred and ninety-five,
from which time all lotteries are prohibited in the State. The forty
thousand dollars per annum now provided by law to be paid by the
Louisiana State lottery company, according to the provisions of its
charter, granted in the year eighteen hundred and. sixty-eight, shall
belong to the charity hospital of New Orleans, and the charter of said
company is recognized as a contract binding on the State for the
period therein specified, except its monopoly clause, which is hereby
abrogated; and all laws contrary to the provisions of this article are
hereby declared null and void; *provided*, said company shall file a
written renunciation of all its monopoly features in the office of the
secretary of State within sixty days after the ratification of this constitution. Of the additional sums raised by licenses on lotteries the
hospital at Shreveport shall receive ten thousand dollars annually, and
the remaining sum shall be divided each year among the several parishes in the State for the benefit of their schools.

ART. 168. In all proceedings or indictments for libel the truth thereof
may be given in evidence. The jury in all criminal cases shall be
judges of the law and of the facts on the question of guilt or innocence, having been charged as to the law applicable to the case by the
presiding judge. D. 3641.

ART. 169. No officer whose salary is fixed by the constitution shall
be allowed any fees or perquisites of office, except where otherwise
provided for by this constitution. D. 138.

ART. 170. The regulation of the sale of alcoholic or spirituous
liquors is declared a police regulation, and the general assembly may
enact laws regulating their sale and use. D. 1211, 1216.

ART. 171. No person who, at any time, may have been a collector
of taxes, whether State, parish or municipal, or who may have been
otherwise entrusted with public money or any portion thereof, shall
be eligible to the general assembly or to any office of honor, profit or
trust under the State government, or any parish or municipality
thereof, until he shall have obtained a discharge for the amount of
such collections and for all public moneys with which he may have
been entrusted.

ART. 172. Gambling is declared to be a vice, and the general
assembly shall enact laws for its suppression. D. 911, 913.

ART. 173. Any person who shall directly or indirectly offer or give
any sum or sums of money, bribe, present, reward, promise or
any other thing to any officer, State, parochial or municipal,
or to any member or officer of the general assembly, with the intent
to induce or influence such officer or member of the general assembly
to appoint any person to office, to vote or exercise any power
in him vested, or to perform any duty of him required

with partiality or favor, the person giving or offering to give, and the officer or member of the general assembly so receiving, any money, bribe, present, reward, promise, contract, obligation or security, with the intent or for the purpose or consideration aforesaid, shall be guilty of bribery, and on being found guilty thereof by any court of competent jurisdiction, or by either house of the general assembly of which he may be a member or officer, shall be forever disqualified from holding any office, State, parochial or municipal, and shall be forever ineligible to a seat in the general assembly; *provided*, that this shall not be so construed as to prevent the general assembly from enacting additional penalties. D. 860, 861, 3962.

ART. 174. Any person may be compelled to testify in any lawful proceeding against any one who may be charged with having committed the offence of bribery, and shall not be permitted to withhold his testimony upon the ground that it may criminate him or subject him to public infamy; but such testimony shall not afterwards be used against him in any judicial proceedings, except for perjury in giving such testimony. D. 860, 861.

ART. 175. The general assembly shall, at its first session, pass laws to protect laborers on buildings, streets, roads, railroads, canals and other similar works against the failure of contractors and sub-contractors to pay their current wages when due and to make the corporaton, company or individual for whose benefit the work is done responsible for their ultimate payment.

ART. 176. No mortgage or privilege on immovable property shall affect third persons unless recorded or registered in the parish where the property is situated, in the manner and within the time as is now or may be prescribed by law, except privileges for expenses of last illness and privileges for taxes, State, parish or municipal; *provided*, such privilege shall lapse in three years. D. 2877, 2888, 3093, 3188, 3189.

ART. 177. Privileges on movable property shall exist without registration for the same, except in such cases as the general assembly may prescribe by law after the adoption of this constitution.

ART. 178. The general assembly shall provide for the interest of State medicine in all its departments, for the protection of the people from unqualified practitioners of medicine; for protecting confidential communications made to medical men by their patients while under professional treatment and for the purpose of such treatment; for the establishment and maintenance of a State Board of Health. D. 3034.

ART. 179. The general assembly shall create a bureau of agriculture, define its objects, designate its officers and fix their salaries, at such time as the financial condition of the State may warrant them, in their judgment, in making such expenditures; *provided*, that such expenditures never exceed ten thousand dollars per annum. Act 1880, No. 56.

THE NEW CANAL AND SHELL ROAD.

ART. 180.* The new basin canal and shell road and their appurtenances shall not be leased nor alienated.

*As amended in 1886.

MILITIA.

ART. 181. The general assembly shall have authority to provide by law how the militia of this State shall be organized, officered, trained, armed and equipped, and of whom it shall consist. D. 2309, 2315.

ART. 182. The officers and men of the militia and volunteer forces shall receive no pay, rations or emoluments when not in active service by authority of the State.

ART. 183. The general assembly may exempt from military services those who belong to religious societies whose tenets forbid them to bear arms; *provided*, a money equivalent for these services shall be exacted. The governor shall have power to call the militia into active service for the preservation of law and order, or when the public service may require it; *provided*, that the police force of any city, town or parish shall not be organized or used as a part of the State militia.

SUFFRAGE AND ELECTION.

ART. 184. In all elections by the people the electors shall vote by ballot; and in all elections by persons in a representative capacity the vote shall be *viva voce*. D. 1379-1435.

ART. 185. Every male citizen of the United States, and every male person of foreign birth who has been naturalized or who may have legally declared his intention to become a citizen of the United States before he offers to vote, who is twenty-one years old or upwards, possessing the following qualifications, shall be an elector and shall be entitled to vote at any election by the people, except as hereinafter provided: 1. He shall be an actual resident of the State at least one year next preceding the election at which he offers to vote. 2. He shall be an actual resident of the parish in which he offers to vote at least six months next preceding the election. 3. He shall be an actual resident of the ward or precinct in which he offers to vote at least thirty days next preceding the election.

ART. 186. The general assembly shall provide by law for the proper enforcement of the provisions of the foregoing article; *provided*, that in the parish of Orleans there shall be a supervisor of registration, who shall be appointed by the governor, by and with the advice and consent of the senate, whose term of office shall be for the period of four years, and whose salary, qualifications and duties shall be prescribed by law. And the general assembly may provide for the registration of voters in other parishes.

ART. 187. The following persons shall not be permitted to register, vote or hold any office or appointment of honor, profit or trust in this State, to-wit: those who shall have been convicted of treason, embezzlement of public funds, malfeasance in office, larceny, bribery, illegal voting or other crime punishable by hard labor or imprisonment in the penitentiary, idiots and insane persons.

ART. 188. No qualification of any kind for suffrage or office, nor any restraint upon the same, on account of race, color or previous condition shall be made by law.

ART. 189. Electors shall, in all cases except for treason, felony or breach of the peace, be privileged from arrest during their attendance on elections, and in going to and returning from the same.

ART. 190. The general assembly shall by law forbid the giving or selling of intoxicating drinks, on the day of election, within one mile of precincts, at any election held within this State.

ART. 191. Until otherwise provided by law the general State election shall be held once every four years on the Tuesday next following the third Monday in April. Presidential electors and members of congress shall be chosen or elected in the manner and the time prescribed by law.

ART. 192. Parochial and the municipal elections in the cities of New Orleans and Shreveport shall be held on the same day as the general State election, and not oftener than once in four years.

ART. 193. For the purpose of voting no person shall be deemed to have gained a residence by reason of his presence, or lost it by reason of his absence, while employed in the service, either civil or military, of this State or of the United States; nor while engaged in the navigation of the waters of the State or the United States, or of the high seas, nor while a student of any institution of learning.

ART. 194. The general assembly shall provide by law for the trial and determination of contested elections of all public officers, whether State, judicial, parochial or municipal. D. 1417-1435.

ART. 195. No person shall be eligible to any office, State, judicial, parochial, municipal or ward, who is not a citizen of this State and a duly qualified elector of the State, judicial district, parish, municipality or ward wherein the functions of said office are to be exercised. And whenever any officer, State, judicial, parochial, municipal or ward, may change his residence from this State, or from the district, parish, municipality or ward in which he holds such office, the same shall thereby be vacated, any declaration of retention of domicile to the contrary notwithstanding.

IMPEACHMENT AND REMOVALS FROM OFFICE.

ART. 196. The governor, lieutenant-governor, secretary of State, auditor, treasurer, attorney-general, superintendent of public education and the judges of all the courts of record in this State, shall be liable to impeachment for high crimes and misdemeanors, for nonfeasance or malfeasance in office, for incompetency, for corruption, favoritism, extortion or oppression in office, or for gross misconduct or habitual drunkenness. D. 1738, 1745.

ART. 197. The house of representatives shall have the sole power of impeachment. All impeachments shall be tried by the senate; when sitting for that purpose the senators shall be upon oath or affirmation, and no person shall be convicted without the concurrence of two-thirds of the senators present. When the governor of the State is on trial the chief-justice or senior associate justice of the supreme court shall preside. Judgment in cases of impeachment shall extend only to removal from office and disqualification from holding any office of honor, trust or profit under the State; but the party, whether convicted or acquitted, shall nevertheless be liable to prosecution, trial and punishment according to law.

ART. 198. All officers against whom articles of impeachment may be preferred shall be suspended from the exercise of the functions of their office during the pendency of such impeachment; and, except in case of the impeachment of the governor, the appointing power shall make a provisional appointment to replace any suspended officer until the decision of the impeachment.

ART. 199. For any reasonable cause the governor shall remove any officer on the address of two-thirds of the members elected to each house of the general assembly. In every such case the cause or causes for which such removal may be required shall be stated at length in the address and inserted in the journal of each house.

ART. 200. For any of the causes specified in article one hundred and ninety-six judges of the courts of appeal, of the district courts throughout the State and of the city courts of the parish of Orleans, may be removed from office by judgment of the supreme court of this State in a suit instituted by the attorney-general or a district attorney, in the name of the State, on his relation. The supreme court is hereby vested with original jurisdiction to try such causes; and it is hereby made the duty of the attorney-general or of any district attorney to institute such suit on the written request and information of fifty citizens and taxpayers residing within the territorial limits of the district or circuit over which the judge against whom the suit is brought exercises the functions of his office   Such suits shall be tried, after citation and ten days' delay for answering, in preference to all other suits, and wherever the court may be sitting; but the pendency of such suit shall not operate a suspension from office. In all cases where the officer sued as above directed shall be acquitted, judgment shall be rendered jointly and *in solido* against the citizens signing the request, for all costs of the suit. Act. 1880, No. 122.

ART. 201. For any of the causes enumerated in article one hundred and ninty-six district attorneys, clerks of court, sheriffs, coroners, recorders, justices of the peace, and all other parish, municipal and ward officers shall be removed by judgment of the district court of the domicile of such officers (in the parish of Orleans, the civil district court); and it shall be the duty of the district attorney, except when the suit is to be brought against himself, to institute suit in the manner directed in article two hundred, on the written request and information of twenty-five resident citizens and taxpayers in the case of district, parish or municipal officers, and of ten resident citizens and taxpayers in the case of ward officers. Such suit shall be brought against a district attorney by the district attorney of an adjoining district, or by counsel appointed by the judge for that purpose. In all such cases the defendant, the State, and the citizens and taxpayers on whose information and at whose request such suit was brought, or any one of them, shall have the right to appeal, both on the law and on the facts, from the judgment of the court. In all cases where the officer sued as above directed shall be acquitted, judgment shall be rendered jointly and *in solido* against the citizens signing the request for all costs of the suit. In cases against district attorneys, clerks, sheriffs and recorders the appeal shall be to the supreme court, and in cases against all other officers the appeal shall be made to the court of appeals of the proper circuit. Such appeals shall be returnable within ten days to the appellate court, wherever it may be sitting or wherever it may hold its next session, and may be transferred by order of the judges of said court to another parish within their circuit, and such appeals shall be tried by preference over all others. In cases of the refusal or neglect of the district attorney or attorney general to institute and prosecute any suit provided for in this and the preceding article, the citizens and taxpayers making the request, or any one of them, shall have the right by mandamus to compel him to perform such duty.

REVENUE AND TAXATION.

ART. 202. The taxing power may be exercised by the general assembly for State purposes, and by parish and municipal corporations, under authority granted to them by the general assembly, for parish and municipal purposes. D. 3233, 3363.

ART. 203. Taxation shall be equal and uniform throughout the territorial limits of the authority levying the tax, and all property shall be taxed in proportion to its value, to be ascertained and directed by law; *provided*, the assessment of all property shall never exceed the actual cash value thereof; *and provided further*, that the taxpayers shall have the right of testing the correctness of their assessments before the courts of justice. In order to arrive at this equality and uniformity the general assembly shall, at its first session after the adoption of this constitution, provide a system of equality and uniformity in assessments, based upon the relative value of property in the different portions of the State. The valuation put upon property for the purposes of State taxation shall be taken as the proper valuation for purposes of local taxation in every subdivision of the State.

ART. 204. The taxing power shall be exercised only to carry on and maintain the government of the State and the public institutions thereof; to educate the children of the State, to pay the principal and interest of the public debt, to suppress insurrection, repel invasion or defend the State in time of war; to supply the citizens who lost a limb or limbs in the military service of the confederate States with substantial artificial limbs during life; and for levee purposes, as hereinafter provided.

ART. 205. The power to tax corporations and corporate property shall never be surrendered nor suspended by act of the general assembly.

ART. 206. The general assembly may levy a license tax, and in such case shall graduate the amount of such tax to be collected from the persons pursuing the several trades, professions, vocations and callings. All persons, associations of persons and corporations pursuing any trade, profession, business or calling, may be rendered liable to such tax, except clerks, laborers, clergymen, schoolteachers, those engaged in agricultural, horticultural, mechanical and mining pursuits, and manufacturers other than those of distilled alcoholic or malt liquors, tobacco and cigars, and cotton seed oil. No political corporation shall impose a greater license tax than is imposed by the general assembly for State purposes.

ART. 207.* The following property shall be exempt from taxation, and no other, viz: All public property, places of religious worship or burial; all charitable institutions; all buildings and property used exclusively for colleges or other school purposes; the real and personal estate of any public library and that of any other literary association used by or connected with such library; all books and philosophical apparatus, and all paintings and statuary of any company or association kept in a public hall; *provided*, the property so exempted be not used or leased for purposes of private or corporate profit or income. There shall also be exempt from taxation household property to the value of five hundred dollars. There shall also be exempt from taxation and license for a period of twenty years from the adoption of this constitution, the capital, machinery and other property employed in the manufacture of textile fabrics, leather, shoes, harness, saddlery, hats, flour, machinery, agricultural implements, manufacture of ice, fertilizers and chemicals, and furniture and other articles of wood, marble or stone, soap, stationery, ink and paper, boat building and chocolate; *provided*, that not less than five hands are employed in any one factory.

ART. 208. The general assembly shall levy an annual poll tax, for the maintenance of public schools, upon every male inhabitant in the State over the age of twenty-one years, which shall never be less than one dollar nor exceed one dollar and a half per capita; and the general assembly shall pass laws to enforce payment of said tax.

ART. 209. The State tax on property for all purposes whatever, including expenses of government, schools, levees and interest, shall not exceed in any one year six mills on the dollar of its assessed valuation, if the ordinance regarding the bonded debt of the State is adopted and ratified by the people; and if said ordinance is not adopted and ratified by the people, said State tax for all purposes aforesaid shall not exceed in any one year five mills on the dollar of the assessed valuation of the property; and no parish or municipal tax for all purposes whatsoever shall exceed ten mills on the dollar of valuation; *provided*, that for the purpose of erecting and constructing public buildings, bridges and works of public improvement, in parishes and municipalities, the rates of taxation herein limited may be increased when the rate of such increase and the purpose for which it is intended shall have been submitted to a vote of the property taxpayers of such parish or municipality entitled to a vote under the election laws of the State, and a majority of same voting at such election shall have voted therefor. Act 1880, No. 88; No. 42, sec. 4; Act 1882, No. 126; 35 A., Duperier's case.

ART. 210. There shall be no forfeiture of property for the nonpayment of taxes, State, levee, district, parochial or municipal; but at the expiration of the year in which they are due the collector shall, without suit, and after giving notice to the delinquent in the manner to be provided by law (which shall not be by publication except in case of unknown owner), advertise for sale the property on which

---

* As amended in 1886.

the taxes are due, in the manner provided for judicial sales; and on the day of sale he shall sell such portion of the property as the debtor shall point out, and in case the debtor shall not point out sufficient property the co'lector shall at once and without further delay sell the least quantity of property which any bidder will buy for the amount of the taxes, interest and costs. The sale shall be without appraisement, and the property sold shall be redeemable at any time for the space of one year, by paying the price given, with twenty per cent. and costs added. No sale of property for taxes shall be annulled for any informality in the proceedings until the price paid, with ten per cent. interest, be tendered to the purchaser. All deeds of sale made, or that may be made by collectors of taxes shall be received by courts in evidence as *prima facie* valid sales. D. 3292–3312.

ART. 211. The tax shall be designated by the year in which it is collectible, and the tax on movable property shall be collected in the year in which the assessment is made. D. 3293.

ART. 212. The legislature shall pass no law postponing the payment of taxes, except in case of overflow, general conflagration, general destruction of the crops or other public calamity. Act 1880, No. 97.

ART. 213. A levee system shall be maintained in the State, and a tax not to exceed one mill may be levied annually on all property subject to taxation, and shall be applied exclusively to the maintenance and repairs of levees.

ART. 214.* The general assembly may divide the State into levee districts, and provide for the appointment or election of levee commissioners in said districts, who shall, in the method and manner to be provided by law, have supervision of the erection, repairs and maintenance of the levees in said districts; to that effect the levee commissioners may levy a tax not to exceed ten mills on the taxable property situated within the alluvial portions of said districts subject to overflow; *provided*, that in case of necessity to raise additional funds for the purpose of constructing, preserving or repairing any levees protecting the lands of a district, the rate of taxation herein limited may be increased when the rate of such increase and the necessity and purpose for which it is intended shall have been submitted to a vote of the property taxpayers of such district, paying taxes for themselves or in any representative capacity, whether resident or non-resident, on property situated within the alluvial portion of said district subject to overflow, and a majority of those in number and value, voting at such election, shall have voted therefor. Act 80, No. 78.

ART. 215. The provisions of the above two articles shall cease to have effect whenever the federal government shall assume permanent control and provide the ways and means for the maintenance of levees in this State. The federal government is authorized to make such geological, topographical, hydrographical and hydrometrical surveys and investigations within the State as may be necessary to carry into effect the act of congress to provide for the appointment of a Mississippi river commission for the improvement of said river

---

*As amended in 1884.

from the head of the passes, near its mouth, to the headwaters, and to construct and protect such public works and improvements as may be ordered by congress under the provisions of said act.

ART. 216. The general assembly shall have power, with the concurrence of an adjacent State or States, to create levee districts, composed of territory partly in this State and partly in such adjacent State or States, and the levee commissioners for such district or districts shall possess all the power provided by article two hundred and fourteen of this constitution.

ART. 217. Corporations companies or associations, organized or domiciled out of this State, but doing business herein, may be licensed by a mode different from that provided for home corporations or companies; *provided*, said different mode of license shall be uniform, upon a graduated system as to all such corporations, companies or associations that transact the same kind of business. D. 735.

ART. 218. All the articles and provisions of this constitution regulating and relating to the collection of State taxes and tax sales shall also apply to and regulate the collection of parish, district and municipal taxes.

HOMESTEADS AND EXEMPTIONS.

ART. 219. There shall be exempt from seizure and sale, by any process whatever, except as herein provided, the homesteads *bona fide* owned by the debtor and occupied by him, consisting of lands, buildings and appurtenances, whether rural or urban; of every head of family or person having a mother or father, a person or persons dependent on him or her for support; also, one work-horse, one wagon or cart, one yoke of oxen, two cows and calves, twenty-five head of hogs, or one thousand pounds of bacon or its equivalent in pork, whether these exempted objects be attached to a homestead or not; and on a farm the necessary quantity of corn and fodder for the current year, and the necessary farming implements to the value of two thousand dollars (D. 1691, 1696); *provided*, that in case the homestead exceeds two thousand dollars in value the beneficiary shall be entitled to that amount in case a sale of the homestead under any legal process realizes more than that sum. No husband shall have the benefit of a homestead whose wife owns and is in actual enjoyment of property or means to the amount of two thousand dollars. Such exemptions to be valid shall be set apart and registered as shall be provided by law. The benefit of this provision may be claimed by the surviving spouse or minor child or children of a deceased beneficiary, if in indigent circumstances.

ART. 220. Laws shall be passed as early as practicable for the setting apart, valuation and registration of property claimed as a homestead. Rights to homesteads or exemptions under laws or contracts, or for debts existing at the time of adoption of this constitution, shall not be impaired, repealed or affected by any provision of is constitution or any laws passed in pursuance thereof. No court ministerial officer of this State shall ever have jurisdiction or auority to enforce any judgment, execution or decree against the operty set apart for a homestead, including such improvements as may be made thereon from time to time; *provided*, the property herein declared to be exempt shall not exceed in value two thousand dollars. This exemption shall not apply to the following cases, to-wit: 1, for the purchase price of said property or any part thereof; 2, for labor and material furnished for building, repairing or improving homesteads; 3, for liabilities incurred by any public officer or fiduciary, or any attorney-at-law, for money collected or received on deposit; 4, for lawful claims for taxes or assessments.

ART. 221. The owner of a homestead shall at any time have the right to supplement his exemption by adding to an amount already set apart, which is less than the whole amount of exemption herein allowed, sufficient to make his homestead and exemption equal to the whole amount allowed by this constitution.

ART. 222. The homestead shall not be susceptible of mortgage, except for the purchase price, labor and material furnished for the building, repairing or improving homestead; nor shall any renunciation or waiver of homestead rights or exemptions be valid. The right to sell any property which shall be recorded as a homestead shall be preserved, but no sale shall destroy or impair any rights of creditors therein.

ART. 223. Equitable laws shall be passed for the protection of creditors against the fraudulent claims of debtors, for the punishment of fraud, and for reaching property and funds of the debtor concealed from the creditor.

PUBLIC EDUCATION.

ART. 224. There shall be free public schools established by the general assembly throughout the State for the education of all the children of the State between the ages of six and eighteen years; and the general assembly shall provide for their establishment, maintenance and support by taxation or otherwise. And all moneys so raised, except the poll tax, shall be distributed to each parish in proportion to the number of children between the ages of six and eighteen years. D. 1217 *et seq*.

ART. 225. There shall be elected by the qualified electors of the State a superintendent of public education, who shall hold his office for the term of four years, and until his successor is qualified. His duties shall be prescribed by law, and he shall receive an annual salary of two thousand dollars. The aggregate annual expenses of his office, including his salary, shall not exceed the sum of three thousand dollars. The general assembly shall provide for the appointment of parish boards of public education for the different parishes. The parish boards may appoint a parish superintendent of public schools in their respective parishes, who shall be *ex officio* secretary of the parish board, and whose salary for his double functions shall not exceed two hundred dollars annually, except that in the parish of Orleans the salary of the parish superintendent shall be fixed by the general assembly, to be paid out of the public school fund accruing to each parish respectively.

ART. 226. The general exercises in the public schools shall be conducted in the English language, and the elementary branches taug therein; *provided*, that these elementary branches may be also taught in the French language in those parishes in the State or localities in said parishes where the French language predominates, if no additional expense is incurred thereby.

ART. 227. The funds derived from the collection of the poll tax shall be applied exclusively to the maintenance of the public schools as organized under this constitution, and shall be applied exclusively to support of the public schools in the parish in which the same shall be collected; and shall be accounted for and paid by the collecting officers directly to the competent school authorities of each parish.

ART. 228. No funds raised for the support of the public schools of the State shall be appropriated to or used for the support of any sectarian schools.

ART. 229. The school funds of this State shall consist of—1, the proceeds of taxation for school purposes, as provided in this constitution; 2, the interest on the proceeds of all public lands heretofore granted by the United States for the use and support of the public schools; 3, of lands and other property which may hereafter be bequeathed, granted or donated to the State, or generally for school purposes; 4, all funds or property, other than unimproved lands, bequeathed or granted to the State, not designated for other purposes; 5, the proceeds of vacant estates falling under the law to the State of Louisiana. The legislature may appropriate to same fund the proceeds, in whole or in part, of public lands not designated for any other purpose, and shall provide that every parish may levy a tax for the public schools therein, which shall not exceed the State tax; *provided*, that with such tax the whole amount of parish taxes shall not exceed the limits of parish taxation fixed by this constitution.

CONCERNING A STATE UNIVERSITY.

ART 230.* An act to foster, maintain and develop the University of Louisiana, to that end to make the Board of Administrators of the Tulane Education Fund, as presently constituted, with the addition of the Governor, Superintendent of Public Education, and Mayor of the city of New Orleans, as *ex-officio* members thereof, the Administrators of the University of Louisiana, which shall hereafter be known as the "Tulane University of Louisiana;" to invest said Tulane Board with all the powers, privileges, franchises and immunities now vested in the Board of Administrators of the University of Louisiana; and with such other powers as may be necessary or pertinent to develop, control, foster and maintain it as a great University in the city of New Orleans. To give to the Administrators of the Tulane Education Fund the control, management and use of all the property of the University of Louisiana, in the city of New Orleans, for the purposes aforesaid: To exempt, in consequence of the terms of this act, and the dedication of its revenues to the purposes stated in this act, all the property, eal and personal, present and future, of the said Board of Administrators of the Tulane Education Fund, from all taxation,

---

amended in 1884.

whether State, parochial or municipal: To make a contract, irrevocable and conclusive, between the State and the Administrators of the Tulane Education Fund, covering the provisions of this act: To enable the said Board of Administrators of the "Tulane Education Fund" to decline to accept the provisions of this act, unless the same, in all its provisions, be ratified and approved by a constitutional amendment, to be submitted at the next general election: To give said Board of Administrators of the "Tulane Education Fund," upon the adoption of said constitutional amendment, not only the full powers of administration over the University of Louisiana conferred by this act, but also the power to create, develop and maintain a great University in the city of New Orleans, which University so to be created shall perpetually be under their full and complete control: To enable said Board, should they act under the provisions of this act, pending the submission of said constitutional amendment, to withdraw and relieve themselves from all the effects of said action should said proposed constitutional amendment be rejected, and to provide for the submission of a constitutional amendment ratifying the provisions of this act to the people of the State at the next general election;

Whereas, Paul Tulane, Esq., formerly a resident of this State, and now of Princeton, New Jersey, with the beneficent purpose of fostering higher education in this State, did, in May, 1882, express to certain citizens of this State his intention to donate for such purposes valuable real estate to him belonging, situate in the city of New Orleans; and,

Whereas, The citizens to whom the intentions of Paul Tulane, Esq., were expressed, did, by act, before Chas. G. Andry, a notary public in the city of New Orleans, organize themselves into a corporation, under the name of the "Administrators of the Tulane Education Fund," with the objects and purposes specified in said act of incorporation; and,

Whereas, Since the formation of said corporation, Paul Tulane, Esq., in the execution of his previously expressed intention, has donated to said Administrators of the "Tulane Education Fund" nearly one million dollars, the revenues whereof are to be used for the promotion and encouragement of intellectual, moral and industrial education, and has expressed his intention to largely increase said donation should this act be adopted; and,

Whereas, The said Board of Administrators of the "Tulane Education Fund," in order to make their work fruitful in results, have expressed their desire to take charge of the University of Louisiana, in the city of New Orleans, and to devote the revenues of the property now owned, or hereafter to be owned, by said Board, to its expansion and development; and upon the adoption of a constitutional amendment to that end, to apply all the revenues of property now owned, or hereafter to be acquired by them, to the creation and development in the city of New Orleans of a great University, whereby the blessings of higher education, intellectual, moral and industrial, ma- given to the youth of this State; and,

Whereas, Under the terms of this action, as proposed by said Board, the property of said Board, and the revenues thereof, will not be used for purpose of private or corporate income or profit, but will be exclusively dedicated to school purposes, and to the service of the State in maintaining and developing the University of Louisiana, an institution recognized in the Constitution, therefore entitling the said property of said Board to exemption from all taxation, both State, parochial and municipal; therefore,

Be it enacted by the General Assembly of the State of Louisiana,

SECTION 1. That the Board of Administrators of the University of Louisiana shall hereafter, instead of the Board appointed as provided by section thirteen hundred and fifty-one (1351) of the Revised Statutes, consist of the seventeen administrators of the " Tulane Education Fund," with power, perpetually, to fill any vacancy in their own number; *provided*, that the said Board shall, on the passage of this statute, recognize by formal notarial act the Governor of the State, the Superintendent of Public Education, and the Mayor of the city of New Orleans, as *ex-officio* members of said Board.

SEC. 2. *Be it further enacted, etc.*, That the Board of Administrators of the " Tulane Education Fund," as Administrators of the University of Louisiana, shall have all the rights, powers, privileges, franchises and immunities, now vested in the Board of Administrators of the University of Louisiana by existing laws. That they shall further have full direction, control, and administration of the University of Louisiana, now established in the city of New Orleans, in all its departments as also of all the property belonging to the State of Louisiana, and now dedicated to or used by the University of Louisiana as well as of all property controlled or used by the said University of Louisiana, and for the purposes thereof, and the Board of Administrators of the University of Louisiana are hereby empowered and directed to turn over to the Board of Administrators of the " Tulane Education Fund" all the property, rights, books, papers and archives now under their administration or control; *provided*, that if the custody of the State library should be transferred to the Tulane University of Louisiana, as herein established by the consolidation of the University of Louisiana at New Orleans with the Board of Administrators of the " Tulane Education Fund," as herein provided for, through the University of Louisiana, at New Orleans, as it now exists, or otherwise, it shall be on the express condition and agreement that the State of Louisiana may resume the custody and control of said State Library, whenever it may be deemed advisable; and provided further, that after the establishment of the " Tulane University of Louisiana," as herein provided for, and after the transfer of the custody of the State Library thereto as aforesaid, if the custody thereof shall be transferred to the "Tulane University of Louisiana," as herein established, then and in that event, the State of Louisiana shall be relieved of and released from all obligations to pay the salary or compensation of the State Librarian or his assistants, as is now or ¬nay hereafter be fixed by law, during the period said State Library y remain in the custody of said "Tulane University of Louisiana;" that during said period the salary or compensation of said State ırarian shall be paid by the " Tulane University of Louisiana."

An inventory shall be made of all the property, movable and immovable, belonging to the University of Louisiana, and transferred by this act to the control and administration of the Administration of the Tulane Education Fund, by two appraisers to be appointed for that purpose by the Governor of the State and sworn, which appraisement shall be filed in the office of the Secretary of State, as evidencing the description and appraised value of the property so transferred, and also in order that the liability of the said Administrators of the Tulane Education Fund may not be extended beyond a return of the property, so transferred, in any contingency; *provided further*, that the property so transferred may not be sold or disposed of, except under legislative sanction: *provided further*, that if the " Tulane University of Louisiana," as herein established, should cease to use the property, and exercise the privileges, franchises and immunities, now under the control and administration of, and enjoyed by the University of Louisiana, as now constituted and transferred by this act for the exclusive purposes intended by this act, then and in that event the State of Louisiana shall have the right to resume the custody, control and administration of said property, and the exercise of said privileges, franchises and immunities.

SEC. 3. *Be it enacted, etc.*, That the said Board of Administrators of the "Tulane Education Fund," shall perpetually as Administrators of the University of Louisiana as above provided, have full and complete control of all the property and rights, and now vested in the University of Louisiana. The said Board shall have the powers above provided in addition to those conferred by its charter, by act passed before Chas. G. Andry, Notary Public, in the city of New Orleans, on the 29th day of May, Anno Domini 1882, including the power to hold and own all real and personal property, now to said Board belonging, or hereafter to be by it acquired, during its corporate existence, for the purposes and objects of its being, or the revenues whereof are to be solely applicable to such purposes.

SEC. 4. *Be it enacted, etc.*, That in honor of Paul Tulane and in recognition of his beneficent gifts and of their dedication to the purposes expressed in this act, the name of the University of Louisiana be and the same is hereby changed to that of the "Tulane University of Louisiana," under which name it shall possess all the powers, privileges, immunities and franchises, now vested in said University of Louisiana, as well as such powers as may flow from this act or may be vested in said Board, under the term of this act, from the adoption of the Constitutional Amendment hereafter referred to. The purpose of this act being to invest the Board of Administrators of the " Tulane Education Fund " with all the rights now vested in the University of Louisiana; to give said Board moreover complete control of said University in all its departments, and in every respect, with all powers necessary or incidental to the exercise of said control. To enable said Board, besides the powers designated by this act, to have irrevocably upon the adoption of said Constitutional Amendment, full power with the rights hereby conferred to create and develop a great University in the city of New Orleans to be named as aforesaid. Said University to be established by the said Board Administrators of the " Tulane Education Fund," to be dedicated the intellectual, moral and industrial education of the youth of the State, in accordance with the Charter of said Board of Administrators of the "Tulane Education Fund."

SEC. 5. *Be it further enacted, etc.*, That in consideration of the agreement of said Board to develop and maintain the University of Louisiana, and thereby dedicate its revenues not to purposes of private or corporate income or profit, but to the public purposes of developing and maintaining the University of Louisiana, all the property of the said Board, present and future, be and the same is hereby recognized as exempt from all taxation, State, parochial and municipal; this exemption to remain in force as long as the revenues of the said Board are directed to the maintenance of the University of Louisiana, as aforesaid, or until said Constitutional Amendment be adopted. The adoption of said amendment shall operate such exemption in consideration of the said Board expending their revenues as aforesaid, or creating, maintaining and developing a great University in the City of New Orleans; *provided*, that the property exempted from taxation by this act shall not exceed in value five millions of dollars, invested in real estate not otherwise exempted, which said value shall be determined in the mode required by law for the assessment and valuation of property subject to taxation, it being the true meaning and intent hereof, that all the property of the Tulane University of Louisiana, of whatsoever character, shall be exempted from taxation, State, parochial and municipal, except the excess of real estate belonging thereto, over and above the value of five million dollars, as above stated.

SEC. 6. *Be it further enacted, etc.*, That in consideration of the vesting of the administration of the University of Louisiana in the said Administrators of the "Tulane Education Fund," of the transfer of the rights, powers, privileges, franchises and immunities of the said University to said Administrators, and of the exemption from all taxation as hereinabove provided, the said Administrators hereby agree and bind themselves, with the revenues and income of the property heretofore given them by Paul Tulane, Esq., as well as from the revenues of all other property, real, personal or mixed, hereafter to be held, owned or controlled by them, for the purposes of education, to develop, foster and maintain, to best of their ability and judgment, the University of Louisiana, hereafter to be known as the "Tulane University of Louisiana," and upon the adoption of the Constitutional Amendment aforesaid, to perpetually use the powers conferred by this act, and all power vested in them, for the purpose of creating and maintaining in the city of New Orleans a great University, devoted to the intellectual, moral and industrial education and advancement of the youth of this State, under the terms of the donation of Paul Tulane, and the previous provisions of this act. The said Board further agree and bind themselves to waive all legal claim upon the State of Louisiana for any appropriation, as provided in the Constitution of this State, in favor of the University of Louisiana. Besides the waiver of the claim, as aforesaid, as an additional nsideration between the parties to this act, the said Board agrees give continuously, in the academic department, free tuiti.on to one ident from each Senatorial and from each Representa' ive district or parish, to be nominated by its member in the General Assembly from among the *bona fide* citizens and residents of his district or parish, who shall comply with the requirements for admission established by said Board. The meaning of this provision being that each member of the General Assembly, whether Senator or Representative, shall have the right of appointing one student, in accordance with the foregoing provisions. The free tuition herein provided for shall continue until each student has graduated from the academic department, unless his scholarship has ceased from other causes. Whenever a scholarship becomes vacant, from any cause, the Senator or Representative who appointed the previous student, or his successor, shall, in the manner prescribed by this section, immediately name a successor.

SEC. 7. *Be it further enacted*, etc., That this act, in all its provisions be and the same is hereby declared to be a contract between the State of Louisiana and the Administrators of the "Tulane Education Fund," irrevocably vesting the said Administrators of the "Tulane Education Fund" with the powers, franchises, rights, immunities and exemptions herein enumerated and hereby granted, and irrevocably binding said administrators to develop, foster and maintain as above provided, the University as aforesaid in the city of New Orleans, subject to and in accordance with the terms of this act.

SEC. 8. *Be it further enacted*, etc., That this act, in all its terms, provisions and stipulations, without in any manner affecting the validity thereof, or casting any doubt upon its constitutionality, be submitted for ratification at the next general election by constitutional amendment, as hereinabove and hereinafter provided.

SEC. 9. *Be it further enacted*, etc., That upon the passage and promulgation of this act the said Administrators of the "Tulane Education Fund," shall have the right to avail themselves of the provisions of this act pending the submission of the constitutional amendment aforesaid. In case they should so elect to do, the said Administrators, upon the passage of this law and the promulgation thereof, shall give notice of such intention to his Excellency, the Governor of this State, which notice shall authorize said Board to act under the provisions of this act and to exercise all the powers, privileges, franchises, immunities and rights which this act confers, and to undertake the performance of the duties by it imposed. In case the said Constitutional Amendment as aforesaid be not ratified, the said Board shall not in any way be held bound by its said action, but shall have the right to relieve itself of all liability growing out of such action by turning over to the Governor of the State, any property received by it from the State, or from the Administrators of the University of Louisiana, under the terms of this act, which to the extent of its imposing any obligation on the said Administrators of the "Tulane Education Fund," shall by said return, become null and void; *provided*, that the said Board may in the event of the defeat of the said Constitutional Amendment continue to secure and to avail themselves of the provision of this act to the full extent that, the same are legal without constitutional enactment.

SEC. 10. *Be it further enacted*, etc., That Sections 1357, 1362, 1363, 1365, 1366, 1367, 1370, 1372, 1373 and 1374 of the Revised Statutes, be and the same are hereby repealed, and that all laws and parts of laws conflicting in any manner with the terms of this act, be and the same are hereby repealed.

SEC. 11. *Be it further enacted, etc.*, That at the next general election to be held in this State, there shall be submitted to the people of the State the following amendment to the Constitution: (The terms of the Act No. [here inserting the number of this act] adopted at the session of the Legislature in the year 1884, are hereby ratified and approved; and all provisions of the Constitution of 1879 repugnant thereto, or in any way impairing the passage thereof, are hereby repealed, so far as the operations of said act are concerned.)

SEC. 12. *Be it further enacted, etc.*, That all electors who desire to vote at said election for said amendment, shall write or print upon their ballots the words: "For the Tulane University amendment," and all electors who desire to vote at said election against said amendment shall write or print upon their ballots the words: "Against the Tulane University amendment."

The Louisiana State university and agricultural and mechanical college, now established and located in the city of Baton Rouge, is hereby recognized, and all revenues derived and to be derived from the sales of land or land scrip, donated by the United States to the State of Louisiana, for the use of a seminary of learning and mechanical and agricultural college, shall be appropriated exclusively to the maintenance and support of said university and agricultural and mechanical college; and the general assembly shall from time to time make such additional appropriations for the maintenance and support of said Louisiana State university and agricultural and mechanical college as the public necessities and the well-being of the people of the State of Louisiana may require, not to exceed ten thousand dollars annually.

ART. 231. The general assembly shall also establish in the city of New Orleans a university for the education of persons of color, provide for its proper government, and shall make an annual appropriation of not less than five thousand dollars nor more than ten thousand dollars for its maintenance and support.

ART. 232. Women over twenty-one years of age shall be eligible to any office of control or management under the school laws of this State.

THE FREE SCHOOL FUND, SEMINARY FUND AND AGRICULTURAL AND MECHANICAL COLLEGE FUND.

ART. 233. The debt due by the State to the free school fund is hereby declared to be the sum of one million one hundred and thirty thousand eight hundred and sixty-seven dollars and fifty-one cents in principal, and shall be placed on the books of the auditor and treasurer to the credit of the several townships entitled to the same; the said principal being the proceeds of the sales of lands heretofore granted by the United States for the use and support of free public schools, which amount shall be held by the State as a loan, and shall be and remain a perpetual fund, on which the State shall pay an annual interest of four per cent. from the first day of January, eighteen hundred and eighty; and that said interest shall be paid to the several townships in the State entitled to the same in accordance with the act of congress, number sixty-eight, approved February fifteenth, eighteen hundred and forty-three; and the bonds of the State heretofore issued, belonging to said fund and sold under act of the general assembly, number eighty-one of eighteen hundred and seventy-two, are hereby declared null and void, and the general assembly shall make no provision for their payment, and may cause them to be destroyed. (D. 1313-1331.) The debt due by the State to the seminary fund is hereby declared to be one hundred and thirty-six thousand dollars, being the proceeds of the sales of lands heretofore granted by the United States to this State for the use of a seminary of learning. And said amount shall be placed to the credit of said fund on the books of the auditor and treasurer of the State as a perpetual loan, and the State shall pay an annual interest of four per cent. on said amount from January first, eighteen hundred and eighty, for the use of said seminary of learning. And the consolidated bonds of the State now held for use of said fund shall be null and void after the first day of January, eighteen hundred and eighty, and the general assembly shall never make any provision for their payment, and they shall be destroyed in such manner as the general assembly may direct. The debt due by the State to the agricultural and mechanical college fund is hereby declared to be the sum of one hundred and eighty-two thousand three hundred and thirteen dollars and three cents, being the proceeds of the sales of lands and land scrip heretofore granted by the United States to this State for the use of a college for the benefit of agriculture and the mechanic arts. Said amounts shall be placed to the credit of said fund on the books of the auditor and treasurer of the State as a perpetual loan, and the State shall pay an annual interest of five per cent. on said amount from January first, eighteen hundred and eighty, for the use of said agricultural and mechanical college. The consolidated bonds of the State now held by the State for the use of said fund shall be null and void after the first day of January, eighteen hundred and eighty, and the general assembly shall never make any provision for their payment, and they shall be destroyed in such manner as the general assembly may direct. The interest provided for by this article shall be paid out of any tax that may be levied and collected for the general purposes of public education.

CORPORATIONS AND CORPORATE RIGHTS.

ART. 234. The general assembly shall not remit the forfeiture of the charter of any corporation now existing, nor renew, alter or amend the same, nor pass any general or special law for the benefit of such corporation, except upon the condition that such corporation shall thereafter hold its charter subject to the provisions of this constitution. C. C. 427-447, 677-746; Act 1880, No. 79.

ART. 235. The exercise of the police power of the State shall never be abridged or so construed as to permit corporations to conduct their business in such manner as to infringe the equal rights of individuals or the general well-being of the State.

ART. 236. No foreign corporation shall do any business in this State without having one or more known places of business, and an authorized agent or agents in the State, upon whom process may be served. D. 735.

ART. 237. No corporation shall engage in any business other than that expressly authorized in its charter or incidental thereto; nor shall it take or hold any real estate for a longer period than ten years, except such as may be necessary and proper for its legitimate business or purposes. C. C. 433; D. 681, 682; Act 1880, No. 79.

ART. 238. No corporation shall issue stock nor bonds except for labor done or money or property actually received; and all fictitious issues of stock shall be void, and any corporation issuing such fictitious stock shall forfeit its charter. C. C. 433; D. 692.

ART. 239. The stock shall not be increased, except in pursuance of general laws, nor without consent of persons holding the larger amount in value of the stock first obtained, at a meeting of stockholders to be held after thirty days' notice given in pursuance of law. D. 687.

ART. 240. The term corporation as used in this constitution shall be construed to include all joint stock companies or associations having any power or privileges not possessed by individuals or partnerships.

ART. 241. It shall be a crime, the nature and punishment of which shall be prescribed by law, for any president, director, manager, cashier, or other officer or owner of any private or public bank or banking institution to assent to the reception of deposits, or the creation of debts by such banking institution after he shall have had knowledge of the fact that it is insolvent or in failing circumstances. Any such officer, agent or manager shall be individually responsible for such deposits so received, and all such debts so created with his assent. D. 809–832.

ART. 242. The general assembly shall have power to enact general laws authorizing the parochial or municipal authorities of the State, under certain circumstances, by a vote of the majority of the property taxpayers in numbers and in value, to levy special taxes in aid of public improvements or railway enterprises; *provided*, that such tax shall not exceed the rate of five mills per annum, nor extend for a longer period than ten years. D. 711-714; Act 1880, No. 78.

ART. 243. Any railroad corporation or association organized for the purpose shall have the right to construct and operate a railroad between any points within this State, and connect at the State line with railroads of other States. Every railroad company shall have the right with its road to intersect, connect with or cross any other railroad, and shall receive and transport each the other's passengers, tonnage and cars, loaded or empty, without delay or discrimination.

ART. 244. Railways heretofore constructed or that may hereafter be constructed in this State are hereby declared public highways, and railroad companies common carriers. D. 466, 1697; C. C. 2745, 2751.

ART. 245. Every railroad or other corporation, organized or doing usiness in this State under the laws or authority thereof, shall have nd maintain a public office or place in this State for the transaction of its business, where transfers of stock shall be made, and where shall be kept for public inspection books, in which shall be recorded the amount of capital stock subscribed, the names of owners of stock, the amount owned by them respectively, the amounts of stock paid and by whom, the transfers of said stock, with the date of transfer, the amount of its assets and liabilities, and the names and places of residence of its officers. C. C. 38.

ART. 246. If any railroad company organized under the laws of this State shall consolidate, by sale or otherwise, with any railroad company organized under the laws of any other State or of the United States, the same shall not thereby become a foreign corporation; but the courts of this State shall retain jurisdiction in all matters which may arise, as if said consolidation had not taken place. In no case shall any consolidation take place except upon public notice of at least sixty days to all stockholders, in such manner as may be provided by law.

ART. 247. General laws shall be enacted providing for the creation of private corporations, and shall therein provide fully for the adequate protection of the public and of the individual stockholder. D. 677-746; C. C. 427-447.

ART. 248. The police juries of the several parishes and the constituted authorities of all incorporated municipalities of the State shall alone have the power of regulating the slaughtering of cattle and other live stock within their respective limits; *provided*, no monopoly or exclusive privilege shall exist in this State, nor such business be restricted to the land or houses of any individual or corporation; *provided*, the ordinances designating the places for slaughtering shall obtain the concurrent approval of the board of health or other sanitary organization. D. 2743, 3033.

PAROCHIAL AFFAIRS AND BOUNDARIES.

ART. 249. The general assembly may establish and organize new parishes, which shall be bodies corporate, with such powers as may be prescribed by law; but no new parish shall contain less than six hundred and twenty-five square miles, nor less than seven thousand inhabitants; nor shall any parish be reduced below that area or number of inhabitants.

ART. 250. All laws changing parish lines or removing parish seats shall, before taking effect, be submitted to the electors of the parish or the parishes to be affected thereby, at a special election held for that purpose, and be adopted by a majority of votes of each parish cast at such election.

ART. 251. Any parish may be dissolved and merged by the general assembly into a contiguous parish or parishes, two-thirds of the qualified electors of the parish proposed to be dissolved voting in favor thereof at an election held for that purpose; *provided*, that each of the parishes into which the dissolved parish proposes to become incorporated consents thereto by a majority of its qualified electors voting therefor.

ART. 252. Whenever a parish shall be enlarged or created from territory contiguous thereto it shall be entitled to a just proportion

the property and assets and liable for a just proportion of the existing debts or liabilities of the parish or parishes from which such territory shall be taken.

THE CITY OF NEW ORLEANS.

ART. 253. The citizens of the city of New Orleans or any political
corporation which may be created within its limits shall have the
right of appointing the several public officers necessary for the
administration of the police of said city, pursuant to the mode of
election which shall be provided by the general assembly.

ART. 254. The general assembly at its next session after the adoption of this constitution shall enact such legislation as may be proper
to liquidate the indebtedness of the city of New Orleans, and apply
its assets to the satisfaction thereof. It shall have authority to cancel
the charter of said city, and remit its inhabitants to another form of
government if necessary. In any such new form of government no
salary shall exceed three thousand five hundred dollars. Act 1880,
No. 74.

ART. 255. The general assembly shall pass necessary laws to prevent sailors or others of the crew of foreign vessels from working on
the wharves and levees of the city of New Orleans; *provided*, there
is no treaty between the United States and foreign powers to the
contrary.

AMENDMENT AND REVISION OF THE CONSTITUTION.

ART. 256. Propositions for the amendment of this constitution
may be made by the general assembly at any session thereof; and if
two-thirds of all the members elected to each house shall concur
therein, after such proposed amendments have been read in such
respective houses, on three separate days, such proposed amendment or amendments, together with the yeas and nays thereon,
shall be entered on the journal, and the secretary of State shall cause
the same to be published in two newspapers published in the parish
of Orleans, and in one paper in each other parish of the State in
which a newspaper is published, for three months preceding the
next election for representatives, at which time the said amendment
or amendments shall be submitted to the electors for their approval
or rejection; and if a majority voting on said amendment or amendments shall approve and ratify the same, then such amendment or
amendments, so approved and ratified, shall become a part of the
constitution. When more than one amendment shall be submitted
at the same time they shall be so submitted as to enable the electors
to vote on each amendment separately. The result of said election
shall be made known by the proclamation of the governor.

SCHEDULE.

ART. 257. The constitution of this State, adopted in eighteen hun-
˄ed and sixty-eight, and all amendments thereto, is declared to be
perseded by this constitution; and in order to carry the same into
ect it is hereby declared and ordained as follows·

ART. 258. All rights, actions, prosecutions, claims and contracts, as well of individuals as of bodies corporate, and all laws in force at the time of the adoption of this constitution and not inconsistent therewith, shall continue as if the said constitution had not been adopted. But the monopoly features in the charter of any corporation now existing in the State, save such as may be contained in the charters of railroad companies, are hereby abolished.

ART. 259. In order that no inconvenience may result to the public service from the taking effect of this constitution, no office shall be superseded thereby; but the laws of the State relative to the duties of the several officers—executive, judicial and military—shall remain in full force, though the same be contrary to this constitution; and the several duties shall be performed by the respective officers of the State, according to the existing laws, until the organization of the government under this constitution, and the entering into office of the new officers to be appointed or elected under said government, and no longer.

ART. 260. Appointments to office by the executive under this constitution shall be made by the governor, to be elected under its authority.

ART. 261. All causes in which appeals have been or may be hereafter taken or now pending in the supreme court, under the constitution of eighteen hundred and sixty-eight, and of which jurisdiction has been vested by this constitution in the courts of appeal, shall, after the adoption of this constitution, be transferred for trial to the court of appeal of the circuit from which the appeal has been or may be taken. All other causes that may be pending in the supreme court, under the constitution of eighteen hundred and sixty-eight, shall be transferred to the supreme court created by this constitution as soon as it shall be organized. All causes that may be pending in all other courts, under the constitution of eighteen hundred and sixty-eight, upon the adoption of this constitution and the organization of the courts created by this constitution, shall be transferred to the courts respectively having jurisdiction thereof under this constitution.

ART. 262. Immediately after the adjournment of this convention the governor shall issue his proclamation, directing the several officers of the State, authorized by law to hold elections for members of the general assembly, to open and hold a poll in every parish in the State, at the places designated by law, upon the first Tuesday in the month of December next, eighteen hundred and seventy-nine, for the purpose of taking the sense of the good people of this State in regard to the adoption or rejection of this constitution; and it shall be the duty of said officers to receive the votes of all persons entitled to vote under the constitution of eighteen hundred and sixty-eight. Each voter shall express his opinion by depositing in the ballot box a ticket, whereon shall be written or printed, "for the constitution," or "against the constitution," or some such words as will distinctly convey the intention of the voter. It shall also be the duty of the governor in his said proclamation to direct the said officers authorized by law to hold elections to open and hold a poll at the above stated time and places for the election of governor, lieutenant-governor, members of the general assembly, secretary of State, attorney-general, State auditor and superintendent of public education, and of all other officers whose election by the people is provided for in this constitution; and the names of the persons voted for shall be written or printed on the same ticket and deposited in the same box as the votes for or against the constitution. And the said election for the adoption or rejection of the constitution and for the said officers shall be conducted and the returns thereof made in conformity with existing laws upon the subject of State elections.   Upon receipt of the said returns, or the last Monday in December, eighteen hundred and seventy-nine, if the returns be not sooner received it shall be the duty of the governor, lieutenant-governor, the secretary of State and the attorney-general, in the presence of all such persons as may choose to attend, to compile the votes given at the said polls for ratification and rejection of this constitution; and if it shall appear from said returns that a majority of all the votes given on the question of adoption and rejection of the constitution is for ratifying this constitution, then it shall be the duty of the governor to make immediate proclamation of that fact, and thenceforth this constitution shall be ordained and established as the constitution of the State of Louisiana, and the general assembly elected in eighteen hundred and seventy-eight shall thereupon be dissolved.   Whether this constitution be adopted or rejected it shall be the duty of the governor to cause to be published in the official paper of the convention the result of the polls, showing the number of votes cast in each parish for and against the said constitution.   If the constitution be ratified it shall be the duty of the secretary of State to examine and compile the returns and publish the result of the election of officers herein ordained, and in the manner provided by existing laws.

ART. 263. The general assembly first elected under this constitution shall convene in the city of New Orleans upon the second Monday in January next, eighteen hundred and eighty, after the election, and the governor and lieutenant-governor elected shall be duly installed in office during the first week of the session, and before it shall be competent for the said general assembly to proceed with the transaction of business beyond their own organization.

ART. 264. The State auditor, attorney-general, secretary of State and superintendent of public education, elected at the first election herein provided for, shall enter upon the discharge of the duties of their respective offices on the second Monday of January, eighteen hundred and eighty, after complying with the requisites of existing laws; and all other officers whose election or appointment is provided for by this constitution shall enter upon the discharge of the duties of their respective offices on the first Monday of April, eighteen hundred and eighty, after complying with the requirements of existing laws; until which period all officers under the constitution of eighteen hundred and sixty-eight shall receive the pay and emoluments provided for under said constitution; *provided*, that the pay of the officers elected or appointed under this constitution shall not commence until after their induction into office.   The State treasurer elected in November, eighteen hundred and seventy-eight, shall continue in office as if elected at the election to be held on the first Tuesday in December, eighteen hundred and seventy-nine; but the salary of said officer shall be as established by this constitution from and after the second Monday in January, eighteen hundred and eighty.

ART. 265. The time of service of all officers chosen by the people at the first election under this constitution shall terminate as though the election had been holden on the first Tuesday after the first Monday in April, eighteen hundred and eighty.

ART. 266. The judges of the courts of appeal, district judges, city judges, district attorney, coroner, clerks of courts, sheriffs, recorder of mortgages and register of conveyances, all of whose election and appointment are provided for by this constitution, in the parish of Orleans, shall only enter on the discharge of the duties of their respective offices on the first Monday of August, eighteen hundred and eighty, and the present incumbents shall continue until then in the performance of the duties of their respective offices and the enjoyment of the emoluments thereof as now prescribed by law.

ART. 267. The general assembly is required to make provision for paying J. H. Gosgrove, printer of the convention, for the balance due him for work done previous to adjournment, and for all work that may be done by him after adjournment of the convention by its direction; and shall make a special appropriation to liquidate the debt which this convention has contracted, authorizing the fiscal agent of the State to negotiate a loan of twenty-five thousand dollars; and also for the payment of such vouchers as may be issued by the chairman of the committee on contingent expenses, under the authority of this convention, in excess of the foregoing appropriation, for the purpose of enabling this convention to complete its work; *provided*, said vouchers are approved by the president of the convention.

ART. 268. There shall not be any municipal election in the cities of New Orleans and Shreveport in December, eighteen hundred and seventy-nine. The general assembly shall provide for a municipal election in the city of New Orleans or such municipal corporations as may be created within the territorial limits of the parish of Orleans during the year eighteen hundred and eighty. The general assembly may fix the time for a municipal election in the city of Shreveport before April, eighteen hundred and eighty-four.

MISCELLANEOUS ORDINANCES.

Relief of Delinquent Taxpayers.

ART. 1. *Be it ordained by the people of the State of Louisiana in convention assembled*, All interests, penalties, costs, fees and charges whatever on taxes and licenses due the State, or any political corporation therein, prior to the first day of January, eighteen hundred and seventy-nine, and yet unpaid, are remitted, and all property forfeited to the State or any political corporation on account of non-payment of taxes or licenses, or to which the State or any political corporation now has a title, shall be redeemable, and the title to the State or any political corporation thereto annulled, upon the payment by the debtor or any interested party of the principal of all taxes and licenses that may be due thereon at the date of redemption, and this right of redemptio·

shall continue until the first day of January, eighteen hundred and eighty-one. In the event the principal of said taxes and licenses is not paid by said time, the interest, penalties, costs, fees and charges hereinbefore remitted shall revive and attach to the property upon which the taxes and licenses are due, and such property shall be then sold in the manner to be provided by law, and the title of the purchasers shall be full and complete; *provided*, that nothing herein contained shall be construed as affecting the rights of third persons who may have purchased property, legally assessed and sold at tax sales, or from the State or any political corporation after the same was legally forfeited to or purchased by the State or such corporation; *and provided further*, that nothing in this ordinance shall be taken as granting any time for the payment of the principal of said taxes and licenses; *and provided further*, that interest shall accrue and be collected on the principal of said delinquent taxes and licenses at the rate of eight per cent. per annum from January first, eighteen hundred and eighty; and on all said taxes and licenses paid a discount of ten per cent. per annum shall be allowed from the date of payment to January first, eighteen hundred and eighty-one. (Act 1880, No. 49, 93, 107.) That all taxes and licenses due the State prior to January first, eighteen hundred and seventy-nine, may be paid as follows: 1. That portion of said taxes and licenses due the general fund and all other funds, except as hereinafter provided, in any valid auditor's warrants outstanding at the date of the adoption of this constitution, except all warrants issued prior to the first of January, eighteen hundred and seventy-four, and also all warrants issued from the first of January, eighteen hundred and seventy-four, to first of January, eighteen hundred and seventy-five, for other purposes than for salaries of constitutional officers, or for the support of charitable institutions for the year eighteen hundred and seventy-four. That at the option of the holders of any of said warrants the said warrants may be funded in bonds of the denomination of five dollars, with interest coupons attached thereto, at the rate of three per cent. per annum interest from the first day of July, eighteen hundred and eighty; the said bonds to be due and payable six years from the first day of January, eighteen hundred and eighty; the said coupons being payable at the State treasury on the first day of February and August of each year. All moneys received in the treasury for all taxes and licenses due the State prior to the first day of January, eighteen hundred and seventy-nine, except such as are otherwise provided for by this ordinance, shall be set aside to pay the interest on said five dollar bonds, and to provide a sinking fund to redeem the same. The bonds above provided and interest coupons shall also be receivable for amounts due to the State for the redemption or purchase of property which has been forfeited or sold to the State for delinquent taxes and licenses of any of the years named in this article. The bonds so issued shall be receivable for the said taxes and licenses and the obligations of the public charitable institutions of the State given for purchase of necessary supplies of food, clothing, medicine and hire of employés. 2. That portion of said taxes and licenses due the interest fund subsequent to January, eighteen hundred and seventy-four, in any matured coupons issued by the State since that date. 3. That portion of said tax due the levee fund since the year eighteen hundred and seventy-one to the year eighteen hundred and seventy-six, inclusive of both years, in any valid warrants issued by the levee company and endorsed by the auditor and treasurer of the State as follows: "Receivable for levee tax due for eighteen hundred and seventy-one to eighteen hundred and seventy-six inclusive;" and the auditor and treasurer are hereby authorized to so endorse warrants issued by the levee company, as provided above, to an amount sufficient to cover the balance due on the judgment recovered by said company in the case entitled Louisiana Levee Company vs. the State of Louisiana, No. 7163 in the supreme court of Louisiana.

Be it further ordained, etc., That no auditor's warrants shall be taken as valid for the purpose of payment of taxes and licenses or for funding, as hereinbefore prescribed, until the same shall have been examined by the auditor, treasurer and attorney-general of the State, and endorsed by them as valid. Said warrants when so endorsed, may be surrendered to said officers and by them registered and canceled; and in lieu thereof said auditor and treasurer shall issue certificates in sums of five, ten, twenty or fifty dollars, as may be desired by the holder of said warrants, which shall be receivable for all taxes and licenses due the State prior to January the first, eighteen hundred and seventy-nine, except the taxes due the interest fund and levee fund.

Be it further ordained, That all taxes and licenses due any parish or municipal corporation prior to January first, eighteen hundred and seventy-nine, may be payable in any valid warrants, scrip or floating indebtedness of said parish or municipal corporation, except judgments.

INDEBTEDNESS OF THE STATE TO ITS FISCAL AGENT.

Be it ordained by the people of the State of Louisiana in convention assembled, That the debt due from the State to its fiscal agent, being in amount one hundred and eighty-seven thousand, seventy-seven dollars and twenty-four cents, subject to such reduction as may result from credits arising out of taxes due to the interest fund since June the thirtieth, eighteen hundred and seventy-nine, which said debt was created under the contract made between the board of liquidators and the fiscal agent, under date of the twenty-fifth of May, eighteen hundred and seventy-seven, and under act number twenty-eight, session of the legislature of eighteen hundred and seventy-eight, is hereby declared to be a valid obligation of the State; and the legislature shall, at its first session after the adoption of this constitution, provide for the payment of the same; and the fiscal agent shall, as a condition precedent to said payment, surrender and deliver to the auditor of the State for cancellation the interest coupons which were taken up and held by said fiscal agent at the time of making the advances which created the said indebtedness; but the interest to be allowed said fiscal agent shall be at the rate of four per cent. per annum until the debt is paid.

LOAN BY FISCAL AGENT.

ARTICLE I. *Be it ordained by the people of the State of Louisiana in convention assembled,* That the fiscal agent of this State shall be ar is hereby empowered, by authority of this convention, to negotiate a loan of twenty-five thousand dollars, or so much thereof as may be necessary, at seven per cent. per annum, to defray the residue of the expenses of this convention not provided for by the act of the general assembly calling this convention, and to enable the convention to complete the work of framing the new constitution.

ART. 2. The said loan shall be evidenced by certificates of indebtedness, signed by the president of this convention and countersigned by the secretary thereof, under seal of this convention, in sums of five hundred dollars or under, bearing seven per cent. per annum interest from the date of such certificates until paid, and payable on the fifteenth day of March, A. D. eighteen hundred and eighty, at the State National Bank of New Orleans, in the city of New Orleans.

ART. 3. The first general assembly convened under this constitution shall make a special appropriation to liquidate the debt which this convention has contracted or may contract, as per ordinance adopted authorizing the fiscal agent of the State to negotiate a loan of twenty-five thousand dollars for the purpose of enabling this convention to complete the work of framing this constitution.

STATE DEBT.*

ARTICLE I. *Be it ordained by the people of the State of Louisiana, as provided by law,* That the State debt ordinance read as follows: That the interest to be paid on the consolidated bonds of the State of Louisiana be and is hereby fixed at two per centum per annum for five years, from January 1, 1880, and four per centum per annum thereafter, payable semi-annually; and there shall be levied an annual tax sufficient for the full payment of said interest, not exceeding three mills, the limit of State tax for all purposes being hereby fixed at six mills, and said bonds and coupons shall be duly stamped: "Interest reduced to two per centum per annum for five years from January 1, 1880, and four per centum per annum thereafter."

ART. 2. That the holders of the consolidated bonds may at any time, in order that the coupons may be paid, present their bonds to the treasurer of the State, or to agents to be appointed by the governor in the city of New York and the other in the city of London, and the said treasurer or agents, as the case may be, shall endorse or stamp thereon the words: "Interest reduced to two per centum per annum for five years from January 1, 1880, and four per centum per annum thereafter," and said treasurer or agents shall endorse or stamp on said coupons the following words: "Interest reduced to two per centum per annum," or "Interest reduced to four per centum per annum," as the case may be."

SEC. 2. *Be it further enacted, etc.,* That the foregoing provisions and articles shall not form any part of the constitution, except as hereafter provided, as follows: At the election, as provided by law, it shall be lawful for each voter to have printed or written on his ballot the words "for amendment to ordinance relative to State debt," or the words, "against amendment to ordinance relative to State debt;"

As amended in 1882.

and in the event that a majority of ballots so cast be for the amendment to ordinance relative to State debt, then the said foregoing provisions and articles of this amendment shall form a part of the constitution, as if the same had been originally so ratified; and if a majority of the ballots so cast shall have on them the words, " against the amendment to ordinance relative to State debt," then said provisions and articles shall form no part of the constitution.

INDEX.